SUPER SCHOOLMASTER

SUPER SCHOOLMASTER

EZRA POUND AS TEACHER, THEN AND NOW

Robert Scholes
and David Ben-Merre

Cover image from Ezra Pound's "Announcements" from "The Egoist," November 1914.

Published by State University of New York Press, Albany

For information, contact State University of New York Press, Albany, NY
www.sunypress.edu

Library of Congress Cataloging-in-Publication Data

Names: Scholes, Robert, author. | Ben-Merre, David, author.
Title: Super schoolmaster : Ezra Pound as teacher, then and now. / Robert Scholes, author | David Ben-Merre, author.
Description: Albany : State University of New York Press, [2021] | Includes bibliographical references and index.
Identifiers: ISBN 9781438481470 (hardcover : alk. paper) | ISBN 9781438481487 (ebook)
Further information is available at the Library of Congress.

10 9 8 7 6 5 4 3 2 1

For Jo Ann (of course)

Contents

Acknowledgments ix

Preface: Back to Basics xi
Robert Scholes

Preface: In a Station xvii
David Ben-Merre

Introduction 1

Chapter 1 Pounding the Academy: The Poet as Student
and Teacher 9

Chapter 2 The Critic as Teacher: Pound's "New Method"
in Scholarship 33

Chapter 3 How to Read Comparatively 61

Chapter 4 Periodical Studies 87

Chapter 5 The Instructor as Propagandist 115

Afterword: Schools of Fish 137
David Ben-Merre

Notes 149

Works Cited 181

Index 189

Acknowledgments

We are tremendously grateful to Carl Klaus and Sean Latham for their encouragement at all stages of this project, and Clifford Wulfman for his generosity in allowing us to reimagine and amplify a chapter from his and Bob's groundbreaking *Modernism in the Magazines* (New Haven: Yale University Press, 2010). We offer a very special thanks to our editor Rebecca Colesworthy, who was also a student of Bob's. Sadly, Bob passed away before she became involved in this project, but he would have been so delighted by this serendipitous turn and ever so thankful—as am I—for her constant help and unrelenting stewardship. To the entire community of Bob's students (from both inside and outside the classroom) and to all those who continually think and rethink the possibilities of modernism—thank you.

Preface

Back to Basics

> Waaal, frankly, I allus thought it would be a good thing to come back
> and put some sort of a college or university into shape to teach the
> young something. Not merely the god damn saw dust and substitutes
> for learnin' and literature they got handed.
>
> —Doob 9–10

So said Ezra Pound in one of his infamous radio broadcasts to the United States during the Second World War—this one dated October 26, 1941, weeks before the United States would enter the war. Even though the contexts of many of his teachings from these years were horribly wrong, I am inclined to believe him and take what he said quite literally. He had been thinking along these lines, and even acting along them, for more than thirty years when he wrote those words and spoke them.

This book began with the faith that there is more to the story of Pound as a teacher than his informal pontificating in Italy. My thoughts were confirmed by the recently published volume of letters from Pound to his parents (excellently edited by A. David Moody, Joanna Moody, and Mary de Rachewiltz) in which his persistent attempts to get academic employment and recognition are fully visible for the first time.[1] These letters might make us reconsider substantial portions of his published work as demonstrations of his pedagogical skill and scholarly strength. My thoughts continued in this direction by contemplating Pound's essay "Small Magazines," which appeared in the *English Journal* for November 1930 (though I did not read it until a bit later). This periodical was then, and still is, the voice of the National Council of Teachers of English.

There are reasons why modernist literature in English made such an impact on the academy, and they are grounded in the academic training of the masters of that literature. T. S. Eliot—that other American academic poet—wrote his dissertation in philosophy, while James Joyce specialized, like Pound, in Romance languages, though he ended up teaching English in a Berlitz school and giving public lectures in Italian on Shakespeare, Defoe, and Blake. Dora Marsden, the founding editor of *The Freewoman* magazine and its successors, had an academic degree and always appeared on the masthead of her magazines as "Dora Marsden, B.A." Virginia Woolf thought and wrote frequently about the way women were disadvantaged in the British educational system, but she, too, taught courses and wrote in an educational mode regularly.

For his part, Pound actually did go to graduate school at the University of Pennsylvania and then got a teaching job at Wabash College in Craw- fordsville, Indiana. As we learn from his letters to his parents, Pound was not an English teacher but rather the entire (newly established) Department of Romance Languages, teaching French to fifth-seven students, Spanish to thirty, and handling another fifteen in advanced French (*EPtP* 57). Pound's career in Crawfordsville was terminated abruptly after he befriended two theatrical women who were stranded there—the first a male impersonator, and the second a refugee from a burlesque show (though reports about the incidents differ). This was the final straw for the Wabash administration, and Pound was forced to resign and abandon his formal teaching career. He did think of himself as a teacher, however, for most of his life, even though he never received the PhD he thought he deserved. From his earliest days in college Pound had sought degrees for learning what he wanted to learn rather than for fulfilling some set of requirements that did not interest him. To the extent that much of his poetry has a distinct scholarly quality and his scholarship is exceptionally lively and creative, he was able to bridge an important gap between the scholar and the poet. And importantly for him, both poetry and scholarship became a means of teaching. The poetry, of course, has been examined extensively—and intensively, too—but the pedagogical Pound can stand a bit more examination.

While it is hard to miss how didactic Pound can be, we are seldom aware of just how educational his purpose is. I remember James Laughlin, the founder of the New Directions Press, once telling me that he got into publishing after visiting Pound in Rapallo, which he referred to as attending the "Ezuversity." And he was neither the first nor the last to study in that school. In a sense, Pound's entire career can be seen as one great pedagogical lesson. In a letter to Laughlin, he noted:

> Just opened ABC Reading. as practical assset to the Jas / consider the number of yung who hv / said that they hv / learned MORE from sd / book than all their schooling. What about drive by STATES to git it into curriCUlumz / even with bait of cheaper reprint. . . . (qtd. in Gordon 216)

Written most likely in 1951, Pound's letter shows the poet's faith in his own abilities as a teacher. While his desire to instruct others never wavered, his methods of doing so did. Those changes are notable even in the few years between the publications of *How to Read* (1931) and *ABC of Reading* (1934), which is very much a revision and extension of the first book with a short anthology set of "Exhibits" included. It is also very specifically designed as a primer: "The present pages should be impersonal enough to serve as a text-book. The author hopes . . . to produce a text book that can also be read 'for pleasure as well as profit' by those who are no longer in school; by those who have not been to school; or by those who in their college days suffered those things which most of my own generation suffered" (11). Pound, of course, had refused to suffer those things and had carved out his own program in comparative literature as a student, defying the English Department at Penn to do so, after getting just what he wanted from Hamilton College. In his introductory note, however, he also has encouraging words for "teachers and professors," saying that he is not trying to make their lives more difficult but "should like to make even their lot and life more exhilarating and to save even them from unnecessary boredom in the class-room" (11). Pound correctly diagnosed one of the major problems with delegating education. Teachers, often overworked, become just as exhausted as their overworked students, uninterested in their own topics and left without any motivation for discovering what is new.

By insisting that his was a textbook, addressed both to students and teachers, Pound was also clearly trying to promote sales. And, over time, this worked pretty well. The book was first published by George Routledge & Sons in London, and the first American publisher was the Yale University Press. There were 2,000 copies printed in England and another thousand in the United States. In 1951, Faber and Faber in England printed 2,670 copies and sent sheets for 3,500 more to New Directions in the United States. In 1960 and 1961 both of these companies issued paperback versions, totaling almost 20,000 new copies. Ultimately Pound reached an audience. My own copy is the New Directions hardcover edition, published in 1951. In contrast, Pound's collection of periodical articles called *Make It New* was printed in England by the Cambridge University Press and published by

Faber and Faber in 1934 and by the Yale University Press with print runs of just 1,600 and 1,000 copies. This book has never been reprinted. The recommendation Pound received to leave "Studies in Contemporary Mentality" out of *Make It New* probably did not help, but the advice he got about making a textbook by expanding *How To Read* into *ABC of Reading* seems to have worked very well. Even so, Pound complained that his publisher had asked him to make English literature "as prominent as possible" in this version of his introductory book but insisted that he couldn't do this and "play fair with the student" (71). In addition to teaching reading, Pound tries in this book to teach writing as well, and he proposes some clever assignments designed to help students become better readers. However, he warns these students that they "cannot learn to write by reading English" (71). He insists forcefully throughout that learning foreign languages makes students better readers and writers of their own. And he is certainly right about this.

In *ABC of Reading* he invites his student readers to challenge his opinions when they have done enough work to justify their own. Well, I have done enough, I believe, to do just that. Fifty years of teaching English have helped me see some of Pound's weaknesses as a teacher and mentor with some clarity. Pound knew best and taught best the literature that he had studied most fully, under the guidance of professors who knew their subject well, which is to say that he knew the Romance languages and literatures better than he knew English and American literature. Pound is good at seeing the things he really looks at but he can't see what he doesn't look at, a criticism of which we all ought to be aware. His *ABC of Reading*, nevertheless, offers some interesting assignments for students, and it is full of brilliant phrases like this one: "Your language is in the care of your writers" (33), a point he makes in more than one way, more than one time. He seems to have really believed that good literature leads to good government: "Rome rose with the idiom of Caesar, Ovid, and Tacitus, she declined in a welter of rhetoric, the diplomat's 'language to conceal thought,' and so forth" (33). His beliefs in the power of literature and in his own power of seeing and understanding are visible in this book and building toward the hubris that preceded his own fall into what he failed to recognize as the sort of rhetoric he should have despised. This process is even more visible in his other primer: *ABC of Economics*, which was published in 1933, the year Pound was writing *ABC of Reading*. In his book on reading, Pound would caution his students against accepting opinions from people who have not "themselves produced notable work" (40), implying (and rightfully so) that he had produced some of that precious stuff himself. He does not offer such a warning in his little primer of economics—for obvious reasons. He is writing about a subject in which he has achieved nothing notable.[2] Writing a book to prove yourself is very different from writing a book because you have already proven yourself to be worthy of being called a teacher.

In his more focused books, and especially in *The Spirit of Romance*, he really knew what he was talking about, had studied it carefully with people who knew a lot about it themselves, and had earned his right to profess in public. Many of his articles, later collected in volumes, are also full of learning and insight. And, as a spotter of contemporary literary and artistic talent, his record is startlingly high. Just think of Robert Frost, D. H. Lawrence, T. S. Eliot, James Joyce, Wyndham Lewis, William Carlos Williams, H. D. [Hilda Doolittle], and Henri Gaudier-Brzeska, who all owe a lot to the teachings of Pound. He also helped other excellent young writers get attention, from Richard Aldington to Louis Zukofsky. In economics, however, he was untaught, and (mis)guided by others, many of whom, though Pound would not admit it, had not produced scholarly works in the field. His main economic guides at the beginning were A. R. Orage, the editor of *The New Age*, with whom Pound disagreed about almost everything else, and Major C. H. Douglas, who, when given the opportunity, had trouble explaining persuasively his own theory of "Social Credit." Pound later learned more about this difficult subject, but much of what he "learned" was both wrong and poisonous, even if it took him to what he believed was the heart of the matter.

When Pound talks about language he is on firm ground, but he does not stick to language, even in this book about reading. He makes a major point in chapter 1, for example, that is based on biology rather than literature. Borrowing, most likely, from the English teacher Lane Cooper's 1917 book on the biologist Louis Agassiz, Pound gives us his version of an anecdote about Agassiz forcing a student to look at a fish over and over until he can describe it to the professor's satisfaction. I bought *ABC of Reading* when I was a graduate student and learned from it. I believe it helped me become a better teacher. About twenty years later, in a book called *Textual Power*, I criticized Pound's use of Agassiz.[3] Now, almost thirty years after that, I am coming back to give Pound credit for being the teacher that he was, and to sort out more carefully his pedagogical strengths and weaknesses.[4]

On a personal note, several years ago I wanted to write a book on Ezra Pound as a teacher. I started that book but then had a stroke. One of my friends, Carl Klaus, thought I should get someone to finish the book for me. I thought about that and wondered who might be able to do such a thing. There was only one person I could think of, but he was working hard on a book of his own. Even so, I asked if, when he had finished the one he was working on, he would be willing to finish the book on Pound. My friend David Ben-Merre said he would do that. And he did.

Robert Scholes

Preface

In a Station

I met Ezra Pound a few years before I met Robert Scholes. I was introduced to Pound, as many were, through his "In a station of the metro" poem—my grade school teacher liking (a little much) those fourteen words. At the time for us, as I imagine they did for others decades earlier, the words meant new possibilities, democratizing poetry in an astonishingly novel way. It was a moment when school could mean more than just school and when our learning could extend beyond 3:30. It wasn't until college that I met Professor Scholes—first as his reader (one of those faces in the crowd), then as his student, then as his friend. And, to those who knew him, he would always insist on simply being called "Bob." His request to continue this manuscript came as a great surprise: twofold in fact, because it meant a sudden invitation to engage with Bob's work—work that we all closely admired—but in a whole new way, and also because I hadn't realized that he had returned to Pound, a central figure of modernism but one who was so often in Bob's crosshairs. I soon learned that this return to Pound meant a return to modernism and its relationship to new media and to new ways of understanding and teaching the world. As I note in the "Afterword," my sense was that Bob wanted to rethink the value of an incredibly problematic poet, especially for the twenty-first century, as those both inside and outside the academy reassess the utility, instruments, and challenges of higher education amid the global proliferation of new technologies and revolutionary ways of distributing and consuming knowledge and culture. Like Pound, Bob could see the social advantages and pedagogical excitement of embracing that which is "new," but he was also wary of the dangers of such commercialized obsessions, wherein the unrelenting forces of modernity could swallow whole cultural histories. Across higher education, we talk about knowing where we are going, but we don't even really know which of the so-called innovative transformations will (or ought to) endure and which are momentary (and monetary) fads. The excitement and the fear of this new modernity are tangible, and the stakes could not be higher.

Super Schoolmaster is our attempt to navigate these many concerns. It brings together Bob's recent thoughts on modernism (*Paradoxy of Modernism*), media studies (*Modernism in the Magazines*, with Clifford Wulfman), ways of learning (*The Crafty Reader, Protocols of Reading*), the digital humanities (the *Modernist Journals Project*), and the future(s) of teaching in the United States (*Textual Power, The Rise and Fall of English*). It is part of Bob's life-long project of rethinking just what was at stake in modernism and why it all matters. Importantly spanning generations of critical thought, Bob's scholarship has moved from narratively centered semiotic and structuralist approaches to a cultural materialism acutely aware of the historical contexts of turn-of-the-century artistic production. At the heart of each of these critical approaches—the self-conscious turns of a life among texts—was a genuine faith in the worth of the humanistic project. The book is also, I imagine, an attempt to come to terms with Ezra Pound—whom Bob often called the "elephant in the room of Modernism"—because the poet still has valuable lessons to pass along, not only about modernism and aesthetic practice but also about the rewards and perils of educational systems.

Bob passed away in December 2016, a few years before this man-uscript's completion.[5] In the relatively short time since, the world seems to have changed so much, too much. And this was the case even before the COVID-19 pandemic began to spread globally.[6] Two more academics noting how terrifying the rhetoric is coming out of the executive branch will, sadly, not tip any scales. Neither will a reminder of the echoes of history—those voices we, not too long ago, thought had been relegated to the caves. It is more than disconcerting to note the parallels between the rhetoric of the 1930s and 1940s—much of which found its way into Pound's mythology—and that we find on the AM dial and in mainstream political speeches today. One is scared to think of tomorrow. Yet to reread Pound at this moment is not only to imagine a fearful tomorrow. The con-nections he makes between history and culture, between his contemporary times and locations across the globe from centuries ago, are all a way for him—and for those still willing to listen—to celebrate the perpetual spirit of life. And it was not just about appreciating a living cultural tradition; it was also about bringing the joy of learning to everyone, as odd as this may sound, given the notorious difficulty of Pound's poetics. These are the crucial values that Bob, with critical distance and a lifetime dedicated to learning, wanted to reexamine because he, like Pound, believed that they were worth preserving no matter how unstable the ground of our world.

In terms of media, methodologies, and reading lists, Bob was as innovative a teacher as he was a scholar. Still, for all this novelty, he could also have a "traditional" sense of modernism—here, the individual Pound battling the oppressive constraints of the institution while all the time endeavoring to build a new one. Call it a paradox, or, rather following Bob's neologism, a "paradoxy" of modernism.[7] And yet it would be dishonest to call Pound the "hero" of this book, however much he is its focus. Why Pound? There are others, many others who have much to say about higher education, other "schoolmasters" who have much to tell us about our predicaments today. It wasn't that Pound was the greatest modernist poet or the finest pedagogical example or that he was at *the* center of what earlier scholars saw as modernism, but rather that he was so integral to a long-standing conception of how the threads of culture, history, politics, and the university were all or could all be woven together at the beginning of the century. But to say that this is a book solely about the past would be to miss the thrust of Pound's import, one that is captured in the paradoxical title of this book: "Super Schoolmaster." Pound could be so scornful of schooling, yet he could also believe in its vitality and importance, and it is in his role as a super schoolmaster that he may have lessons to teach us, particularly at this moment.[8]

While we illuminate many of those lessons here, readers looking for solutions to all the ills of twenty-first-century education, however, will not find quick-fix answers in this book. Instead, we offer a new vantage point to view Pound's contradictory career, wide-ranging thought, innovative poetics, and alarming politics by following his extensive thinking about the practices of teaching and the processes of learning beyond the walls of the academy. Those familiar with Pound will hopefully recognize further connections among his vast body of work, his continual advocacy for what we now view as the humanities—or what he saw as a transgenerational, transnational culture—and the opportunities and pitfalls of education in the twentieth and twenty-first centuries. And readers new to Pound will be introduced not only to how he figures as a key modernist figure but moreover, as Paul Stasi and Josephine Park's recent collection articulates (albeit in a different way), to how central he is to understanding and imparting the possibilities of culture today.[9]

The special character of *Super Schoolmaster* also should not be over-looked. This is a book that captures the final thoughts of one of the most important modernist scholars of our time. For those modernists who would scoff at yet another book about Pound, my hope is that they might still find some value in understanding why Professor Scholes felt the need to return to him. We detail the book chapters further in the "Introduction," but I wanted to say something brief about our collaborative process here. Before his stroke, Bob drafted much of these first three chapters. He wanted to include chapter 4 as a reimagined version of sections of his and Clifford Wulfman's influential *Modernism in the Magazines*, now recontextualized in terms of Pound's pedagogy. Most of the close readings of Pound's essays in these chapters are Bob's, while most of the critical contextualization is my own. Moving into a specific moment in Pound's epic verse, chapter 5 was my own attempt to describe the perils of where Pound's "teachings" had ended up. The last couple years with this manuscript have been a collaborative effort—if you will—with various readers, who have helped lend a coherence to the project as well as place it within critical discussions today. As the collaboration continued, Bob and I found that we did not always agree about Pound, but both of us were convinced of his importance, then and now.

Readers familiar with Bob as a teacher or author will hear his voice, especially his later one, in the personal turns and colloquial phrasings, which I have tried to maintain throughout. What can sometimes read on a rhetorical level as whimsiness or informality, or on a theoretical level as indecisiveness, was never meant as glibness or a desire to avoid the question. Rather, it was always part of his aspiration to democratize the reading experience, a process he encouraged in his classes as much as in his texts. Bob was invested, at times, in letting contradictions sit, in recognizing the very complex patterns in modernism and in individual authors who were pulled in extraordinarily different ways by the revolutionary developments of the twentieth century. This, we might say, was the pedagogical rather than the polemical element of his approach. He and Pound (when at his best) could both stress this process of looking, of thinking through a question rather than searching for a simple answer—each with the faith that the deeper awareness often resided in uncertainty. Our book, similarly, works by drawing connections, trying to get at what Pound would call the "luminous detail"—all with the purpose of showing just how central teaching was to this central modernist figure. Pound could be blind to his own ideological politics (well beyond his fascism), but at the same time he could anticipate questions that would become central to critical theory, whose practitioners, one must confess, have not always addressed those questions in ways he would have admired. Readers looking for a comprehensive book on Pound's contributions to the history of literary theory or critical pedagogy, however, might be a little disappointed.[10] While connections with developments in the theory and politics of teaching are noted throughout, we have produced mainly a biblio-biographical account of Pound's pedagogy through what we have identified as significant thematic clusters, with an eye toward higher education and especially the place of the humanities today. The book's argument is straightforward: that we ought to reconsider Pound, modernism, and possibilities of higher education broadly conceived—then and now—in light of Pound's frequently insightful thoughts on teaching and learning. If we cannot offer much-needed solutions to our many current predicaments, we hope to put Pound into conversation with others as a first step to understanding where we stand.

For my part, I am fortunate to have had both Ezra Pound and Robert Scholes as teachers—more personally grateful for the introspection and generosity of the latter. To Bob, who would blanch at the thought of being mentioned here (and then again in the Afterword), I will have to offer one final apology. However much Bob wanted this book to be solely about Pound, I have found it difficult to ignore that teacher who would, for all his students, go out as far as Cho-fu-Sa.

I confess that I could not have finished the book Bob wanted to write, but my hope is that I was able to finish the book he taught me how to write.

David Ben-Merre

Introduction

It is always tempting just to ignore Ezra Pound. Pound, though, would not sit still for that, and neither should we. As Leonard W. Doob puts it, in his introduction to the poet's wartime radio broadcasts, "If Pound was not always totally accepted, at least he was unavoidably there" (ix). Wearing the various but inescapably interrelated hats of poet, scholar, cultural advocate, and fascist apologist, Pound has famously been the shibboleth at the center of modernist studies. By the account of some literary scholars (Hugh Kenner, Christine Brooke-Rose), he is believed to be central to the story of the time, and by others (Helen Vendler, Harold Bloom) to be a myth or a fraud perpetrated upon cultural history, a name that can only be whispered in New Haven to this day.[1] "No consensus on Pound's reputation has yet emerged," Ira B. Nadel writes, "but the very debate is credit to the activist poetics Pound promoted. Poets do not observe, he insisted: they engage with social and political change."[2]

Pound was at once a brilliant poet, resolute mentor, and extraordinary promoter of the arts. And, yet, according to some at the time and others today, he could also be a spiteful counselor and, at worst, a type of intellectual charlatan.[3] However one understands Pound, he was, at the very least, a very different voice at the onset of a very different generation of artists, intellectuals, and students. Our book makes the claim that this "unavoidable" presence is as true for Pound's pedagogical methods as it is for Pound's modernist aesthetic. Even T. S. Eliot could make such a claim in his introduction to Pound's *Literary Essays*, where he would write that Pound "has always been, first and foremost, a teacher and campaigner" (xii).[4] Pound's instruction reveals much about literature and culture in general, as well as his own unmistakable sense of the literary marketplace early in the century. But it is the lessons *of* Pound alongside the lessons *by* him that

1

show, in a way we might otherwise ignore, the tenuous relationship between our generally altruistic educational intentions and what is often a precarious process of ideological indoctrination. As he wrote in *ABC of Reading* (and might have reminded even himself on more than one occasion), "The teacher or lecturer is a danger. He very seldom recognizes his nature or his position" (83). If Pound could be said to be a dangerous mentor—in both the positive and negative senses of pushing his disciples to imagine previously unheard-of possibilities for what he called "Kulchur"—then he also could be said to be a troublemaker of a student. As he wrote, "I fought every university regulation and every professor who tried to make me learn anything except this, or who bothered me with 'requirements' for degrees" (Stock 34).

Many readers of Pound—writers and critics both—have pointed out how the poetry itself functioned as a type of pedagogy. Hugh Kenner, for one, called Pound a "poet at the blackboard."[5] Despite a few recent efforts to recognize the pedagogical Pound—such as Gail McDonald's excellent *Learning to Be Modern* (1993)[6] and Steven G. Yao and Michael Coyle's diverse collection *Ezra Pound and Education* (2012)—recent scholarship on Pound has mostly focused on the question of how we ought to weigh his poetry against his fascist speeches and writing, and this seems to be a topic ever of relevance.[7] Those aspects of his life cannot—must not—ever be ignored, but they might be importantly recontextualized in light of his educational impulses, which anticipate contemporary trends in higher education generally and in the humanities specifically.

Pound's pedagogical concerns were oriented in different temporal directions. He wanted to preserve the cultural treasures of the past for future generations, and he was also concerned with ongoing institutional tendencies, which were harmfully affecting the teaching and intellectual work of humanists and scholars in literary studies. This was true for his day, and it is perhaps even more true for us today. Recent calls to reform higher education on both the left and the right, as well as the growth of massive open online courses (MOOCs) and vocational colleges, show how Pound's early concerns about faceless, detached, and unaware academic settings remain prevalent in vastly different political circles. A university system that had no awareness of or interest in how the energy of contemporary life was rooted in a vibrant historical soil was of no appeal to Pound, and he was wary of social systems that were motivated by economic rather than humanistic decisions. Looking back from the twenty-first century, we might be alarmed, as Pound would have been, by the growing investment of both governmental and business interests in education, which seem to reduce and compartmentalize the disciplines. Much is now at stake, and much of the present and future decisions are not even moderately informed by those people who day-in-and-day-out spend their time in the classroom. Pointing to the 2006 Spellings Commission Report, Steven G. Yao and Michael Coyle note that in "the context of a contemporary ideological environment in which the federal government has sought to assert more direct control over higher education in the United States, and where state governments call for the dissolution of Boards of Trustees and advocate running state university systems directly from the statehouse, a renewed consideration of one of America's great cultural and pedagogical iconoclasts seems all the more timely and pressing" (xxiv).

It seems both easy and difficult to imagine what Pound would have made of the current state of the humanities and, even more specifically, of literary studies. There is a lot of overlap between his critiques and anger at out-of-touch professors who know much about their specialty and not as much about its social relevance or, moreover, about why their idiosyncratic work ought to matter to twenty-year-olds seeking jobs in a marketplace that has a very different valuing system than, say, a medievalist with a red pen. Universities, often called by Pound "beaneries," would continually come under indictment, as would many of the scholarly methods employed in those spaces.[8] Pound would not have been partial to what, today, is called "Theory" (especially as much of it derives from what he saw as the contaminated minds of thinkers like Karl Marx and Sigmund Freud), though we may guess that he would have been charmed by its early guises.[9] (This would not be too far afield from the experiences Pound had with his many modernist "isms" in the first few decades of the twentieth century.) He also, without any contradiction here, would have railed against the "historicist turn" in literary studies, much of which he would have seen as a repackaged incarnation of the scholarly philology he learned to detest at school.

Although he might not find many self-acknowledging theoretical neighbors, Pound is, at heart, a manner of humanist. In a 1912 article he published in the *New Age* (one to which we return later), Pound writes, "Our life is, in so far as it is worth living, made up in great part of things indefinite, impalpable; and it is precisely because the arts present us these things that we—humanity—cannot get on without the arts" (*NA* 10.13:298). "Knowledge," he later writes in his *Guide to Kulchur*, "is to know man" (98), and teaching others means rousing them into wanting to know man too: "I suspect that the error in educational systems has been the cutting off of learning from appetite" (98). Pound knew that a college was most successful when both the students and teachers wanted to be there. Moreover, being a part of a humanistic global "kulchur" did not mean merely being well educated institutionally. His *Guide* preambles with the following: "This book is not written for the over-fed. It is written for men who have not been able to afford an university education or for young men, whether or not threatened with universities, who want to know more at the age of fifty than I know today . . ." (6). Worthy intentions notwithstanding, as can be the problematic case with much humanism, the proprietor here assumes that others share his knowledge and expectations of what a human ought to entail. Pound, for his part, was a master of sharing his knowledge, and nothing significant remained out of his ken: "Russia is not a civilized nation" (158), "Mussolini a great man" (105), and "For fish, try Taormina" (113).

What follows in the next five chapters are the various guises of Ezra Pound, "Super Schoolmaster." This epithet (the book's title) comes from a review of one of Pound's books in *The Dial*, in which the reviewer, one of the editors of the magazine, situated Pound this way in his concluding paragraph: "Is nobody aware that a contemporary writer is actually giving a course on the Comparative Literature of the Present, that a first rate literary man, a poet, with the rarest gift for translation, is bothering to teach school?"[10] Pound was a revolutionary schoolmaster in vastly different ways. His unwavering advocacy for "comparative" methods in education heralds the rise in academia of interdisciplinary programs and collaborative fields today. He wanted to study and teach people about popular periodicals because he understood their ideological relationship to social life. Culture was not a dusty collection of books and magazines; it was living, breathing, tied into the very fabric of contemporary being.[11] And the beauty of it all was not to be found in the methods of his teachers—that mired study of insignificant detail and "endless pondering over some utterly unanswerable question of textual criticism."[12] Instead, Pound would later propose his own version of "the grisly roots of ideas that are in action," which, following a correspondence with the ethnographer Leo Frobenius, he would come to call the "Paideuma" (*Guide to Kulchur* 58). Different from the Zeitgeist ("the tints of mental air and the idées reçues"), the "Paideuma" (etymologically linked to teaching and education [Gr.]) allowed Pound to go right to the core of a historical moment. This would become not only a scholarly method but also a pedagogical one.

At a time when the prejudices of many in academia insisted that all cultural values stemmed entirely from the West, he turned Eastward, introducing poets and philosophers to audiences who otherwise would never have learned about them. He individually mentored aspiring writers he admired, even giving a lot of his time to teach those whose talents he doubted.[13] In terms of academic institutions, he was shocked "that it took ideas an appallingly long time to filter through to the population," telling a professor at the University of Pennsylvania that there was a "Time Lag, between real culture and that TAUGHT" (Carpenter 522). Hence, he campaigned for the inclusion of contemporary writers and artists—as both objects of study and potential faculty members—in colleges because they knew how art could still animate the souls of the young.[14] In this, he anticipates the precipitous rise of creative writing programs in the United States, even though he was none too keen on their institutionalization. His literary criticism and cultural essays, his mentorship of other writers, and his promotion of the arts in both small journals and more extensive primers were all means by which the poet Pound could act as the professor he believed he could be. Indeed, as early as thirty years ago, the writer and publisher of *New Directions* press, James Laughlin, was explaining how Pound's oeuvre was, in the end, a pedagogical method. "Pound was a born a teacher," Laughlin writes, noting that a "great teacher presents verities and compares them so that students can judge for themselves" (34, 35).[15] Pound's pedagogy, for Laughlin, reached students widely in the guises of introductory books, edited anthologies, literary reviews, editorial work with journals, literary networking, translations, manifestoes, dreams of future colleges, and the "'tutorial' of his letters—instructions that reached hundreds of students, voluntary or involuntary" (50).[16]

Although still roughly chronological in scope, our book is organized thematically, following different aspects of Pound the schoolmaster. Readers looking for enumerated lists of Pound's "best teaching practices" will be at a loss here. Rather than provide such detached bullet points, each chapter in its own way tries to get at the "luminous detail"—that tidbit of cultural history that goes right to the core of the matter—of a specifically Poundian pedagogy. We begin the first chapter early on, recounting Pound's early experiences as a student—looking at why he developed such a distaste for the way that literature was read and taught—and then examining his brief foray into teaching at an academic institution. These early experiences at school were formative for him as a poet, scholar, and teacher. And, while he easily made the material his own, he was never able to adjust or reform the institution in a way that suited his needs. Although he would continually look for opportunities to be awarded graduate degrees he thought were owed to him, he mostly broke ties with American universities. His "instruction," therefore, needed to find new outlets if he was going to challenge the phil-ological way of reading he had been taught. Our second chapter examines Pound's "New Method in Scholarship" by considering *The Spirit of Romance* (a book that sprang from Pound's first lectures) alongside his pieces in *The New Age* called *I Gather the Limbs of Osiris*. In these works, Pound presents what will become his "comparative" method, elucidating for the scholar and pedagogue new phrases such as his "resembling unlikeness" and his more well-known "luminous detail," likened by Pound in *I Gather . . .* to that which "governed knowledge as the switchboard the electric circuit."

Our third chapter follows Pound's pedagogical criticism by considering the poet's incursions into comparative education. While his books *Pavannes and Divisions*, *Instigations*, and *How to Read* were intellectually expansive instructional texts on culture meant for larger, mostly nonacademic audiences, he also retained the hope that they could lay the groundwork for future curricular studies.[17] This is no less the case for Pound's literary anthologies. If the "luminous detail" was akin to a cultural vortex or switchboard, then the anthological arrangement of poems and translations became, for Pound, a vast circuitry, dynamic yet held together by a common center. Jumping ahead a few years, the third chapter concludes by considering Pound's engagement with Eastern culture in light of his and Marcella Spann's (his protégé and muse) anthology *Confucius to Cummings*, which shows just how international Pound's comparative method could be. To educate the masses on a global scale, Pound would also work with numerous small subscription periodicals (writing, editing, and promoting other writers). The fourth chapter details such avenues through which Pound could both promote the new arts and save literary tradition from the dusty halls of academe. (This chapter is a revision and amplification of a chapter in Clifford Wulfman and Robert Scholes's *Modernism in the Magazines*.)

It would have been difficult, in the early part of the century, to predict Pound's precipitous movement into economic/political theory and subsequent wartime radio broadcasts, but, looking back from today, it is easy to see—given his views and personality—how he got there. Our fifth chapter tries to negotiate how the poet-propagandist, who by this time might be considered one of the worst possible role models for a teacher, might, beyond all the hateful rhetoric, still have something valuable to impart. This chapter details the road Pound took to the broadcasts, to the cage in a prisoner-of-war camp, and finally to St. Elizabeths psychiatric hospital, which are all now inescapable aspects of his story. Rather than list the instances of pedagogy throughout the *Cantos*, we focus on one moment—one "luminous detail"—that sheds a great light on the difficult history.[18] Here we proceed with the faith, as Pound confesses toward the very end of his *Cantos*, that "it coheres all right," even if the poet's notes do not. If the *Cantos* "cohered" the way Pound thought the world did, they wouldn't be worth reading, and the learning experience—the struggle, the insights, the labor—would be empty. Poetry is what challenges, not what is—perhaps that is the great lesson of Pound's aesthetic pedagogy, even if he didn't always remember it.

At St. Elizabeths, Pound still fancied himself a schoolmaster, but he was, in Leon Surette's words, "incompetent as a teacher and propagandist of economic theory" (*Pound in Purgatory* 138). Pound was never one to apologize, and even many of his postwar teachings (informal ones to disciples who visited him at the hospital) betray not altogether dangerous motives but the sense that the schoolmaster had contented himself reciting his old lectures. The opposite endeavor—looking *reflexively* at the ways in which art and knowledge, creativity and tradition continually reproduce the world around us—seems the better pedagogical practice for today, and, excluding conspiratorial economic theories (granted, a big exclusion), was one Pound continually endorsed.[19] Still, it is important to understand why and how the "school" of Pound was so instrumental in shaping our cultural attitudes of the twentieth and twenty-first centuries and in seeing, upon reflection, different possibilities for the future. After all, many of Pound's students were unwitting, and their rebelliousness against their "Super Schoolmaster" laid the grounds for new methods and deeper relationships yet to be explored. Pound contradicted himself often, penned letters a hundred years ago as kids send text messages today, and would have found a home for himself nowadays on the AM dial. We do not know whether or not Ezra Pound would enjoy this book. We can only offer that, as for everything else, he would have had something to say about it, and it would have been instructive.

CHAPTER 1

Pounding the Academy

The Poet as Student and Teacher

[Pound] could not keep himself from teaching. In one way or another he was always teaching.

—James Laughlin, 34

After moving at a very early age from the territory of Idaho to Pennsylvania, Ezra Pound began his schooling at the hands, interestingly enough, of a Miss Elliott. Humphrey Carpenter recounts that the young schoolboy, mockingly called "professor," "irritated his first schoolmates with evidence of precociousness: 'I . . . used polysyllables'" (26, 22). A few years hence, he entered the Wyncote Public School. A. David Moody mentions a photograph from the time in which, unlike most of his classmates, Pound appears "serious and considering" (I 6).[1] Pound's earliest letters from there show a personal concern (or a belief that his parents were concerned) with his schoolwork. Writing home in February 1898 from Wyncote, he told of a grade of 75 3/7 in arithmetic ("I went over them all twice and thought I proved them") but reminded his parents that his average would still be around 90. A few months later, with Pound now attending the Cheltenham Military Academy, he spoke of upcoming exams and a "declamation contest, which [he] hope[d] to win" (*EPtP* 5). Appended to this letter was some schoolboy verse:

Four more days until vacation
Then we leave this ———plantation,

No more Latin, no more Greek
No more smoking on the sneak,
No more lessons, no more books
No more teachers sour looks
No more spelling no more grammar
Nor more of the profeshiun crammer (5)

This harmless ditty about school (not too significant though perhaps a welcome window into the turn-of-the-century classroom) shows just how comfortable Pound seems to have been with the youthfully rebellious rhetoric of his classmates. (Pound at this time also always seemed to be aware of what he called his "careless" writing—idiosyncrasies of spelling, which he would later consciously adopt as small jests throughout his poetry, letters, and prose.) In fact, the first letter we have of Pound to his parents (a month before Pound's tenth birthday) has him signing off apologetically with the following appeal, which very well reads like it could have come from today's iPhone: "As nobody has looked over this pleas excuse mistakes" (1). Unlike nearly everything else he would end up writing at the time, teachers would not be looking over and judging this letter.

In 1901, at the age of fifteen, Pound started college at the University of Pennsylvania. He later described his time there in a letter to the poet and eminent anthology editor Louis Untermeyer:

> Entered U. P. Penn at 15 with intention of studying comparative values in literature (poetry) and began doing so unbeknown to the faculty. 1902 enrolled as a special student to avoid irrelevant subjects. . . . (*EP to LU*, 15)

Think of it. Pound told Untermeyer of his "intention of studying comparative values in literature" *in 1901*. Granted, given the date of his letter to Untermeyer (1930), the word "comparative" was most likely an afterthought, but there can be no doubt that the program Pound followed was a sequence in what is now called comparative literature.[2] As it happened so often in his case, part of his academic difficulty was that he was well ahead of the learning curve of the rest of his world. (The first department of comparative literature in this country—at Harvard—was established in 1906.) He tried changing to a special student at Penn to take the courses he wanted rather than those required by an academic system he detested because, in his view, it restricted learning. He did not avoid all requirements, but he got to take a lot of the courses he wanted to study. In 1902 and 1903, he took five courses in Latin, three in history, two in philosophy, and a required English composition course, in which he got grades of B in both semesters. He also took a compulsory course in nineteenth-century English fiction.

A hundred years ago, though, such a course was taught very differently than we have come to know it today (the study of themes, forms, discourses) or even as it was known seventy years ago. As K. K. Ruthven writes, "Pound entered the American academy at one of its more productive moments of crisis, and . . . some of the misgivings he had about what happened to him there are not unrelated to what were recent and contemporary debates about the nature and aims of the humanities" (10). Just a couple years after Pound was born, on the other side of the Atlantic, academics were already debating the scholarly value of teaching "literature." Edward Freeman, a professor at Oxford College, could forestall the study of literature there by arguing that "we are told that the study of literature 'cultivates the taste, educates the sympathies and enlarges the mind.' These are all excellent things, only we cannot examine tastes and sympathies. Examiners must have technical and positive information to examine" (qtd. in Barry 14). Similar debates would be held in American universities for the next few decades. "Teachers who seemed merely to waffle on about literature and culture for a living," Ruthven notes, "were therefore easy targets for another breed of scholar who believed that the only way for humanities subjects to justify their existence in a modern university was by introducing scientific methods into humanistic inquiry" (8). University professors, in turn, who did not want to be accused of emotional shillyshallying resorted to a Germanic style of philology to make literary study as rigorous as classics.[3] And this became how institutionalized English was mostly practiced in the day.

The emphasis on philology was one of the things Pound detested most about how literature was taught to him (this notwithstanding the great irony that Pound's own obscure allusions and dated references would eventually create their own philological industry of a sort).[4] He uses the term philology, as J. Mark Smith explains it, "not only as a body of knowledge concerning defunct languages, or as an institutionally transmitted and endorsed expertise in the deciphering of such languages . . . but as an archive of historical usage charged with synchronic possibility" (770).[5] Pound was critical of this scholarly and pedagogical method from the start. As he wrote a few years later in a blistering local venue:

> Scholars of classic Latin, bound to the Germanic ideal of schol-
> arship, [who] are no longer able as of old to fill themselves with
> the beauty of the classics, and by the very force of that beauty

inspire their students to read Latin widely and for pleasure; nor are they able to make students see clearly whereof classic beauty consists. The scholar is compelled to spend most of his time learning what his author wore and ate, and in endless pondering over some utterly unanswerable question of textual criticism. . . . The scholar is bowed down to this Germanic ideal of scholarship, the life work of whose servants consists in gathering blocks to build a pyramid that will be of no especial use except as a monument, and whose greatest reward is the possibility that the servant may have his name inscribed on the under side of some half-prominent stone, where by a chance—a slender one—some future stone-gatherer will find it. ("Raphaelite Latin" 31)

What's more, American teachers were not even good philologists. Pound called their scholarship a "parody of German philology" (*Letters* 196), and he called its practitioners "sterile professors [expounding] a pasteurized, Bostonized imitation of Leipzig" ("The Renaissance" 87). Under this system, "[s]pecialists," as Ruthven writes, quoting Pound's *Guide to Kulchur* and the *Cantos*, "accordingly became 'book-fools,' licensed to spend their time 'obscuring the texts with philology'" (13). One of Pound's most damning critiques of literary philology comes through in *How to Read*, published originally in the *New York Herald Tribune* in 1929 and then as its own book in 1931. (We discuss this book more fully in chapter 3.) "Literary instruction in our 'institutions of learning,'" Pound writes, "was, at the beginning of this century, cumbrous and inefficient" (5). In a footnote to the reprinted version of this essay, Pound would substitute the phrase "institutions for the obstruction of learning" (*Literary Essays* 15). The "dead and uncorrelated system" of education "lacked sense and co-ordination" and "the dimension of depth" (*How* 7, 5, 13).

Pound's words about the stagnation of intellectual and aesthetic engagement with the literary can hold true in some quarters of academia today, where it is very easy for an instructor, having lost all inquisitiveness in the marvel of literature, to continue preaching from his or her yellowing notes of forty years ago. Pound writes, "[i]n extenuation of their miscalculations we may admit that any error or clumsiness of method has sunk into, or been hammered into one man, over a period of years, probably continues as an error—not merely passively, but as an error still being propagated, consciously or unconsciously, by a number of educators, from laziness, from habits, or from natural cussedness" (7–8). Lassitude is the enemy of learning, of art, and—one can see how Pound's thinking would trail off into dangerous territory here—of commerce. Movement and dynamism are central. Anything else, as he would write in his Canto 45, is "CONTRA NATURAM." But before Pound had arrived there, he would still decry the torpor of the German philological method: "One was asked to remember what some critic (deceased) had said, scarcely to consider whether his views were still valid, or ever had been very intelligent" (7). The method "decoys intelligent people away from the central issues of their times by offering them the lure of becoming authorities on marginal specialisms such as 'ablauts, hair-length, foraminifera,' and spending the rest of their professional lives in th[is] kind of stultifying 'research' " (Ruthven 12). In short, such "education" destroyed the beauty of the arts and was an impediment to learning and enjoyment, which, as Pound understood them, ought to be the enduring motivations of teachers and students alike.[6]

It was not so much a question of the work that Pound did not want to (or could not) do, but, rather, the work that he thought needed to be done.[7] Pound was disenchanted, in Ruthven's words, with "two sets of assumptions, one about what constituted knowledge in the humanities, and the other about the most appropriate ways of institutionalizing that knowledge" (7–8). He did not want to avoid Latin, though he did avoid Greek for the most part.[8] He really wanted to study comparative values. He wanted criticism, not philology, to be the rigorous heart of literary study. Here, too, he was ahead of the curve. The later "New Criticism" would, in part, be a response to his efforts and those of T. S. Eliot (who would distance himself from it), but it could only happen after that work had been done, along with a serious new literature that required rigorous criticism and interpretation—literature that included T. S. Eliot's *The Waste Land*, James Joyce's *Ulysses*, Virginia Woolf's *The Waves*, and ultimately Pound's *The Cantos* as well. But while the New Critical methods emphasized the autonomy of the aesthetic object, Pound would continually note its relationship to politics and history. Hence, the mid-century (and after) popularity of Pound among poets and opposition figures and his notable absence from institutions of higher education.

Feeling that he had reached a dead end at Penn, Pound sought another way toward an academic degree.[9] Advised, as David Moody speculates persuasively, by Carlos Tracy Chester, a graduate of Hamilton College in upstate New York, Pound took the train to Clinton and met with the president of Hamilton—the Dickensianly-named Dr. Melanchthon Woolsey

Stryker—who admitted him, gave him credit for his work at Penn, and allowed him to study what he wanted, insisting on only a small number of required courses. Pound, in turn, followed the "Latin-Scientific Course," which allowed German and French to replace Greek as a requirement.

The faculty was also accommodating. An excellent professor of French, William Pierce Sheppard, gave him a special course in Provençal, and the German professor, Herman Brandt, allowed him to skip the prose and concentrate on German poetry. Pound's social life at school, however, was not much better than it had been at Penn.[10] He had trouble making friends, but he did not seem to mind. Shortly after his arrival in Hamilton, he wrote to ask his father to speak to the vice provost at Penn and find out if he could get credit there for the work he was doing as an undergraduate (*EPtP* 13). That is, he was thinking about returning from college to the university "where I belong," as he put it. He thought things over during the summer after his first year at Hamilton, and wrote to his mother to point out that "at the end of senior year there I shall be able to speak French, German & Spanish fairly well & have my reading knowledge of Italian in reserve" (20–21). He felt that if he returned to Penn he would have "no foreign language in useful shape" (21), and it was clear that having a real command of the main European languages was his academic goal. So he returned to Hamilton for another year in 1904. He seemed to be very busy and professed as much to his parents: "With double French, anglo-saxon, Spanish, analytics & three hours of Prex's hot air I expect to come home a corpse" (23). A letter to his mother tells us a number of things about his academic life:

> This being the first evening I have had time to breathe I went down & saw Dr. Wood for a while. Talked his trip abroad for a while & then went down and talked books etc. with Bib [Prof. Ibbotson].
>
> Find Anglo-Saxon very fascinating. Also French of Descartes & Pascal. Eng. Lit. Comedy before Shakespeare. & Junior French. Tragedy. Corneille's "Cid" just now. . . .
>
> Altogether I expect to have about time enough to take ½ breath every 75 hours & 1/3 sneeze to [sic] every 150 weeks. However the work is very fascinating, & if I can get it done in any respectable manner it will be very nice.
>
> Only I expect to come home on ice. (23)

This message shows just how comfortable Pound was with the faculty of the college. "With Ibbotson," Moody writes, Pound "felt free to drop in casually, even at late hours. . . . They would smoke and talk together by the fire" (I 23). Other letters to his parents are similarly full of comments about his visits to the homes of his teachers. Hamilton was a small college in those days, with fewer than two hundred students and just eighteen faculty members. Almost all of the students lived in fraternities. Pound, who tried for a fraternity but was not admitted (most likely because of a blackballing from students who knew him at Penn), lived a different kind of life than did most of the undergraduates (Carpenter 47). His social life involved his mentors as much as his fellow students—if not more. He had nicknames for most of the faculty (like "Bib") that he used in his letters home, and he spent a lot of time outside classes talking with them. Pound would carry this individual style of mentorship with him throughout his teaching life. (There are many things one can say about Pound's tutelage—and we say a lot more about it later—but one thing he was not was selfish with his time.) He was also engaged in class topics, if not so much in class requirements. In the letter above, he uses the expression "very fascinating" twice to describe courses that few of his fellow students were likely to have regarded in this way. He also complains to his mother about how hard he is working, but the last lines quoted above almost make a youthful poem ("nice" / "ice") in which academic pleasures and pains are blended neatly. He really seems to want to learn what he is studying, no matter how hard it will be to do it "in a respectable manner."

In November 1904 he took a "little vacation," as he called it in a letter to his father, going to Ithaca, the site of Cornell University, where he was able to "spend yesterday P. M. in the library looking up Celtic philology & translations of the Vedas" (*EPtP* 32). A few weeks later, he was telling his mother, "I find I'm requiring more exactness of myself which I suppose is good—(& the first sign of scholasticism?)" (40). That January, he began informally teaching some fellow students: "We began today by dissecting Emerson's 'Self-reliance'. It happened to be a freshman 'rhet' assignment. So I butted in & helped 'em tear it out" (42). By February, he was able to report that he had "gathered a very decent gang of freshman who have begun to meet here decently & in order on Tuesday evenings" (45). In later letters, he refers to this group as his "kindergarten." He met with the group regularly, "teaching" and learning various subjects in various ways: "Charming evening with Bill [Prof. Shepard]. have gathered stuff to start my studies in Provencal & extended work in Old French & learned what books I must gather from the four corners of the earth" (48).

Pound's way of learning at Hamilton was strongly based on personal relationships with the faculty there, as this passage from a letter to his mother amply demonstrates:

Evening. Called on Bill he was pleased with what I had been about during the week & is willing to give me more Dante which is not catalogued next term. as this is not usual called on Little Greek [Prof. Edward Fitch] who has charge of schedules in general & he brought forth his wife that I might be well received & seemed well disposed to the Dante arrangement.

Going my homeward way at 10 P.M. I noticed Bib's lights ablaze & knowing that he is still mostly college boy despite his family and professorship I dropped in & we smoked & ate & talked for an hour or two longer. All three calls were very pleasant. (49)

With the cooperation of the faculty, Pound was turning Hamilton into the sort of college that he wanted to attend, and into a kind of model for what he thought a college ought to be—a place where a student could really learn something.

Pound was following his intuitive feeling that the way to learn how to be a poet was to study the techniques of earlier poets. That is, he felt that a certain kind of scholarship was essential for someone who wanted to do creative work. He learned a lot from Professor Ibbotson's course in Anglo-Saxon, for example, which went beyond philology to the technique of Old English poetry. He was also interested in the lives of the early poets, especially the troubadours of Provence, and in the way that their poetry connected their sometimes chaotic lives to a rigorous technique of versification. The "values" in "comparative values" were technical and personal, aesthetic and ethical. Not exactly "beauty" and "truth," but form and life were, for Pound, the essential matters of a literary education. And the purpose of a literary education was to produce people who could use language with a high degree of skill. Ruthven writes, "By subverting what the official education system offered him, he managed to develop concurrently a theory of transhistorical and universal literary value which would enable him, as he was to phrase it in his first book of criticism, to 'weigh Theocritus and Mr Yeats with one balance'" (6; *The Spirit of Romance* vi). Here we find another major difference between the type of school Pound envisioned and what the New Criticism that followed him espoused. For Pound, one learned to read in order to write like those whose work one read. For the New Critics, one learned to read to appreciate rather than to emulate and challenge. Pound was an academic with an agenda far different from that of most degree-granting institutions—to put learning in the service of creativity. At this time, Pound was also thinking of teaching beyond Hamilton, even applying for a job at Central High School in Philadelphia, jokingly telling his mother that he would take a "position as a bellboy" (59). He also thought of teaching at the Cheltenham Military Academy, where he had gone to school as a boy: "I could hold down Latin at Cheltenham with less trouble than any other job I could get . . . [but] will try kindergarten if you like better" (62). He graduated from Hamilton in 1905 with a PhB instead of an AB.

Rather than begin a teaching career (his prospects were still slim), Pound decided to register as a candidate for the PhD at Penn. During the next academic year, he took courses toward the MA in Romance languages and lived at home, studying Provençal, Old French, Italian, and Spanish, and taking a seminar in the Latin authors Catullus and Martial. Still, for reasons both personal and professional, Pound was not always able to study the authors he really wanted to study.[11] After he completed work for the MA, Pound was helped by Hugo Rennert, one of his professors, to get a fellowship that paid tuition and $500 for work on a PhD, and he began research for a dissertation on the *gracioso* (clown or jester) in the plays of Lope de Vega, under the direction of Rennert (see Carpenter 58–65; Moody I 27–33).

In the spring of 1906, Pound sailed for Europe to carry on his research in the libraries of Madrid, Paris, and London. After landing in Gibraltar, he moved on to Madrid, where he worked in the library when it wasn't closed for the frequent feast days, writing to his mother on May 20 to say that he had "Finished Lope's 'Castelvines y Monteses' his treatment of the Romeo & Juliet story, and have squeezed several thesis pages out of that & the Francesilla" (*EPtP* 77). At the end of May, he reported that he was about to "finish a sort of bibliography of Lope's inedited mss. this week and get out of the heat" (79), telling his father a few days later that he had "just finished a report on over sixty unpublished or little known mss. of Lope's plays in the Bibliotecca National & feel learned as hell" (80). He then went on to Paris, where he was disappointed in the library but loved the old bookshops, writing reviews of two books by Péladan he found there—reviews that were published in the September *Book News Monthly*: *Origine etesthetique de la tragédie* and *Le secret des troubadours* (83). Off to London, he found the British Museum "very important not only for major work but for minor" (85). In July, he returned to the United States and his studies at Penn, but everything there took a turn for the worse. What happened then is neatly summed up by the editors of his letters:

> According to the doctoral degree requirements he now needed
> to add a further dozen credits to the dozen earned for the MA.

> In the fall he did six courses with Rennert, all in the Romance literatures—Old Provençal, Old French, Early Italian Poets, Dante, Old Spanish, Spanish Drama—and a further course in French Phonetics for which he received no credit. In the Spring he signed up for five courses in the English Department, fell out with the professors, and refused to submit himself to examination by them. His Harrison Fellowship was not renewed, and he abandoned the doctorate. (*EPtP* 86)

"I have spatted with nearly everybody," Pound wrote, but the final straw might have been when he, in his own words, "achieved the distinction of being the only student [who] flunked in J[osiah] P[enniman]'s course in the history of literary criticism" (qtd. in Stock 61).[12] Although Pound would confess a boredom of sorts with the doctoral requirements, he would staunchly defend his interest in the arts—something he thought no one at Penn truly understood. "So far as I know," he writes, "I was the only student who was making any attempt to understand the subject of literary criticism and the only student with any interest in the subject" (qtd. in Stock 61; see also Moody I 29–30). Although he quit Penn at this point, he tried more than once in the future—usually enlisting the help of his father—to pry that doctorate out of the university, but these attempts were always blocked by the English faculty.[13]

Finding himself out of graduate school in 1907, Pound began his teaching career at Wabash College in Crawfordsville, Indiana, comprising the entirety of its Romance Languages department: "Wabash nailed & everything most delightful. whole d—d dept. French, Spanish & Italian to run as I bang please" (*EPtP* 87). Not surprisingly, during his time there, he was not a teacher like any other, and much of his instruction took place informally outside the classroom.[14] "Secret of teaching is a bit theatrical," he later wrote to T. C. Wilson: "Simply act the best prof you have known. The irritation of fools won't come from stewddents *but* from the 'orthorities'" (September 24, 1933; Paige 248). The orthorities would indeed soon get irritated; this, following his landladies' complaints to the college about certain guests (theatrical women) the young teacher housed. Moody speculates that this event was contrived by Pound, and Carpenter surmises that Dr. Mackintosh, the president of Wabash College, "and the Trustees had other reasons besides the actress for wishing to see the back of [Pound]. The college magazine had pointed out his repeated absences from chapel, and there was his constant smoking and his language, even a horrid rumour that he put rum in his tea" (81).[15] But, as Emily Mitchell Wallace has convincingly argued after studying the Wabash administrative archive, Pound's relationship with the college was not as strained as scholars have come to believe.[16] Pound, though, always liked to run things as he bang pleased, and he could not get away with doing everything he pleased at Wabash, and his hospitality led to the termination of his formal academic career. If Pound wanted to be a "super schoolmaster," he would have to find a place other than a university to do it—however much he kept his thoughts on reforming the institution.

He headed for Europe in March 1908, and proceeded from Gibraltar to Venice, where he had his first book of poems published at his own expense and met a Miss Norton whose father (Charles Eliot Norton) was, as Pound said, "our foremost American Dante scholar" with another relative (Charles William Eliot) who "has a gentle little job as President of Harvard" (*EPtP* 112). He also began teaching Italian to tourists and noted that there might be an academic job for him at the University of Idaho. While in Venice, he sent articles and stories to American magazines, telling his father that he "had learned a little of what they [the magazines] don't want" (116). He also kept thinking of getting that PhD, writing to the registrar of Baliol College, Oxford "for particulars as to the Doctorate" (118). When his book of poems was printed, he urged his parents to generate publicity for it back home, suggesting that the Philadelphia newspapers might notice "another University man in the Literary Field. Mr. E. P. Sometime Fellow in U. Penn. a promising magazine writer, etc." (121).

Writing to his father about a possible academic post in Moscow, Idaho, he said

1st I can teach romance languages

2nd I can teach em to just as many people as can be packed into a class room.

3rd I don't give a rip whether I ever teach romance languages

4th Let the mountain come to Mo'ammed. . . .

6th Such details as Ph. D. are of no weight at all against a bit of personality. the sort that gets the gang together and makes things move. (125)

Mixed feelings about both an academic post and the doctorate come through in the letters, as these matters were clearly never very far from his mind. He wanted an advanced degree because it had eluded him and because he knew it would open up many doors, but if he wasn't going to get it, then, to steal a phrase he liked to use, be d——d with it! There were other ways to go about things, and Pound, possibly more than anyone else in his vast circles over the years, was able to "make things move." He quite properly understood that the PhD did not guarantee good teaching, which depended more on personal qualities and an ability to break out of the tedious modes of the institution. However, though he often mocked the degree he wanted, he never mocked the learning he gained and cherished. When his time in Venice came to an end in August, he moved on toward London, where he hoped, among other things, to meet a poet he really admired, W. B. Yeats. As it happened, he also had plans for teaching there. He describes how this materialized in the "Post-Post-Script" to the 1968 edition of his book, first published in 1910, *The Spirit of Romance*:

> A fellow named Smith put me on the road which led to the publication of this book. . . . he gave me a note to a man named Sullivan who had something to do with the Covent Garden Market. I do not know how, but he persuaded the London Polytechnic to let me give a round of lectures there: The Development of Literature in Renaissance Europe. These were a very raw summary of things in Rennart's Seminar at the University of Pennsylvania; out of their condensation, this volume. (9)

The title and author as they were given in that first edition of 1910 are also significant for our purposes: "*The Spirit of Romance: An Attempt to Define Somewhat the Charm of the Pre-Renaissance Literature of Latin Europe*, by Ezra Pound, M. A." Like Dora Marsden, the founding editor of *The Freewoman* magazine and its successors, who would always appear on the masthead of her magazines as "Dora Marsden, B.A." (rare for a woman at the time), Pound wanted his academic standing to be visible at the head of his work. This urge was balanced, however, by his use of that very unacademic word "*Charm*" in the title of his book, which was, as he says, a "condensation" of what he had said in his lectures.

When he arrived in London, he wrote to his father, "I've got a fool idea that I'm going to make good in this bloomin village" (*EPtP* 128), and he did make good, ultimately. His success was partly social. That is, he met people and impressed them, and his lectures became a part of that process.

People he had met socially came to hear him speak, and those who heard him speak extended further invitations where he could meet other people. As he told his father, "If I can hang on here in London I can get literary position that would take ten years at home. . . . I don't think I'll need more than one London season" (130), as though literary achievement were a fiscal year. (He wasn't wrong about this.) All the time, though, he continued to think of academic as well as social success: "If I could get enough into my head to take my Doctorate at the Sorbonne it would not be a bad thing" (132). Clearly, he saw his stay in London as a campaign, which he was waging on several fronts, one being social and another academic.[17] He thought at that time that his lectures for the Polytechnic, which were getting scheduled, might lead to a stable appointment: "If I get permanently into the Polytechnique. It'll mean that I get 3 or 4 months a year in London" (135). "Of course," he added, "this is all a pipe dream."

Some of his dreams, though, were quite specific and not unrealistic. He hoped, for example, that a contract from the Polytechnic might be used to convince "the Univ extension" back home to give him some teaching work, and he also told his father that "if I can meet the right people, the results may not be too long delayed" (138). He kept his parents closely informed, because he still depended on them for funds, which they duly sent him, along with whatever else he requested. The Polytechnic had a brochure printed announcing Pound's first series of lectures, described as "A Short Introductory Course on The Development of the Literature of Southern Europe . . . by Ezra Pound, M.A. (Sometime Fellow in the University of Pennsylvania)" (140–41). Clearly his academic credentials, such as they were, remained an important aspect of his campaign to conquer London. There were fifty-five people at his first lecture, he reported, as an indication that he was beginning to make his mark. He also now had a serious publisher, Elkin Matthews, interested in his work and ready to publish *Personae* in the spring. He received social invitations from people who had attended his lectures, and he reported to his mother that he had had tea with a certain "Mrs. Shakespear who is undoubtedly the most charming woman in London" (156). Mrs. (Olivia) Shakespear, a playwright and novelist, would ultimately become his mother-in-law.

Pound's social network kept expanding in 1909. He met the poet and scholar Lawrence Binyon (who was also offering public lectures) in February and was introduced at a Poet's Club dinner by Elkin Mathews. During this time, he also kept trying to land academic work near Philadelphia, asking his father to look into Temple University for the winter and Princeton for the summer. Meanwhile, in London, he met some "friends of Yeats" and reported that he was "getting much closer to people" (159). One of those people was May Sinclair, whose *Mary Olivier* would later be serialized alongside *Ulysses* in *The Little Review*. (Sinclair became an enthusiast of both Pound and Joyce.) In his letters, Pound keeps weighing the relative merits of staying in London to meet important literary people and coming back to the United States and teaching at some place like Temple (164). However much he thought of returning home, his social life in London was clearly beginning to pay off. His "Sestina Altaforte" appeared in *The English Review* in June, along with a review of his *Personae*, preparing the way for his "Ballad of the Goodly Fere" in October, which brought him considerable attention, none as important as that from the editor of that magazine, Ford Madox Hueffer (later Ford), who became a lifelong friend and supporter.[18] Pound still speculated about teaching summer school at Princeton and returning in the fall for more lectures at the Polytechnic. Clearly he saw the academic side, the poetic side, and the social side of his life as working together toward a common goal not only of recognition, but also of giving him the ability to champion, unlike most of his teachers, what was so great about the arts.

By this time, he had met what he called "the New Age Crowd," who wanted to feature a review of his new book of poems, *Personae*, and he finally met Yeats and spent "about five hours" with him at the end of April, reminding his parents in a later letter that "Yeats is the greatest poet of our time" (170, 171). While he and his father corresponded about "a Trinity job" (Trinity College in Hartford), *Personae* was reviewed in *The New Age* by F. S. Flint, leading to Pound's meetings with a group of young poets who gathered around the writer T. E. Hulme. (Hulme, too, had academic leanings, lectured on Henri Bergson, and later defended abstraction in visual art in the pages of *The New Age*.) The group was seriously interested in aesthetic theory, knew a good deal about European culture, and had quasi-academic discussions that paved the way for the movement later known as Imagisme. At the end of July, Pound was crowing about having been lampooned in *Punch* and moaning about having to give "21 be d—d lectures at Polytec" (177). His campaign was advancing on all fronts. By August he was attending gatherings at Violet Hunt and F. M. Hueffer's "South Lodge," where people like the novelist Rebecca West and the painter and future collaborator of Pound, Wyndham Lewis, were likely to turn up.

Writing to his mother, he told her he was working on the "Beginnings of romance poetry"—which he clearly thought of as both a series of lectures and a book—and that he was finding the work interesting. He also made a revealing statement about his methodology: "it will have to cauterize the germanists & surpass them in accuracy. or at least equal them. & yet seem careless (all this is not for general quotation)" (184; *mit Entschuldigungen*). The pedagogical desire to be both accurate and rhetorically "careless" feels a bit oxymoronic, but it describes Pound's future writings well. He also asks for books from home to support his research and alternately complains about the work he is doing and revels in it. In October he reported that "Hueffer & Miss Hunt are trying to stir up the very very gifted to have me lecture privately" (197). Then, in November, he conferred with his father about the possibility of a "Rhodes Scholarship from Idaho," which would have made him a student at Oxford, if he had received it. In December he noted that he had earned some money from "private teaching." The academic side of his life remained quite visible during this period of his development, and he was soon discussing with his mother an article on the proposed establishment of an American Academy, a topic to which he would return again and again:

> of course an academy never has a beneficial effect on art. But it gives the dam'd canaille something to bow down to & thereby makes life easier for the artist, especially for the artist who is a bit of a hypocrite. . . . I suppose I'll join the dam thing when I'm asked—adv. mighty force adv. (209)

In December he gave a talk at the Poet's Club, where he had once listened to George Bernard Shaw and Hilaire Belloc, telling his parents that the talk was taken from the second chapter of the book he was working on in connection with his Polytechnic lectures. His talks were becoming the foundation of a new pedagogical method. His parents, of course, were still hoping he might come home from London. He complied to the extent of saying that he would apply for a fellowship at Penn, observing that "I suppose no decent job is open 'till I take their rotten Ph. D." (212), and asking again about possible openings at Princeton. He also answered a question—for his mother, but also for himself—about his work on *The Spirit of Romance*: "The book as discipline? humph ! ! yes it does solidify the lecture material. Delivering 'notions' to an audience is an uninteresting performance but it does not bore me much" (213). One can see in his choice of word "notions" how far he had strayed from the philological method he was taught, and how very unapologetic he was about his pedagogical wandering. He wrote his mother shortly after that:

> In case the U. P. should not feel sufficient need of me to overcome its natural repugnance: Please insert the following "ad" in some reputable daily.

POET
Out of a Job

Specialties: incisive speech, sarcasm, meditations, irony (at special rates), ze grande manair, (to order) will do travel, or stand unhitched while being fed. Price 1£ per. hr.—special rates for steady customers.

Now that ought to dew the job tidy like.

And he added that his life was going on as usual: "Classes, lectures, scholarly prose works, proofs of Canzoni—regular routine. plus a certain amount of tea & conversation. Harmless variety of existence" (216–17). Before it would become a regular practice, Pound knew that the university would be the place for the modern poet to land a job. He applied for the fellowship at Penn, and, although his dissertation director tried to help, the director could not prevail against the belief of the faculty that Pound was not "intending to continue as a professor" (219). The department's assessment of Pound was no doubt partly accurate (as Pound certainly would not have wanted to continue as a normal professor), but it missed Pound's genuine interest in teaching and scholarship. He had, in fact, applied for what he called "a better job at Hobart College. Geneva. N. Y." (219), which he also did not get. Unable to land a job in that academy, he started envisioning the sort of place that might actually employ him.

In 1912 he wrote a series of articles about the United States for *The New Age* in two series: the first called *Patria Mia* and the second, dropping the Latin, simply *America: Chances and Remedies*. The articles covered a wide range of subjects (and we return to them later on), but we want to touch briefly on his musings on a "respectable college of the arts" (*NA* 11.25:588), which he thought would be a perfect fit for a major city like New York, Chicago, or San Francisco. Pound imagined a school of "one hundred members, chosen from all the arts, sculptors, painters, dramatists, musical composers, architects, scholars of the art of verse, engravers, etc." The inclusion of "scholars of the art of verse" is the uniquely Poundian touch, because they are the only representatives of verbal art on the list. No doubt he saw this as a role for himself—or someone like him, if any such person existed. But he wanted a school of the arts where artists in different media could learn from one another. Pointing out that it was possible in the United States to get "subsidised for 'research,'" but not for verbal art, he urged the creation of "an efficient college of the arts, an institution not unlike a 'graduate school' without professors." In literary studies, we now have specialized programs in "creative writing," to be sure, but Pound wanted a mixture of the arts, and he wanted people learned in the traditions of those arts to be among the artist-teachers in his ideal college. University departments, as they were, stifled such discussions across the arts. Pound also felt that American artists were simply copying European artists in every field but architecture, and he was looking for an academic way of dealing with that problem. He found a homely parable to describe it:

> It is not enough that the artist have impulse, he must be in a position to know what has been done and what is yet to do. He must not be like the plough-boy on the lonely farm who spent his youth devising agricultural machinery and found when he went out into the world that all his machines had been invented before he was born. (588)

Pound's words—reminiscent of Eliot's in "Tradition and the Individual talent"—could be a cautionary tale for students of every culture and every generation, including, perhaps, for a younger Pound himself. Here, though, Pound sought to combat this feeling of torpidity, the sense that students arrive at college enthusiastic for learning only to find themselves after a few months with no real reason for continuing to learn. He proposed various remedies for this, such as putting "the actual artist" in university seminars, or establishing what he called "The super college." Assuming that his readers might think his proposal crazy, he added, "have patience, I may be nevertheless in the grip of my lucid interval" (*NA* 13.2:34).

A few years later, Pound put his proposal in print, advertising it as though it were on its way (most likely to help with fundraising). The 1914 "Announcement," taking up two pages in Harriet Shaw Weaver and Dora Marsden's *The Egoist*, is a remarkable vision for academic instruction, especially considering that Europe was just a few months into the Great War. In it, Pound aims "at an intellectual status no lower than that attained by the courts of the Italian Renaissance." (Its value is such that we hasten to print it in its entirety.)[19]

everything. In fact, says the first husband, "she has devoured your soul" . . . "as savages devour their enemies." He, too, has experienced the sweating capacity of the creature and has no illusions left about her real nature. These plays of his, in spite of their big cargo of strong meat, are not dramatic. They are dissection, not soul-movement as in Ibsen's plays. Still, they will be read by the complete misogynist, who in the reading thereof will grow as young and lusty as an eagle. They will be distributed in tens of thousands by the Anti-Suffs. They will be compared with Ibsen's by students who are undecided whether women are angels (Ibsen) or men are gods (Strindberg). And they will be avoided by the Victorian young Miss with a silk shoe and a simper.

HUNTLY CARTER.

PRELIMINARY ANNOUNCEMENT OF THE COLLEGE OF ARTS.*

IT has been noted by certain authors that London is the capital of the world, and "Art is a matter of capitals." At present many American students who would have sought Vienna or Prague or some continental city are disturbed by war. To these The College of Arts offers a temporary refuge and a permanent centre.

We draw the attention of new students to the fact that no course of study is complete without one or more years in London. Scholarly research is often but wasted time if it has not been first arranged and oriented in the British Museum.

The London collections are if not unrivalled at least unsurpassed. The Louvre has the Venus and the Victory but the general collection of sculpture in the Museum here is, as a whole, the finer collection. The National Gallery is smaller than the Louvre but it contains no rubbish.

Without chauvinism we can very easily claim that study in London is at least as advantageous as study elsewhere, and that a year's study in London by no means prevents earlier or later study in other capitals.

The American student coming abroad is usually presented with two systems of study, firstly, that of "institutions" for the most part academic, sterile, professorial; secondly, instruction by private teachers often most excellent, often the reverse.

The College of Arts offers contact with artists of established position, creative minds, men for the most part who have already suffered in the cause of their art. Recognising the interaction of the arts, the inter-stimulous, and inter-enlightenment, we have gathered the arts together, we recommend that each student shall undertake some second or auxiliary subject, though this is in all cases left to his own inclination. We recognise that certain genius runs deep and often in one groove only, and that some minds move in the language of one medium only. But this does not hold true for the general student. For him and for many of the masters our art is the constant illuminator of another, a constant refreshment.

The college prepares two sorts of instruction; one for those who intend a career in some single art, who desire practical and technical instruction, a second for those who believe that learning is an adornment, a gracious and useless pleasure, that is to say for serious art students and for the better sort of dilettanti.

The cost of instruction will vary from £20 to £100, depending on how much the student wishes to do himself and how much he wishes to have done for him. We recognise that the great majority of students now coming to Europe are musical students, the next most numerous class are painters and sculptors; we nevertheless, believe that there are various other studies which would be pursued if students knew where to go for instruction.

* This interesting prospectus comes to hand. Its value is such that we hasten to print it entire.

We try not to duplicate courses given in formal institutions like the University of London, or purely utilitarian courses like those of Berlitz. London is itself a larger university, and the best specialists are perhaps only approachable in chance conversation. We aim at an intellectual status no lower than that attained by the courts of the Italian Renaissance.

Our organisation is not unlike that of a University graduate-school, and is intended to supplement the graduate instruction in "arts." This instruction is offered to anyone who wants it, not merely to those holding philological degrees.

A knowledge of morphology is not essential to the appreciation of literature, even the literature of a forgotten age or decade.

M. Arnold Dolmetsch's position in the world of music is unique, and all music lovers are so well aware of it, that one need not here pause to proclaim it. Painting and sculpture are taught by the most advanced and brilliant men of our decade, but if any student desires instruction in the earlier forms of the art, instruction in representative painting awaits him. The faculty as arranged to date, though it is still but a partial faculty, is perhaps our best prospectus.

SCULPTURE.

Atelier of Sculpture　...　...　...　GAUDIER-BRZESKA.

PAINTING.

Atelier of Painting　...　...　...　WYNDHAM LEWIS
　Assistant, and Director of the Atelier, H. SANDERS.
Atelier of Design　...　...　EDWARD WADSWORTH
Representational Painting (miniature)
Private instruction　...　...　...　MATHILDE HUHN
Portraiture, and the History of Occidental Painting
REGINALD WILENSKI
　(Writer on the History of the Fine Arts to
　　　"The Athenæum")
Etching and Dry Point　...　...　WM. P. ROBINS

MUSIC.

ANCIENT MUSIC ...　...　...　... ARNOLD DOLMETSCH
MODERN INSTRUMENTS:
　Violin　...　...　... SENYEI (arrangement pending)
　'Cello　...　...　...　...　...　FELIX SALMOND
　　　Assistant, BEATRICE EVELINE.
　Piano　...　...　...　...　... K. R. HEYMAN
　　　Assistant, GLADYS HAMILTON.
Voice　...　...　...　...　... ROBERT DE BROUCE
Diseuse　...　...　...　...　...　AUGEITE FÖRET
Lecturer on modern Russian Composers ... EDWIN EVANS

LETTERS.

Comparative Poetry ...　...　... EZRA POUND, M.A.
　Author of "Personæ," "Exultations," "The
　Spirit of Romance" (a study of the mediæval
　poetry of latin Europe), "The Approach to
　Paris" (a series of papers dealing with the
　contemporary poetry of France, "New
　Age"), etc., translator of Guido Caval-
　canti's "Ballate" and of the "Canzoni of
　Arnaut Daniel"; Contributor to "The
　Quarterly Review," "The Fortnightly Re-
　view," etc., Sometime Fellow in Romanics
　of the University of Pennsylvania, now in
　charge of the late Ernest Fenollosa's papers
　dealing with Chinese lyric poetry and the
　Japanese stage.

Russian Novelists　... IVAN KORSHUNE (JOHN COURNOS)
　Translator of various tales by Gogol,
　Korolenko, Dostoyevsky, Gorky. Turgenev,
　Chekov, Andreyev, Sologub, Remizov, etc.
　(World's Masterpiece series), Contributor to
　"The Forum," "Lippincott's," "The
　Mask," etc.

Figure 1.1. Pound's "Preliminary Announcement" in *The Egoist* page 1/2.

Russian Contemporary Thought   ZINAIDA VANGEROWA
    Published works: Seven volumes of essays in
    Russian. Contributor to "The Fortnightly
    Review," etc.

Dramatic-Criticism   ...   CECIL INSLEE-DURRIAN
    Late dramatic critic of "The New York
    Tribune," general European representative
    of the Oliver Morosco Company (Los Angeles
    and New York).

PHOTOGRAPHY.

Studio   ...   .   ALVIN LANGDON COBURN

CRAFTS.

(in course of arrangement).

Silver and Ornament ...   ...   LABORATORY SANDHEIM
Pottery   ...   .
Furniture and Reproduction...
Book-binding (Plain Letter Illuminating, Tool-
    work, Inlay, Restoration) ... G. SUTCLIFFE
Printing   ...   .   CHAS. T. JACOBI (Man-
    aging Partner of the
    Chiswick Press).

Engraving, Wood-cut ...   ...
Metalwork   ...   .
Enamel   ...   .
Jewels   ...   .
    "The Crafts become the Fine Arts when men of
    sufficient culture maintain them."

THE DANCE.

XVI. Century Dances   ...   ...   MRS. DOLMETSCH

Communications should be addressed to the Secre-
tarial Offices, 5, Holland Place Chambers, Kensington,
London, W., to Vaughn Baron, Sec.

As a supplement to the various courses in arts and
crafts, we point out the value of individual research in,
and study of, the various collections of the South
Kensington and British Museums. We will en-
deavour to save the student's time by giving general
direction for such work, and initiation in method, apart
from the usual assistance offered by the regular Museum
officials.

In certain rare cases, the American college student,
desiring more than his degree, will find it possible to
spend his Junior or Sophomore year in London and
return to his own University for graduation. Those
desiring to do this should of course submit to us their
plans of study, together with a clear statement of their
requirements for graduation at the home college. Such
students will have to possess rather more than average
intelligence.

If intending to take graduate work for higher degrees,
they may, however, find that this form of recess will give
them a distinct advantage over their colleagues, such
as fully to compensate for the inconvenience and derangement of undergraduate studies. It is always open
to them, to fill in routine courses by application to the
University of London (that is to say, ordinary mathe-
matics or classics) pursuing said courses in conjunction
with their special work with the College of Arts.

(End of Prospectus).

REMARKS.—The college should come as a boon to
various and numerous students who would otherwise be
fugging about in continental pensions, meeting one
single teacher who probably wishes them in the inferno,
and dependent for the rest on fellow boarders and public
amusements.

Secondly, it would seem designed to form itself into
a centre of intelligent and intellectual activity, rather
than a cramming factory where certain data are pushed
into the student regardless of his abilities or predilections.

We note with interest that M. Dolmetsch's book on
"The Interpretation of The Music of the XVII. and
XVIII. centuries" is announced as about to appear.

THE THEATRE.

THE theatre is the staging for emotion; has been,
    must be. . . .
Emotion invariably translates itself into action,
immediate or deferred;
Never in words.
Words are a waste product of emotion and do not
concern it.
Thus the intellectual drama is not drama at all.
It is the "acting version" of a novel.
This much for Shakespeare.
The new school Strindberg.—Tchekhov.

    *   *   *

A fool is not known as such by his words.
His actions are the clue to his madness.
Similarly the hero, the villain.
The secret springs which move them and which the
dramatist considers himself bound to expose have but a
literary value and do not concern us when shown upon
the stage.
The idea that they interest even is mistaken.
A successful play however is a valuable property.
There are also actors and actresses.
A play of pure emotion would need a tithe of the
present cast of a play, a hundredth of the expense in
staging. . . .
Hence its impracticability.

    *   *   *

The successful playwright, Shakespeare, Tchekhov
later, discovered that without action of some sort, no
play "will go." That is, a play without some spec-
tacular interest. No two senses may be concentrated
without one losing somewhat in intensity. A sonata
cannot be criticised and heard intensely at the same
moment. Nor the music of a ballet when the choreo-
graphy is overloaded.
The only form of drama which evades these mistakes
is that made by "Marionettes." That is, conven-
tionalised figures which do not draw attention to their
idiosyncrasies; placed in a neutral environment which
does not detract from the evocation of a pure emotion.
For hundreds of years this has been understood.
It must not be lost sight of.

THE EVOCATION OF RACE MEMORIES.

Art no longer attempts to elevate. So rare indeed
is it to meet one who believes in a utilitarian art that it
was a profound shock for me to hear lately, "but I don't
see what use your poetry is."
Not attempting to elevate, Art becomes entirely a
factor for the suggestion of emotions; thoughts.
With the old artists, too often it was merely a hitting
of the same nail after it had impinged, thus driving it
into a groove where the vibrations were deadened
instead of merely a first tap which would have caused
the whole of the receptive material to vibrate (the
liberation of a complex).
It is conceivable that a smell of musk wafted through
a theatre would affect an audience more poignantly,
more profoundly, than anything they had before then
experienced. For all plays are amenable to intellectual
criticism of whatever kind. Hamlet to a single
single member of the audience who does not wish it.
This insidious smell of musk penetrates deeper into the
mind through the senses, until the body is rapt into
those vague splendid imaginings which are the flutterings
of memories of man and the earth when they were young.
Who knows why a leaf pittering along a starlit path
fills one with a sense of impending tragedy which sur-
passes all the poignancy made by poets telling of great
loves? An empty stage, quite dark; the rustling of a few
leaves—— I can conceive nothing which could affect me
more poignantly, more profoundly.
I want to take a theatre in London, using for the plays
either human marionettes of the Dutch-doll type or naked
humans, or to clothe them in a sort of cylindrical gar-
ment. The plays will be the completion of a cycle dealing
with the primitive emotions, of which Fear is one, these
being I think the simplest for the evocation of race

Figure 1.2. Pound's "Preliminary Announcement" in *The Egoist* page 2/2.

Passing off what was really an opinion essay as a "Preliminary Announcement," the editors gave Pound his forum. He begins early on by noting that "[a]t present many American students who would have sought Vienna or Prague or some continental city are disturbed by war. To these The College of Arts offers a temporary refuge and a permanent centre" (413). Betraying his own partial (albeit enthusiastic) leanings, Pound calls "[s]cholarly research" a "wasted time if it has not been first arranged and oriented in the British Museum." Here, we see the hands-on vision Pound had for his college. Culture in a textbook was not enough—this, notwithstanding Pound's own introductory textbooks (discussed later) and the half-pride he took in Yeats's suggestion that he was "trying to provide a portable substitute for the British Museum'" (Paige 257). Pound's college would be beneficial to both the future artist and the interested bon vivant. "The college prepares two sorts of instruction," he writes, "one for those who intend a career in some single art, who desire practical and technical instruction, a second for those who believe that learning is an adornment, a gracious and useless pleasure, that is to say for serious art students and for the better sort of dilettanti."

After upbraiding the American academic "institution" he knew as "sterile" and "professorial," he endorsed a tutorial system for his own college, because "instruction by private teachers [was] often most excellent." Not-so-subtly attacking scholars for inexperience with their very own subject matter, he writes that "The College of Arts offers contact with artists of established position, creative minds, men for the most part who have already suffered in the cause of their art." Pound's "sufferers" included such luminaries as Wyndham Lewis and the French sculptor and artist Henri Gaudier-Brzeska, and the college would offer diverse topics in the history and philosophy of art and in the practicalities of crafting. These included areas like "Etching and Dry Point," "Book-binding," and "Russian Contemporary Thought." (Pound had not yet corralled enough people to volunteer their names for each topic.) Naturally, the lengthiest blurb, under "Comparative Poetry," belongs to the now-titled "EZRA POUND, M.A." Pound would be welcoming, offering instruction "to anyone who wants it, not merely to those holding philological degrees," even including American college students so long as they "possess rather more than average intelligence" (413, 414).

The prospectus is followed by an editorial statement (penned most likely by the same hand), which takes a few more jabs at academic institutions—or "cramming factor[ies] where certain data are pushed into the student regardless of his abilities or predilections"—and its faculty, "who probably wishes [students] in the inferno" (414). Pound's "college" is not unlike hands-on scholarly summer programs run by various American universities and European institutes today, but it does differ considerably with respect to the faculty-artists. Pound is really envisioning what arts and humanities schools might be today. One can see how the frequent social gatherings—the meetings of artists and writers, the lecturers on contemporary culture—that Pound had recently attended had made such a dream—if not the college itself—possible. Had he the funding, this is the college Pound would have established, as, in his estimation, it would have "compensate[d] for the inconvenience and derangement of undergraduate studies" (414). As to whether he would have had the patience to stick with it (and all of its inevitable technical and administrative hurdles), one cannot but speculate.

In other venues, Pound continued to offer shrewd critiques of the way graduate degrees were granted in the United States: "After devising the new castes, to wit, of Professors who could meet a creative artist without being made to appear ridiculous, and of artists who could meet a decently informed professor without being shown for charlatans, I would consider the matter of the thesis" (*NA* 13.4:83). Whether or not Pound took his own thoughts to heart here, he is aware of a problematic tension between the scholar-teacher and the artist-creator. As many students, some faculty, and a good deal of the public critics of academia complain (for different personal and political reasons), today's literary and cultural theorists can "miss the point" of art. This is not a position we endorse, but it is not wholly without merit. As one example, we might note how many academic scholars of the last few generations have, while searching for the meaning of a literary text, spurned the author's intention. Although authors' comments about their own work are not necessarily the most profound remarks on the subject, ignoring them does risk appearing ridiculous, especially to those students new to the university classroom or to those readers outside the academy's walls. On the other hand, Pound was also aware of the ease of the fraudulent artist who could claim creative brilliance without having any sense of history or technique—the "you just don't understand my art" claim, also familiar, perhaps, today in classrooms, studios, and publishing houses across the country.

As to the graduate thesis itself, Pound had some very interesting things to say:

> The "Thesis" as an institution may need some explanation to the present reader; be it known then that in the United States of America, possibly in the United States of Brazil, in France,

Germany, and most civilised countries except England, the seats of learning confer the higher degree of "Doctor of Philosophy" in most cases upon students who have never studied and who never intend to study any philosophy, but no matter, it is an old custom and worthy of reverence, and it dates from the time when people did study philosophy and the liberal arts. "Ph.D." after your name implies that you have done at least three years' hard work on some two or three special branches of learning after and above what you did for your baccalaureate degree, and part of this work is a thesis which is supposed to make some new contribution to the pre-existing sum of knowledge.

Now this is a very fine system, it is a tremendous machinery for accumulating minute information, and I speak of it, and in especial of its inventor, with nothing save the deepest respect. But this system implies that after every hundred or so of such theses there should come a super thesis, the product of some intelligent person capable of efficient synthesis. (*NA* 13.4:83)

Pound was aware that the thesis, which is "supposed to make some new contribution to the pre-existing sum of knowledge," would soon lose its sharpness while still maintaining its prominence. More than with what would become the industry of doctoral programs, Pound was concerned with the difference between "studying" and "accumulating minute information," the latter of which doctoral programs in the philological mode promoted, in Pound's view, for no necessary reason. He sought, instead, the "super thesis," which was not so much an original contribution to intellectual history but an "efficient synthesis" of existing cultural knowledge. The task—to borrow a word from a draft to one of his final *Cantos* (then resigned to a hopeful sense of failure)—was about making it "cohere" (816). He went on to point out that "good introductory works are sadly lacking"—a defect he clearly intended to remedy himself—before he had more to say about the thesis itself:

The usual doctor's thesis is dull, is badly written, the candidate usually has to pay for the printing of the required copies, as even the special journals will not be bothered with the average thesis.

My suggestion is the very simple one that the thesis be briefed, that the results, with due introduction and with due explanation of their bearing on the whole of the science or on the particular period of history, be published in some newspaper of standing, which should become in some measure the organ of the university. Secondly, that the minutae of the thesis be typewritten and placed in the university library to be printed only if they happen to be of general interest or if the results and conclusions of the thesis based upon them are called into question.

He understood the system then in place very well. The custom of having students pay to publish their theses has gone away (except for initial copies), replaced to a great extent by university press monographs, and, thanks to online media possibilities, we now have incipient versions of the print-on-demand concept for dissertations. We are not likely to adopt the idea of newspaper publication, but the proliferation of academic journals has covered that aspect of Pound's proposal fairly well. When Pound writes that "the usual doctor's thesis is dull" and "badly written," he means not only a monotony of language but moreover a lifelessness of thought, something without an "efficient synthesis." (As though the world would desire another thesis on what Dorothy Sayers would later call "an entirely original and revolutionary theory about funerary rites."[20]) Pound ultimately points to a problem with the expectations that doctoral students produce an original scholarly monograph, a challenge that still exists today.[21] Given the typical readership of such monographs, we might say that an audience of twenty was not Pound's goal.

Likewise of note is Pound's concern for education and for the proper conduct of academic life, which he cared about, understood, and wanted to improve. He also wanted, in some way, to be a part of it. His notion of the super-college was a sort of dream, but his criticism of actual graduate programs was very real, as was his desire to get that PhD from Penn. He sought it again in 1920, asking the faculty to take his by-then substantial body of work in poetry and criticism as sufficient to grant him that doctorate, which he both wanted and, at some level, disdained. When it became clear that Penn would not budge, Pound wrote to his father, expressing some of his complex feelings on the matter:

The point is, do the blackguards want to hang up on that mere formality, <u>despite</u> my record of published work. Remember this is as much an enquiry into the psychology of the University // scientifically valuable as a record of the Spirit of the Age // as a desire on my part to possess a futile decoration which I shd. use only about once in 10 years.

> It will be quite as <u>valuable</u> to learn that they will accord no
> credit <u>whatever</u> on my last 12 years of work, as to receive any
> leniencies or courtesies they might offer. (*EPtP* 466; underlines
> in original)

For the out-of-luck former student, the PhD became a "futile decoration."
Pound's desires, as well as his memory, could be selective. He notes incred-
ulously that Wharton Barker (a trustee at Penn and family friend) "seems
to think I asked for a degree & was refused" (466).[22] True, Pound had
quit, but he later had been refused the degree and then honorary degree
he sought. Threatening that "[t]here'd be a high mortality list . . . if I <u>shd</u>
return & continue my studies <u>in</u> <u>course</u>," he asks, "[h]ave they considered
<u>that</u> contingency?" (466). He then adds a racial slur and signs off with "Love
to you & mother." A few months later, Pound wrote to Barker, telling him
that the faculty's objections were philosophical—that the professors had a
"prejudice against the right of contemporary literature to exist" and that
Professor Penniman especially never forgave Pound "for wanting to think,
and for preferring the search for sound criteria to a parroting of dead men's
opinion" (467).

In 1929, the alumni secretary at Penn made the mistake of sending Pound a flyer, probably asking for funds. His reply expressed a lot
of pent-up anger at his supposed "soul mother." Among other things, he
observed that "The matter of keeping up one more otiose institution in a
retrograde country seems to me to be the affair of those still bamboozled by
mendicancy, rhetoric, and circular letters." He concluded with a postscript
to this effect: "All the U. of P. or your god damn college or any other god
damn American college does or will do for a man of letters is to ask him to
go away without breaking the silence" (Paige 225). Although Pound would
eventually get an honorary degree from Hamilton College years later, his
disdain for the American university culture was set, and being a man of
letters no longer necessitated having letters after his name. Pound's feelings
about the United States became grounded more and more in his feelings
about the American academic world, and they were getting angrier and
angrier. They would finally boil over in his radio broadcasts in the 1940s.
Importantly, though, even in those radio talks, as we will see, he was still
brooding about the state of university education in the United States. In
the chapters that follow, we look at those works of his that are not just
criticism but also are clearly intended as instruction, starting with that first
set of lectures that became a book: *The Spirit of Romance*.

CHAPTER 2

The Critic as Teacher

Pound's "New Method" in Scholarship

Chiefly impressed by lack of correlation between different depts. and lack either of general survey of literature or any coherent interest in literature as such. . . .

—Pound to Louis Untermeyer (qtd. in Robbins 15)

What kind of pedagogue was Pound? This entire book is designed to address that question—if not entirely to answer it. The present chapter, which takes up *The Spirit of Romance* and *I Gather the Limbs of Osiris*, is concerned with one piece of the larger puzzle. Each of these works introduces new pedagogical phrases (such as the famous "luminous detail" or the lesser-known "resembling unlikeness"), and each demonstrates Pound's evolving "comparative" method of teaching, whether he moves across time or culture or artistic medium to get at the heart of a work. Many of Pound's musings about art here (despite his claims) can seem a bit flowery or unsubstantiated, but that style is a deliberate reply to his educational upbringing. He believes that looser, metaphorical, lively, and direct engagements with a work of art get closer to the meaning of that work and to life itself than could any philological monograph.[1] We know that he was taking what he had learned at both Hamilton and Penn and putting his own stamp on that material. This chapter considers the shape of that stamp.

By looking into *The Spirit of Romance*—the book he made out of his lectures at the London Polytechnic in 1910 when he was just twenty-five years old—we can get a line on his teaching style, his methodology, and his strengths and weaknesses in presenting his thoughts and feelings to an audience. There are traces of the lecturer in the book, but the book, as he admitted, was an attempt to "solidify the lecture material," so that it became less important to "seem careless," as he had boasted about the lectures. The book comes to us now after several reprints, so that we find a series of prefaces in the most recent edition along with dated notes added at later times, often admitting deficiencies or recording changes of opinion since that first publication of 1910. One thing emerges clearly from even a cursory engagement with this text, and that is that Pound was not simply acting as a scholar or a critic. He had already developed a theory of literature that is both proclaimed and embodied in the course of these lecture/chapters. This theory begins by Pound's insisting in the 1910 preface that what he is doing is not philology, and humbly allowing that "only by courtesy can it be said to be a study in comparative literature" (5).[2] Pound's work is characterized by a blend of humility and arrogance that is uniquely his. It is based on his sense that he knew enough to know what he did not know.

Pound's theory was not just a theory of literature. It was a theory of art, and it included a hierarchy in which poetry stood above other forms of literature. Pound wants to distance himself from that other academic poet, the Inspector of Schools, Matthew Arnold.[3] In particular, he rejects Arnold's notion that poetry should be a criticism of life: "Poetry is about as much a 'criticism of life' as red-hot iron is a criticism of fire" (222).[4] That is, for Pound, poetry was an intensification of life, not a withdrawal from it. That statement, however, incongruously comes at the end of the book, which begins with a Latin phrase: "Praefatorio ad Lectorem Electum" or Preface for the Chosen Reader, which is, to say the least, an odd way to end. Surely a preface ought to be for all readers, not a withdrawal from them. And we do not know who may be supposed to have chosen the person who is actually reading it. The Latin itself might repel some potential readers, but it might also attract some, marking them as among the elect, self-selected to read Pound's words. The game he is playing—and it is a game—is a sort of seduction by apparent indifference. We know this schoolteacher wanted an audience. He counted them. And we know he wanted readers. He courted them. But it is important to him, apparently, to seem indifferent. Pound forces us to think, in many ways, and he rewards us with instructive language that has memorable moments—like that red-hot iron of poetry. Good poetry, like good teaching, ought to breathe in the fire of life.

It is also important to him to make large claims, to utter bold statements, like "The aim of the present work is to instruct. Its ambition is to instruct painlessly." Actually, the ambition is a bit more complex. It is to make the pain of instruction pleasurable. Just before this remark, Pound made some statements that can serve to illustrate his complex intentions. Let us look at them:

- Art is a joyous thing.

- I would in all seriousness plead for a greater levity, a more befitting levity, in our study of the arts.

- Good art never bores one. By that I mean that it is the business of the artist to prevent ennui; in the literary art, to relieve, refresh, revive the mind of the reader—at reasonable intervals—with some form of ecstasy, by some splendor of thought, some presentation of sheer beauty, some lightning turn of phrase—laughter is no mean ecstasy. Good art begins with an escape from dullness.

There are several things going on in these statements, and they are intricately interconnected. First of all, Pound claims that his subject matter itself—art—is a thing of joy. He will not be discussing some academic, boring thing, like Matthew Arnold's "high seriousness." Instead, he will present something joyful, which his readers should welcome. Second, he implies that his way of approaching this pleasure will be far from solemn. It will involve levity—a levity more appropriate to the joy of art than, say, the solemn philological approach current in those universities he wanted to infiltrate. Finally, what he says about the ability of verbal art to refresh or revive the mind of the reader extends by implication to his own way of discussing that art. He will engage and amuse us—at reasonable intervals, though not all the time. Pound is trying to raise the whole academic process to a higher level by seeing the object of literary study as joyful and by moving the method of such study toward some occasional "splendor of thought" or "lightning turn of phrase." He turns such phrases himself repeatedly in this book, as in "laughter is no mean ecstasy."

After the preface, the book proceeds in a largely chronological order. He will be discussing the beginnings of poetry in those dialects of Latin that became distinct languages around the end of the first millennium AD:

"Provençal, Italian, Spanish, French, Portuguese, Catalan, Roumanian and Romansch" (12). But he starts by going back to the Latin of the second century AD to examine two threads that will be important in his view of the Romance verbal art: a thread of stylistic floridity combined with narrative fantasy, and a thread of erotic intensity combined with technical innovation. His examples of these two threads are the *Metamorphoses* or *Golden Ass* of Apuleius, and the *Pervigilium Veneris*. As he admits, Pound is following the Oxford professor John William Mackail on this track, though he does not always agree with him; he concludes, though, by agreeing that, after the *Pervigilium*, "song did not awake until the Provençal viol aroused it" (21), which enables him to make a smooth transition to the next chapter on the Provençal poet Arnaut Daniel. Pound did not merely rely on Mackail. He depended on the professor and drew on him deeply in this chapter. In one of the later notes, Pound admitted the extent of his indebtedness, saying this about one of his observations on Apuleius:

> I take it this was mere parroting of Mackail. did not *know*; but
> I had to get through my introduction and in general get to and
> at the subject of the book I was trying to write. The statement
> is correct enough and does no injury to the reader. (12)

Pound can be both flippant and grateful at once, and whether he is quickly dismissing Mackail or his own preface is up in the air. Either way, he soon moves along to his chapter on "Il Miglior Fabbro," a phrase that attracted attention fifteen years later when T. S. Eliot added it after the epigraph in an edition of *The Waste Land*. Pound translates it in his chapter as "the better craftsman."[5] It was applied to Arnaut by a poet encountered by Dante in Purgatory, who, when praised, points to Arnaut and utters those words. In a sense, these are the types of student-teacher relationships that Pound admires. The sixth chapter of Pound's book (in 1910) is devoted to Dante, but he is also present in most of the chapters preceding that one. As Virgil guided Dante through Hell and much of Purgatory, Dante guides Pound from the second chapter until the middle of this book. *The Spirit of Romance*'s "middle way" follows Dante's *De Vulgari Eloquentia*, as well as passages in the *Commedia* that concern poets who wrote in the modern languages of Europe. And there are several such moves in *The Spirit of Romance*. Just as Beatrice replaced Virgil as Dante's guide in the *Purgatorio*, Dante has replaced Mackail as Pound's guide to the poetry of Provence. Here we see an important pedagogical movement, for Pound, back into the poetry itself. But when it comes to Dante's *Commedia*, Pound leans on W. P. Ker, who was Oxford Professor of Poetry a few years after MacKail, as a guide with whom he sometimes quarrels.

What would it mean to take Arnaut as a teacher? Pound begins the chapter on this poet by admitting that "[s]ome temperamental sympathy may prejudice me in favor of this age. I lay no claim to dispassionate judgment" (22). He then informs us that Dante, in his "*Treatise on the Common Speech*" (*De Vulgari Eloquentia*), situates Arnaut as "the type of writers on love" (23), adding that Petrarch called him the "gran maestro d'amor" (25). For Pound, however, it is Arnaut's technical skill that is especially interesting, and by technical skill Pound means not so much the complicated verse forms that he himself imitated in his early poetry, but something much harder to imitate—what Pound calls "his refusal to use the 'journalese' of his day," and "his aversion from an obvious vocabulary." He sums up the source of Arnaut's difficulty this way: "He is not content with conventional phrase, or with words that do not convey his exact meaning; and his words are therefore harder to find in dictionaries" (25). Years later, in a radio broadcast, Pound would mock his own expertise in Arnaut Daniel, observing that any postdoctoral student could do that sort of thing. But it is clear that Arnaut—and Dante—were important to him as writers "whose diction and metaphor are occasionally so vivid as to seem harsh in literal translation" (25). Pound's method in this chapter, apropos of a teacher starting out, is to quote extensively in the original, to translate frequently, and to cite Dante regularly for support. The quotation that best sums up the qualities he admired in Arnaut is probably this one:

Ieu sui Arnant qu'amas l'aura
E chatz le lebre ab lo bou
E nadi contra suberna

I am Arnaut who loves the wind,
And chases the hare with the ox,
And swims against the torrent.[6]

Pound enjoys swimming against the torrent as much as he relishes being a part of it. One of the qualities that makes him an often attractive critic and teacher in his younger years is his ability to see things from more than one side. In all the arts—and he later reviewed music and visual art for *The New Age*—he looks for innovation, but he also admires craftsmanship

and praises it even when used in traditional manners. He covers the ground
of Provençal poetry thoroughly—so thoroughly, in fact, that he later adds
a note (probably in the 1930s) at the start of the next chapter with this
disclaimer: "*The patient reader is welcome to gnaw at the following chapter;
when she can no longer stand it, we offer the postscript on p. 141*" (64). In
the 1968 edition, there is no postscript on that page, and just what he was
referring to is by no means certain. More interesting, perhaps, is that he
assumes a female reader. One is unsure what to make of this. It may reflect
his actual memory of the composition of his lecture audience, or it may
echo his often gendered division between the producers and consumers of
culture, or, among other things, it may be a misogynistic comment about
the assumed attention spans of a female readership.[7] While more recent
critics have focused on such significant moments in Pound—moments that
betray his and his age's and perhaps "modernism's" ideological assumptions
about the gendered subjectivity of the artist—Pound doesn't linger on such
matters. Instead, chapter 4 has him moving into territory where Dante had
not ventured—the Spanish *Poema del Cid* (which he prefers to the French
Chanson de Roland).

Pound is, at this stage of his career, a different kind of academic—not
really a teacher in the general sense—but a promoter of learning, urging his
students to learn what they need to read for themselves. His praise of the
Cid is partly a defense of its verse against charges of crudeness but mainly
has to do with the poem's characterizations and dramatic structure. For a
defense of the verse, he must have had in mind (as he admits in a note to
a later edition) the views of one of his old teachers at Penn:

> As to "irregular" metre, I can still see Dr. Rennert manicuring his
> finger nails in seminar, pausing in that operation, looking over
> his spectacles and in his plaintive falsetto, apropos someone who
> had attempted to reprint the *Cid* with ten syllables in *every* line:
> "Naow effa man had sense enough to write a beautiful poem like
> this is, wudn't yeow think he wudda had sense enough to be able
> to keount ep to ten on his fingers *ef he'da wanted tew?*" (67n)

Though Pound respects the verse, it is not the main reason for his admiration of the poem. He finds in it scenes and speeches "not unworthy of
Greek tragedy," and he adds, "[t]his drawing to the life, the variety of actors
who are individuals, not figures, gives the *Poema* much of its vitality; as
the Spanish sense of tableaus and dramatic setting give it so much of its

charm" (67). This leads him to a theoretical statement about the role of visualization in poetry:

> As in the Greek, or, indeed, as in most moving poetry, the simple lines demand from us who read, a completion of the detail, a fulfillment or crystallization of beauty implied. The poet must never infringe upon the painter's function; the picture must exist around the words; the words must not attempt too far at being brush strokes. (68)

Pound is not quite a "reader-response" theorist, but his contention that works make a "demand" on us and that the reader participate in the "crystallization of beauty" is remarkable, especially so for a "teacher" at the time. In a later note, he would call this a "[v]ery dangerous statement" (68), but it appears in the original with no qualification. The danger for the later Pound, one gathers, comes from the reliance on the reader to play a creative role in interpreting the poem. Here is where we see a great conflict in the schoolmaster. Pound is equally inviting and suspicious of readers; all the time, though, he keeps trying to teach them how to do their job properly. About half the time, he seems to trust his reader—his student—alone with the artwork, in that only in such an encounter can beauty manifest itself. He is also, on this point, confronting the question—crucial to his theory of poetry—of whether the poet should represent or evoke, a question still asked and, perhaps, too easily resolved in many writing programs today.[8] In the course of these discussions, Pound has occasion to theorize once again, observing that the romances "belong to that vast body of pleasant literature which one should read when one feels younger than twenty" (82). Note that this twenty-five-year-old does not say when one *is* younger than twenty, but when one *feels* oneself that age. Still, he goes on to make a point we can recognize as typical of his theory of the arts: "Great art is made to call forth, or create, an ecstasy. The finer the quality of this ecstasy, the finer the art; only secondary art relies on its pleasantness" (82).

One thing we can learn from reading this early work of Pound is how well he knows the poetry of certain English predecessors. In the course of the book he has occasion to mention and often praise the translations of these early works not only by the Scottish poet Andrew Lang (who "was born in order that he might translate it perfectly" [84]), but also by the scholar of folklore Jessie Weston (whose 1920 *From Ritual to Romance* was instrumental for early modernist poets and scholars), the University of

Chicago Chaucer scholar Edith Rickert, the Irish dramatist John Millington Synge, and the English poets Dante Gabriel Rossetti, Robert Browning, Thomas Hardy, and even Algernon Charles Swinburne—with whom he had a conflicted relationship. At this point we should, perhaps, reflect on the apparent contradiction between the relegation of the "pleasant" to a secondary status and the elevation of the "gay" *Aucassin and Nicolette* to a position alongside *Tristan* and the *Cid*. Pound has stressed levity and joy from the beginning of this book, but these should not be confused with mere pleasantness, which he associates with escape from realities. Great comedy, like a great teacher, on the other hand, faces life head-on. Pound's apparent self-contradictions—and they are frequent—show an educator still sorting out his ideas.

Pound begins this chapter by noting that "The Albigensian Crusade, a sordid robbery cloaking itself in religious pretense, had ended the *gai savoir* in Southern France. The art of the Troubadours meets with philosophy at Bologna and a new era of lyric poetry is begun" (101). Bologna was important, not only because of its university, but because Guido Buinicelli of that city is credited by Pound with "bringing to perfection" the form of a single stanza from the longer canzone poems, so that it might stand alone. This new form was what we have learned to call the sonnet. Pound also credits Guido with adding the voice of the soul to that of the eyes and the heart heard in the poetry of Provence: "The Tuscan bookworms find themselves in the groves of philosophy, God becomes interesting, and speculation, with open eyes and a rather didactic voice, is boon companion to the bard" (104). The academic Pound has a stylistic grace and energy that enable him to express this rather didactic point about literary history in a memorable fashion. He turns the learned Tuscans into worms and puts them in a divine grove so that the abstraction "speculation"—a problematic word for the later Pound—can turn into a blessing. This enables him to conclude that "Thought, which in Provence had confined itself to the manner, now makes conquest of the matter of verse" (104).

Guido Cavalcanti, the thirteenth-century Italian troubadour, is the central figure of this chapter, standing to Dante, as Pound puts it, as Christopher Marlowe did to Shakespeare, and he adds that "Dante himself never wrote lines more poignant, or more intensely poetic that did this Cavalcanti" (110). Pound *feels* this poetry. His academic pronouncements are driven by an intense emotional connection to the material. This is one of the things that makes him a good teacher in this book. He is not afraid to say that "After a few hours with the originals, criticism becomes a vain thing" (111). The teacher in Pound progresses from facts to an experience of the work itself. Seeing the move from Provence to Italy as a move from a "cult of the emotions" to "a cult of the harmonies of the mind," Pound praises the best of Tuscan poetry as appealing "by its truth, by its subtlety, and by its refined exactness" (116).[9]

The next chapter, called "Il Maestro" in 1910 and simply "Dante" in current editions, reveals Pound's method, which is not the sort of explicative criticism that would become the chosen mode of his New Critical followers. He tells his readers to read Dante, but he does not do it for them. Urging us to regard Dante's Hell, Purgatory, and Heaven as "states [of mind], and not places," Pound goes on to say that "[i]t is therefore expedient in reading the *Commedia* to regard Dante's descriptions of the actions and conditions of the shades as descriptions of men's mental states in life, in which they are, after death, compelled to continue" (128). Leading us through Dante's poem, summarizing a bit, quoting the original, and providing translations of passages he especially admires, Pound still fears that he cannot do justice to the poem for readers without Italian. One of the most revealing passages in this book comes in the middle of the Dante chapter:

> Any sincere criticism of the highest poetry must resolve itself into a sort of profession of faith. The critic must begin with a "*credo*" and his opinion will be received in part for the intelligence he may seem to possess, and in part for his earnestness. Certain of Dante's supremacies are comprehensible only to such as know Italian and have themselves attained a certain proficiency in the poetic art. An *ipse dixit* is not necessarily valueless. The penalty for remaining a layman is that one must at times accept a specialist's opinion. No one ever took the trouble to become a specialist for the bare pleasure of ramming his *ipse dixit* down the general throat. (154)

Unapologetically, he tells us that to appreciate Dante's achievement properly we must learn Italian and become proficient in writing poetry ourselves. He offers us his *credo*, which is to say what he believes, hoping that he has conveyed enough of his intelligence and earnestness to persuade us to share his belief because he himself had said it—*ipse dixit* (a personal, unproven assertion). But he is not going to interpret for us. Learning means being able to discover for oneself; Pound, here, merely wants us to learn enough language and enough about composing poems to share his pleasure in Dante's work. In doing so, he does not address the problem of *how* we should read (he will tackle that in later works), for in 1910 he was content to quote, translate, point to splendors, and theorize about the nature of artistic beauty.

In discussing Dante, he turns to the visual arts for examples of what he describes as two kinds of beauty. One, exemplified by Edward Burne-Jones, delights us immediately with its beauty. The other, exemplified by James Whistler, puzzles the viewer at first but leads that viewer to find new beauty in natural things. "Thus, there are works of art which are beautiful objects and works of art which are keys or passwords admitting one to a deeper knowledge, to a finer perception of beauty; Dante's work is of the second sort" (154). The schoolmaster wants artworks to spark curiosity in his audience, not just provide them with a simple answer. We are so used to the teacher as explicator, reading on behalf of the student, that Pound's avoidance of this—his turning to "faith"—is a bit shocking, as if it were his belief that the great poets do not need to be "interpreted." Very importantly, they only need to be read, because they speak directly to us. In the course of this chapter, he tries to help us appreciate Dante by comparing him with English poets such as Wordsworth, Milton, Shelley, and Browning—usually to Dante's benefit, but without denying the value of the other poets' work. He names only one writer as Dante's equal: Shakespeare, who was born three hundred years after Dante and worked mainly in a very different mode. And he points out that both Dante and Shakespeare came at a fortunate moment for the craft in which they worked, following predecessors who had blazed a trail of technical skill that they could then adopt and surpass, to "set their own inimitable light atop of the mountain" (162).

After a fascinating chapter on François Villon—the fifteenth-century French criminal turned poet—Pound turns to the writer on whom he almost wrote his dissertation: Lope de Vega.[10] The chapter gives Pound a chance to rethink some of his earlier academic work and to theorize about the difference between poetry and drama. "The aims of poetry and drama differ essentially in this," he writes, "poetry presents itself to the individual, drama presents itself to a collection of individuals. It cannot be understood too clearly that the first requirement of a play is that it hold the audience" (179).[11] This distinction is important because Lope wrote something like two thousand plays (yes, two thousand!), which means that Lope could not be giving the language of his plays the kind of attention that his contemporary Shakespeare gave to his. Also important is Pound's stance that Shakespeare was the "consummation" of a tradition, while Lope was the founder of one. Accordingly and necessarily, there would be more unevenness in the work of the latter. Lope's play about Henry III, for instance, though it "contains one of the tensest scenes of all romantic drama," is mostly "delightful comedy" (185). Pound treats this play at length, translating and summarizing, before concluding that "[i]n reading a play of Lope's it is always worth while to notice which character precipitates the action. Sometimes the entire movement is projected by the gracioso" (193). Pound, of course, was working on the gracioso in Lope's plays for that dissertation he never finished. He makes much of that clown or jester in this chapter, praising Lope's use of the figure "solely for comic relief and with a fine precision" (193). We can see how scholarship and teaching come together for the explicator here, as Pound cites H. A. Rennert's (his Penn teacher's) *Life of Lope de Vega* as the source for much of his information.[12]

Thinking of the achievements and limitations of the great sixteenth-century Portuguese poet Luís de Camoens,[13] Pound finds himself returning once more to an objection with Matthew Arnold's notion of poetry as a criticism of life:

> . . . true poetry is in much closer relation to the best of music, of painting, and of sculpture, than to any part of literature which is not true poetry; if, however, Arnold considered poetry as a part of literature, then his definition of literature as "criticism of life" is the one notable blasphemy that was born of his mind's frigidity.
>
> The spirit of the arts is dynamic. The arts are not passive, nor static, nor, in a sense, are they reflective, though reflection may assist at their birth.
>
> Poetry is about as much a "criticism of life" as red-hot iron is a criticism of fire. (222)

Pound's dismissal of Arnold's "blasphemy" also betrays an enduring resentment for his own teachers' philological methods, which, in his view, were passive and certainly not fire-borne. *The Spirit of Romance* was published in the United States shortly after the British version and has been republished a number of times since then, indicating that it has held its scholastic interest for a long time, with the last newly edited edition appearing in 2005. From the 1910 edition, however, we can learn a good deal about the young Pound's academic methods. The Pound who is found in this book looks like a born teacher, but a different type of teacher—more animated, less fearful of institutional reprimand—than we often see in higher education today. This was probably more visible in the lectures, but the written version provides plenty of evidence of his pedagogical craft. He provides information for his audience but holds them with his enthusiasm for the subject and the energy of his prose. He points to the virtues of the poets he discusses, and to the limitations of some, but he is mainly an advocate, telling the reader to pay attention, learn languages, and even get a feeling for poetry by learning how to write it. What he does not do is explicate much. He is not here a "close" or "intrinsic" reader in the New Critical sense. His best efforts in this direction are to be found in his summaries of character and situation in the *Poema del Cid* and the plays of Lope de Vega, which are clear and engaging, serving as exemplars of the narrative and dramatic values by which he has come to his appreciation of these works and their authors. In other cases, he tends to rely on the *ipse dixit* a bit too heavily. But this is only the first of his many efforts at teaching readers something he thought they should know. We track this tendency through his next pedagogical efforts, starting with a series of articles he wrote for *The New Age* in 1911 and 1912.

∾

Pound's second extended scholarly work never made it into print as a book, though he clearly thought of it as one. It first appeared as a sequence of articles under the common title of *I Gather the Limbs of Osiris* in *The New Age* magazine.[14] (We have seen in chapter 1 that Pound met what he called "The New Age Crowd" in 1909.[15]) Throughout the articles, we find Pound as scholar, creator, and teacher—a unified persona that remained central to his work for his entire life, because it responded to his deepest impulses for unity. Because not all detail was of equal value, Pound sought to teach his readership a new method for discovering what was crucial in a work of art.

It all began in November 1911. The first article in the series was a bit strange, and the strangeness started with the title: *I Gather the Limbs of Osiris*. The date of this publication may be important, because the Egyptian festivals in honor of the God Osiris began in November. Perhaps more significant is the myth itself—a death and resurrection motif, which is found in other belief systems. Osiris was the lord of the underworld, whose body was hacked into pieces by a jealous relative. Those pieces were carefully retrieved by his wife, Isis, whose devotion impressed the gods so much that they revived the dead Osiris and restored him to his position. For Pound, poetry itself was Osiris, and he was the faithful spouse who might bring the limbs of this lord back to life. But he let his ambitions hide behind his title, so that, as usual, only those who understood would understand. He was challenging readers to attend to him—and to poetry. (We can recognize this similar strategy in his Latin "Preface for the Chosen Reader" in *The Spirit of Romance*.) Hence, the first article is not an article at all but a poem almost a thousand years old: the Old English "Seafarer," which Pound translated for the occasion, though the roots of this translation go all the way back to his course in Anglo-Saxon with "Bib" at Hamilton College.

This poem, then, was one of the limbs of Osiris that Pound was gathering. In the pages of the magazine, however, the poem did not stand alone. A note from the editor appeared before the first seven of the articles: "(Under this heading Mr. Pound will contribute expositions and translations in illustration of "The New Method" in scholarship—THE EDITOR)" (*NA* 10.5:107). After the poem, Pound added his own note, complete with typos both noticed and overlooked:

> PHILOLOGICAL NOTE—The text of this poem is rather confused. I have rejected half of line 76, read "Angles" for angels in line 78, and stopped translating before the passage about the soul and the longer lines beginning, "Mickle is the fear of the Almighty," and ending in a dignified but platitudinous address to the Deity: "World's elder, eminent creator, in all ages, amen." There are many conjectures as to how the text came into its present from [sic]. It seems most likely that a fragment of the original poem, clear through about the first thirty lines, and thereafter increasingly illegible, fell into the hands of a monk with literary ambitions, who filled in the gaps with his own guesses and "improvements." The groundwork may have been a longer narrative poem, but the "lyric," as I have accepted it, divides fairly well into "The Trials of the Sea its Lure and the Lament for Age."[16] (*NA* 10.5:107)

Given Pound's own monkishness with translation, the critique feels amusing, however much Pound's instinct was often the right one. As the note makes clear, Pound has not only translated this poem, but added his own "guesses and improvements." That is, the creator/translator has been preceded by a scholar/critic, who has extracted what he calls a "lyric" from a longer text that is a result of monkish meddling. But what was so "new" about "'The New Method' in scholarship"?

The answer to this question, implied in this first article of the series, was presented more explicitly in the next installment and those that followed. He gave the second article this subtitle: "A RATHER DULL INTRODUC-TION"—and how like Pound it was to provide the introduction in the second segment of the series rather than at the start, where introductions usually reside, and to preempt our response by telling us in advance that it will be dull, which, of course, it isn't. The main feature of the new method was to be a focus on what he called "the Luminous Detail," as opposed to the "multitudinous detail" of current scholarship and the "sentiment and generalization" of the recent past. Actually, there was a fair amount of sentiment and generalization in *The Spirit of Romance*, as we have seen, but Pound was still seeking a New Method in pedagogical writing. The method of Luminous Detail is a near equivalent on the academic side to what Imagism would become on the creative side, but Imagism (or *Imagisme*) had not yet been developed and promoted in 1911 (though its roots, as we know, lay in those meetings of Pound, Flint, Hulme, and other young poets back in 1910). The luminous detail, as Pound explained regularly in these articles, was something that artists discovered in the world and, like teachers, made intelligible to their audience.[17] And scholar-critics for Pound ought to be emulating this search and finding the luminous details in the works they studied. Pound was teaching these critics how to read better. He very specifically saw the method of the arts as a model for the method of scholarship, but he also saw the methods of scholarship as essential for the arts. "The artist seeks out the luminous detail and presents it. He does not comment." Needless to say, the scholar must comment, but "scholarship has erred in presenting all detail as if of equal import" (*NA* 10.6:130). Both the scholar and the artist must select rather than simply assemble details.

Pound's famous short poem of 1913, "In a Station of the Metro," is an example of finding the luminous detail (note the original spacing, absent from most anthologized versions):[18]

> The apparition   of these faces   in the crowd :
> Petals   on a wet, black   bough .

Pound later explained exactly how he had found this luminous detail, well after the experience that triggered the emotion he sought to capture in words. The detail in this case was the image of flower petals on a wet, black bough, which became a way of describing the impression made on him by beautiful faces in a subway crowd. An experience was suddenly turned into an "apparition." The luminous detail, then, functioned in both scholarship and creative work. He concluded the second article of *I Gather the Limbs of Osiris* by mentioning how his scholarly work on *The Spirit of Romance* had an impact on his own creative work: "I have allowed it to impinge on my own poetry in 'Canzoni,' which is a great fault in the eyes of those critics who think I should be more interested in the poetry which I write myself than in 'fine poetry as a whole.' Personally, I think the *corpus poetarum* of more importance than any cell or phalange, and shall continue in sin." Again, we see Pound's determination in the face of critique, specifically the insistence of others that creative and scholarly organs didn't belong to the same body.

This organic frame sounds like something quite different from the luminous detail. Pound has a habit of making a strong argument that may conflict with other strong arguments he has made in other places. Our task, it seems, is to determine whether these are simply self-contradictions or a teacher groping his way toward some more complex conclusion. For Pound, as for T. S. Eliot, the only real way to "make it new" as an artist was to have a deep and rich understanding of literary history, or what Pound called "the media and the traditions of the art."[19] He took both creative work and scholarship with the utmost seriousness, and his long engagement with the academic world was an attempt to improve the education it delivered. One thing that is clear already is Pound's belief that a teacher needs to be able to explain how poetry works so that students can appreciate those moments when it is at its best. To that extent, the body of poetry and the luminous detail support one another.

The third article in the series begins with this statement:

> GUIDO CAVALCANTI, born A.D. 1250, greatest of Dante's precursors in Tuscany. His poetry is interesting, apart from its beauty, for his exact psychology, for an attempt to render emotions precisely; emotions, uncommon, perhaps, save in a land of sun, where the soul and the senses are joined in a union different, may be, from that which occurs in other countries. He, first in Tuscany, chose the "Ballata," the popular song, and raised it to the purposes of "high poetry." His mind was in a way the matrix against which the mind of the young Dante formed itself. (*NA* 10.7:155)

This statement, which is a compressed version of his work on Guido in *The Spirit of Romance*, serves here as an introduction to five translations by Pound of poems by the Tuscan poet. In the statement above, Pound demonstrates his knowledge of the period, and in his translations he shows his command of poetry itself. He tries to capture the form as well as the sense of Guido's songs, as in this version of Ballata IX:

> In a wood-way found I once a shepherdess
> More fair than stars are was she to my seeming.
>
> Her hair was wavy somewhat, like dull gold.
> Eyes? Love-worn, and her face like some pale rose.
> With a small twig she kept her lambs in hold
> And bare her feet were bar the dew-drop's gloze;
> She sang as one whom made love holdeth close,
> And joy was on her for an ornament. . . .

This is not the modern world, to be sure, and while the story may be familiar, many of these images are not clichés. The shepherdess controls her lambs with a small twig rather than the predictable large staff. She is alluring but not an image of perfection, and the speaker's modest request "for kisses only" leads apparently to something more, clothed in elegant images and surprising rhymes, almost-rhymes, and rhythms. This shepherdess may have been a goddess—of love perhaps, or even poetry—whose embrace makes the world more colorful and sweeter. Pound's ability to draw us into this medieval world of Tuscan verse lends force and credibility to his scholarly and critical claims. If we read the *Selected Prose* version only, we encounter the claims without the demonstration of skill that supports them, and that impoverishes the critical work. The two—scholarship and creation—go together for Pound, whose methods do not always fit our ways of categorizing written texts. Pound's insistence that one must become a poet oneself to some extent to understand poetic achievement may not be correct, but it is one of his most fundamental and consistent positions as a teacher of poetry. With examples like this, we can see what he means.

Having reminded us of his credentials as a translator through his versions of Guido's poems, he returns to the academic side in the fourth article, coming back to the "luminous detail" he had discussed, and he tells us that he thought of this series as parts of a book, even while it was appearing as articles. He also calls this article "A BEGINNING," which seems a strange title for the fourth piece in a series, but Pound is always beginning again, going back to first principles, starting over with new terms and metaphors in an attempt to teach us what he feels we really need to know. In this case, he imagines a man, ignorant of painting, thrust into a room full of masterpieces from all the ages of art, trying to assign aesthetic value to the works. Such a man would be lost, Pound feels, and compares him to another man, "thoroughly trained in some other branch of knowledge," among objects in a field far different from the one he knows, like Pound himself in a room full of engines. He would not understand them, but he would realize that he lacked the knowledge to achieve understanding, and he would seek that knowledge.

In the world of the arts, Pound points out,

> we must know, at least, a little of the various stages by which that art has grown from what it was to what it is. This is simply restatement of what ought to be in every text-book, and has nothing to do with any "new method." The handiest way to some knowledge of these "various stages" is, however, by "the new method"—that of luminous detail. (*NA* 10.8:179)

This clarifies a number of things that had been dark before. It is clear that Pound is talking about a pedagogical method, a manner of teaching and learning, and that the "luminous detail" is, in educational matters, simply a shortcut, a way of conveying knowledge about the history of an art that is more efficient than simply trying to cover everything. He then proceeds to illustrate the method by describing two kinds of artists or authors, whom he calls the "symptomatic" and the "donative." The symptomatic artist "registers" things, does what his predecessors had been doing. The donative artist "draws down" into his art something that was not there before. "His forbears may have led up to him; he is never a disconnected phenomenon, but he does take some step further. He discovers, or, better, 'he discriminates.'" (The language prefigures Pound's desire for the "efficient thesis.") The pedagogical problem is, then, how to help students recognize artistic discrimination when they see it.

At this point in his argument, Pound reminds us that, in his translations of "The Seafarer" and the poems of Guido, he has given us samples of very different kinds of "fine poetry." And he announces that in the next article he will show us a third kind of poetic beauty in the canzoni of Arnaut Daniel, adding this:

That beauty is, or would be if you read Provençal, a thing apparent, at least, a thing not to be helped or thrust upon you by any
prose of mine. In the translations (to follow next week) I give
that beauty—reproduced, that is, as nearly as I can reproduce it
in English—for what it is worth. What I must now do as the
scholar—in pursuance of my announced "method" is to justify
my use of Arnaut's work as a strategic position, as "luminous
detail." (179)

Pound treads a critical-pedagogical line closely here. On one hand, he insists
that beauty is "a thing apparent," and, on the other, he believes that he, as
the teacher, can guide the lay reader to the beauty.[20] Next, Pound explains
how Arnaut grew into a strong poetic tradition in Provence, adding something to that tradition:

Arnaut discriminated between rhyme and rhyme.
    He perceived, that is, that the beauty to be gotten from
a similarity of line-terminations depends not upon their multi-
plicity, but upon their action the one upon the other; not upon
frequency, but upon the manner of sequence and combination.
The effect of "lais" in mono-rhyme, or of a canzon in which a
few rhymes appear too often, is monotonous, is monotonous
beyond the point where monotony is charming or interesting.
Arnaut uses what for want of a better term I call polyphonic
rhyme. (179)

Taking his readership as a metaphorical class, Pound teaches about the
distinction between empty technique and meaningful poetic skill. It is not
just enough to rhyme. Rhyme needs to have a purpose. To this lesson,
Pound adds that Arnaut tightened the structure of Provençal verse, so that
each word makes "some special contribution to the effect of the whole."
His organicist aesthetic here is very close pedagogically to the New Critics.
Finally, he credits this poet with a special sense of the musicality of verse,
generating a tighter relationship among words, rhythm, and music, along
with a "precision of observation and reference" that earned the admiration
of Dante. The real test, however, will come in the next article, when Pound
will present his own translations of Arnaut's verse.
    The fifth article is subtitled "Four Early Poems of Arnaut Daniel" and
begins with two paragraphs of introduction in which Pound explains the

relationship between the form he has used and the originals, and he tells us something about Arnaut's world, comparing it with the rather different medievalism of certain British writers of the nineteenth century. About the form of the first two poems, the teacher has this to say:

> The poem runs on four rhymes. Their order in the stanzas changes. Whether I have transgressed in translating with three rhymes and an assonance cannot be determined until we know more twelfth-century orthography and the various dialects of Provençe. The second poem has a rhythm like a sea-chanty, and is almost more like an estampida or dance form than a canzon. It is an interesting experiment in "elevens" and a strong changing caesura. All the poems must be considered as things to *sing*. (*NA* 10.9:201)

One can see how Pound's admiration for Arnaut is also bound up in the early poet's personality. About Arnaut the person, Pound tells us that he was

> a very real, very much alive young man who has kicked over the traces, told his instructors to go to hell, put his title "En" ("Sir") in his wallet, and set out to see life as a jongleur. He will see no stags with crosses growing from their foreheads, he will not fly to an imprisoned lady in the form of a hawk; he will, I think, preserve through life a pleasing sense of humour, he will dine often with the Coeur de Lion, he will form some sort of friendship with that dyspeptic curmudgeon, En Bertrans de Born, fourth holder in the tower of Altaforte. But this sort of thing belongs to the novelists and not to a pedagogue. (201)

Obviously Pound, who had, in a manner of speaking, told his own instructors at Penn to go to hell, in order to go abroad and live as a poet, feels a personal sympathy for Arnaut, who had done something similar eight hundred years earlier, but he catches himself rhapsodizing, and retreats to the position of pedagogue. What does and does not belong to the pedagogue, though, seems a matter of contention for this schoolmaster, who clearly also delighted in this role of the "novelist." He gives us a line from the original of one of Arnaut's poems, "Bona es vida / pos joia la mante," which he translates colloquially as "Bully is living / where joy can back it up." In the full translation of the poem, however, he offers a very different version of the line, constrained by the intricate rhyme scheme he is imitating:

Aye, life's a high thing
　　　Where joy's his maintenance,
Who cries 'tis wry thing
　　　Hath danced never my dance,
I can advance
　　　No blame against fate's tithing
For my good chance
Hath deemed the best thing my thing.

As a mere "pedagogue," Pound intricately and effectively provides a version in English that lets us feel the music of the poem and the lively humor of the young poet. He is teaching us how to hear what he elsewhere calls the "joy" in Arnaut. Using the mastery he has, quite unlike his teachers operating in the philological mode, he enables us to share in the pleasures of the poetry. This is no mean achievement, and it requires the pedagogue to be a poet and still be willing to accept the humble role of teacher—to put his poetry in the service of instruction. This is an admirable aspect of Pound, and it prepares the way for his return to scholarship in the next article, "On Virtue."

In this article, Pound does not refer to proper behavior but to something much deeper: "*virtu*"—the quality that distinguishes one individual from another. "It is the artist's business to find his own *virtu*" (*NA* 10.10:224), he writes, and then proceeds to offer four literary artists as examples of writers who, like Arnaut setting out, found their own *virtu* and were donative rather than symptomatic, adding something special to the traditions they inherited: Homer, Dante, Chaucer, and Shakespeare. Describing their special qualities, he modestly admits, "I doubt not that a person of wider reading could make a better arrangement of names than this is, but I must talk from my corner of the things that I know." This is, of course, a rather safe list, unlikely to generate much opposition then or now, but it does serve to illustrate Pound's thoughts on both "virtue" and "donation." Turning back in the next issue to Arnaut—a poet less familiar to the readers of *The New Age*—Pound offers a brief introduction on the relationship between words and music in Provençal verse.[21] He notes that "the poems in the old manuscripts are written straight along like prose," adding that he "print[s] the verses in this form only better to indicate the rhyme scheme." He then indicates how the reader should group the lines in reading them, using what he calls the stanza "where my translation of the movement is the most felicitous" as his example. It is almost as if the teacher, comfortable with the malleability in the rhythm of the verse, were providing a teaching exercise for his class. The scholar, the translator, the poet, and the critic are all coming together as one person—the schoolmaster.

"Canzon: of the Trades and Love" shows a teacher delving further into his subject. Here Pound tries to show his students the subtleties of Arnaut's verse with a long introduction to a poem, which begins with an attempt to describe the delicacy of metaphors and includes an admission: "I have translated it badly even if my idiom does mean about the same as the Provençal" (*NA* 10.12:274). He goes on to discuss Arnaut's learning ("His Latin was, let us say, no better than mine") and then to take us deeper into the complexities of determining Arnaut's intentions from an imperfect manuscript in an unsettled language. Perhaps the most interesting feature of this poem for our purposes is the conclusion, which Pound had translated before in *The Spirit of Romance*. Comparing the two versions can tell us something about how conscientious Pound is in his attempt to convey the qualities of the original as vigorously as possible:

Original: Ieu sui Arnant qu'amas l'aura
E chatz le lebre ab lo bou
E nadi contra suberna

First version: I am Arnaut who loves the wind,
And chases the hare with the ox,
And swims against the torrent.

Second version: I, Arnaut, love the wind, doing
My hare-hunts on an ox-cart,
And I swim against the torrent.

The second version is not more literal, but it has been adjusted to the schoolmaster's current purpose, which is to demonstrate how Arnaut's verse sounded. That is, these three concluding lines of the poem now rhyme with the concluding three lines of the previous six stanzas. The final words of the last three lines of the fifth, for example, are "going," "smart," and "warrant," which jingle nicely with "doing," "cart," and "torrent." Pound is teaching students of poetry—aficionados and future poets alike—to read with their ears. This does not sound so revolutionary nowadays, but, compared with many of Pound's teachers, it was. All of this prepares us for the ninth article, "On Technique."

Notably a defense, this article attends to the form in which an artwork appears and the history of the medium in which such work takes shape. It is "mildly unthinkable," says Pound, that a child with no training might hear Ferruccio Busoni play Frederic Chopin and hire a hall to perform "what she thinks sounds somewhat the same" (*NA* 10.13:297). And he adds, "No great composer has, so far as I know, boasted an ignorance of musical tradition or thought himself less a musician because he could play Mozart correctly." Still, with respect to poetry, he argues, many people are proud of their ignorance and blindly attack either free verse or symmetrical form.[22] Often, as in the above quotation, Pound insists that people know something about a subject they plan to discuss. (Pound himself would not always follow this rule.) Other times, as we shall see in the next chapter, Pound seeks to provide shortcuts, so that people would not have to do as much work. Whatever the takeaway about preparedness, Pound's point in this article is clear: technique is not static, but something that changes with cultural transformations. The great epic poems emerged from worlds with higher degrees of cultural uniformity than can be found in modernity. The need for technical skill persists, but the forms must change to meet changing conditions: "As for the arts and their technique—technique is the means of conveying an exact impression of exactly what one means in such a way as to exhilarate" (298). These means are not set and never have been settled, and technical skill is not sufficient in itself to produce art at the highest levels.

Making a powerful case for the importance of all the arts, Pound writes,

> Our life is, in so far as it is worth living, made up in great part of things indefinite, impalpable; and it is precisely because the arts present us these things that we—humanity—cannot get on without the arts. The picture that suggests indefinite poems, the line of verse that means a gallery of paintings, the modulation that suggests a score of metaphors and is contained in none: it is these things that touch us nearly that "matter." (298)

This is the schoolmaster at his finest—open but not vague, engaged but not heavy-handed—embracing the "comparative method" he advocated for in college, and laying the foundation for future ways to teach the arts in school.

Speaking of the art of poetry in particular, he admits that he is "trying to say something about the masterly use of words, and it is not easy." There is a "Technique of Content," which comes from a poetic tradition controlled and applied by an artist of genius, and a lesser "technique of manner," which is nonetheless valuable as a gauge of sincerity. These two techniques, we can see, correspond to the donative and symptomatic kinds of poet Pound has already described. They are predictable ways to talk about art, but with a slight Poundian twist: what is clearer now for this teacher who is still working out his method is that the higher form depends upon the lower.

> If technique is thus the protection of the public, the sign manual by which it distinguishes between the serious artist and the disagreeable young person expressing its haedinus egotism, it is no less a protection to the artist himself during the most crucial period of his development. I speak now of technique seriously studied, of a searching into cause and effect, into the purposes of sound and rhythm as such, not—not by any means—of a conscientious and clever imitation of the master of the moment, of the poet in vogue.
>
> How many have I seen, how many have we all of us known, young, with promising poetic insides, who produce one book and die of it? For in our time, at least, the little public that does read new poetry is not twice bored by the same aspirant, and if a man's first book has not in it some sign of a serious struggle with the basis of the art he has small likelihood of meeting them in a second.[23] (298)

Pound insists on technique, even as he preaches originality. Imagine the rhetorical confidence of this twenty-six-year-old teacher to speak of the "how many have we all of us known" and declaiming "the disagreeable young person expressing its haedinus egotism"—a phrase likely apposite, for many of Pound's Penn professors, to describe Pound himself. Perhaps this closeness to home allows Pound, here, to be spot on. His sense of the new, young writer is not wrong in any measure, and the "serious struggle" he speaks of is the writer's education, which—whether formal or not, self-taught or coached—enables the writer to come to grips with both cultural tradition and contemporary social relevance. Turning into a writing teacher, the schoolmaster then advises the young poets to understand that no one cares to hear, in strained iambics, that he feels sprightly in spring, is uncomfortable when his sexual desires are ungratified and that he has read about human brotherhood in last year's magazines. But let a man once convince thirty people that he has some faint chance of finding, or that he, at least, is determined and ready to suffer all drudgery in attempting to find, some entanglement of words so subtle, so crafty that they can be read or heard without yawning. . . . —let thirty or a dozen people believe this, and the man of whom they believe it will find friendship where he had little expected it, and delightful things will befall him suddenly and with no other explanation. (299)

Pound is conflicted. He wants a wide audience but has resigned himself to being comfortable with a small but serious following. His and others' art would still be meaningful even if that grand lecture hall never materialized. Having started by talking to readers, he finishes this article by addressing writers (some of whom are college students looking for a different sort of artistic education). Clearly he feels that it was crucial for them to understand one another, and for writers to write as readers and for readers to read, to the extent that they are able, as writers. This multidimensional approach to the arts is what Pound found lacking in his own academic instruction.

The series continues with Pound seeking to connect with other interested parties—not the reader and writer, but "the poet and the musician" (*NA* 10.15:344). Some verse is written to be sung, and some is written to be spoken or read silently. About the proper relation of poetry to music, Pound begins by admitting defeat: "it seems to me not only futile, but very nearly impossible, to lay down any principles whatever for the regulation of their conjunctions" (343). Futility, however, is not an obstacle. After admitting defeat, Pound goes on to tackle the problem anyway, offering some principles he feels most poets and musicians would agree make sense—that the words should be intelligible when sung, that they should not be much distorted, and that the rhythm of poetry should not be "unreasonably ruined" when set to music. ("Unreasonably"—what a word for Pound to use here!) The poet knows well that those who translate from one language to another or from one medium to another cannot help but do damage. He just asks that it not be excessive. He can also hear a poetic cadence that is beyond the metrical. Avoiding a discussion that he admits "would be, perhaps, too technical for these pages," he offers Arnaut Daniel's verse as a model of words that, when sung to the tunes he wrote for them, "lose neither in beauty nor in intelligibility."

The eleventh article, untitled, continues the discussion of the relationship between words and music, with Pound noting that he has been asked about how much he adds or changes in his translations.[24] "The Seafarer," he tells us, was "as nearly literal, I think, as any translation can be." Nor has he tried, in the case of Arnaut, "to ornament the text" (*NA* 10.16:369). However, he feels that, having given us a sense of Arnaut's rhyme schemes, he should now try to show us the "internal thought-form" or "thought-progress" of one of his poems by providing a prose version of a canzon, after which he seems to admit defeat with respect to this entire project: "I am not in the least sure that I have yet made clear the reasons for my writing these articles." Recovering quickly from these doubts, however, he insists on a "unity of intention" in his own "rambling discourses," a "luminous detail," if you will, that he himself has wholly yet to discover (370). This article is perhaps the most revealing of the set, in that he keeps floundering into admissions of failure and then rallying to claim a sort of success:

> As far as the "living art" goes, I should like to break up *cliché,* to disintegrate these magnetised groups that stand between the reader of poetry and the drive of it. . . . For it is not until poetry lives again "close to the thing" that it will be a vital part of contemporary life. As long as the poet says not what he, at the very crux of a clarified conception, means, but is content to say something ornate and approximate, just so long will serious people, intently alive, consider poetry as balderdash. . . .
>
> And the only way to escape from rhetoric and frilled paper decoration is through beauty—"beauty of the thing," certainly, but besides that, "beauty of the means." I mean by that that one must call a spade a spade in form so exactly adjusted, in a metric in itself so seductive, that the statement will not bore the auditor. Or again, since I seem to flounder in my attempt at utterance, we must have a simplicity and directness of utterance, which is different from the simplicity and directness of daily speech, which is more "curial," more dignified. This difference, this dignity, cannot be conferred by florid adjectives or elaborate hyperbole; it must be conveyed by art, and by the art of the

verse structure, by something which exalts the reader, making
him feel that he is in contact with something arranged more
finely than the commonplace. (370)

The exactness of language, which Pound had fleetingly found in the "image"
and would eventually find in the ideogram, has an important social and
pedagogical component: it needs to live "close to the thing." As any writing
teacher knows, part of the project involves breaking up the wonderfully
phrased "magnetized groups" of words, or clichés, which uncritically and
unimaginatively attract verb to noun. Despite a little clichéd language of his
own in this passage, Pound can still advocate forcefully for that linguistic
space striving to be "close to the thing," even if this teacher-as-a-model-of-
learner is "flounder[ing]" (or performing as much for effect) like his imagined
students in his "attempt at utterance." Pressing on, he moves from cliché to
paradox: "Works of art attract by a resembling unlikeness." He is nearing
Viktor Shklovsky and the Russian Formalist concept of defamiliarization
here but hasn't quite arrived.[25] Moving back to technique, he asks, "Is
my direction the right one?" and then insists that it is. Technique, rightly
understood, is not "suavity of exterior" but "the clinch of expression on
the thing intended to be expressed." This sounds flighty, but it is point on.
Reminding us that he has spent six months of his life translating poems
by "a man living in what one of my more genial critics calls 'a very dead
past,'" he asks if this was justifiable for anyone not a philologist. Addressing
his own doubts, Pound rationalizes that a poet needs to learn technique
from the best examples available, and he defends Arnaut as being just that.
   But this emphasis on what the verbal artist needs is a shift from the
focus of the opening articles, which stressed "The New Method in Scholarship" and "the Luminous Detail." In his final paragraphs, Pound seems aware
that they have gone missing, and he raises the question of "the scholastic
bearing" of what he has been saying. He admits that this is less important
to him than the artistic, but he did, after all, begin with the scholastic, so
he feels obliged to give it some attention, saying, as he gets to the end,
"[i]n this paragraph I wish to be strictly pedagogical." Then, without using
the phrase again, he makes it clear that Arnaut Daniel's work has meant
to serve as a luminous detail, a key that can unlock for us—his non-
institutionalized students—a larger world of poetry:

Arnaut was at the centre of the thing. So intimate a study of
nearly any other troubadour would bore one, and might not

> throw much light on the work of the others; having analysed or even read an analysis of Arnaut, any other Provençal canzon is clearer to one. Knowing him I mean, one can read the rest of Provençal poetry with as little need for special introductions and annotation as one has in reading the Victorians. We know in reading, let us say, [Bertran] de Born, what part is personal, what part is technical, how good it is in manner, how good in matter. And this method of study seems to me the one in which the critic or professor presents the energetic part of his knowledge, the method by which the audience becomes most intelligent of or the most sensitive to the subject or period discussed. (370)

Returning to his perfectly reasonable insistence that professors be "energetic," Pound links the absorption of knowledge not to scholarly erudition but to audience engagement. It is worth noting at this point that Pound's "luminous detail" resembles in certain respects the "touchstones" of Matthew Arnold, in that both are meant as pedagogical shortcuts, ways of approaching one poet by means of another. But there are differences. Arnold was offering single lines of Shakespeare and other poets as a way of evaluating the work of others, regardless of their time and place. Pound presents a larger sample of one poet as a way of understanding and placing others working in a similar culture. Both Arnold and Pound admired Dante, but Pound uses Dante's opinion of Arnaut to help situate Arnaut and a whole poetic tradition. Dante learned from Arnaut and built on his achievement. Pound was not only after "the best that is known and thought in the world" and he, at least on this occasion, did not need to label the "critical faculty [as] lower than the inventive."[26] Both Pound and Arnold were teachers, and both could be essentializing in advocating for their own brands of humanism, however different their methods were. While Arnold searched for the poet who could capture a deep-seeded "humanness," Pound believed in a comparative method and a poetry that could illuminate an era, and not all eras were the same. While Arnold was after something more universal, Pound saw that history changed the possibilities available to poets.

The final article in the series is called "Three Canzoni of Arnaut Daniel" and consists of poetic translations by Pound that we should now be in a position to appreciate, finding for ourselves the luminous details that made his work so important for Dante—and for Pound. The success or failure of the entire series depends, then, on whether we can understand and appreciate Arnaut's poems in Pound's verse translations, and, like all teachers, Pound will have to be judged by what his students have actually learned. The limbs of Osiris have been gathered. Where are we now? It feels as though Pound has indeed taught us something, without having quite accomplished what he promised at the beginning (the comprehensiveness of "a new method"). Still, this series is not without its own luminous details, and, like any good teacher, his enthusiasm for the poetry he presents can be contagious. *The New Age* had an exceptionally lively section of letters to the editor at the end of every issue. During the period in which Pound's *Osiris* articles appeared there were controversies raging in these pages about modern art, feminism, socialism, suffrage, the art of the novel, and Henri Bergson—but Pound's articles unfortunately went mostly unnoticed at the time.[27] He stayed on with the journal until he left London in 1920, ultimately reviewing art under the pen name of B. H. Dias and music under William Atheling. While he would never again publish something as wide-ranging in scope in *The New Age*, his books over the next decades would continue to develop his comparative methodology, and that is where we now turn.

CHAPTER 3

How to Read Comparatively

Keep on remindin 'em that we ain't bolcheviks, but only the terrifyin' voice of civilization, kulchuh, refinement, aesthetic perception.

—Pound to Harriet Monroe, December 27, 1931
(qtd. in Paige 237)

Although meant mostly for non-academic audiences, many of Pound's scholarly books had strong pedagogical and curricular implications. This chapter considers a handful of those books, including one of his later poetry anthologies. As the decades under question progressed, Pound's comparative methodology (originally confined to mostly literary matters) would turn into a global vision and become, in an astonishing and dangerous way, historically, socially, and politically comprehensive.

In 1918 and 1920, Pound published two books with strong pedagogical elements. His book of 1918, *Pavannes and Divisions*, had two parts, as the title suggests—a more creative part and a more critical or pedagogical part. The "pavanne" was a slow dance form, used in earlier times, but it had come back into use in modern music as a name for short compositions by Gabriel Fauré, Claude Debussy, Maurice Ravel, and others. "Divisions," on the other hand, suggests something more mathematically exact—peculiar, because his distinctly human critical and pedagogical efforts are anything but mathematical. The pieces collected here appeared mainly in magazines between 1912 and 1916, but he sometimes adds later thoughts from 1917 as well. He begins with a section called "A Retrospect" in which he returns to the debates about Imagism, which took place from 1912 through 1914.

Looking back, Pound reminds us of the three key principles that he, H.D., and Richard Aldington agreed upon in 1912: direct treatment of the subject, avoidance of excess words, and musical rather than metronomic rhythm. This is pretty much how "Imagism" is taught to this day. Just how serious Pound was about the movement remains in doubt, but it is not doubtful how much he acted as the teacher, "conducting a literary kindergarten" back then.[1]

It is clear throughout his work that Pound has two main pedagogical modes—teaching readers of literature and teaching potential creators of it—and these two modes are clearly visible in the "Divisions" section of this book. The discussions of Imagism are mainly aimed at poets or potential poets for whom he reprints his "Donts" from *Poetry* magazine, reminding his readers to pay no attention to critics who have written nothing "notable" themselves.[2] One of the persistent motifs in this volume is a comparison of artists with scientists; Pound maintains that both are trying to discover things, but in different spheres.[3] He also protests more than once that he really does not want to be writing about art, insisting that he "would rather play tennis" (103).[4] Pound, for his part, did play a lot of tennis in London and later in Rapallo, but he also kept writing about verbal art, believing that "The more every man knows about poetry, the better" (105). While it is easy to see the personal and political motives of such a statement, we would be remiss if we did not allow that Pound the teacher was also speaking genuinely here.

In a note added in 1917, he observes that he has in fact written a lot about art, sculpture, painting, and poetry, but he thinks it would be better for people to look at the artists and writers he has written about, rather than read him or any other critic: "All the critic can do for the reader or audience or spectator is to focus his gaze or audition. Rightly or wrongly I think my blasts and essays have done their work and that more people are now likely to go to the sources than are likely to read this book" (109). One gathers that he was half-sincere in saying this, but he also clearly thought he was writing for an audience, and he tried very hard to reach and persuade his readers, recommending books to them. He proposes to "treat my strange reader as if he were a new friend come into the room, intent on ransacking my bookshelf" (110).[5] This pattern would simply be extended in his next book, *Instigations*.

Writing about Remy de Gourmont in *Pavannes and Divisions*, Pound offers praise in particular for his fairness and then observes that "we all have our moments off guard when we become unfair, and partisan, and personal in our spite, and intolerant" (116). He knew this about himself in 1915, but did not always remember it as he got older. In a piece on the early music specialist Arnold Dolmetsch, Pound concludes with a speculation that points toward those later years. Wondering why fine things like Dolmetsch's work always seem to go on in corners, he moves toward a larger social perspective:

> Is it that the aristocracy, which ought to set the fashion, is too weakened and too unreal to perform the due functions of "aristocracy"? Is it that nature can, in fact, only produce a certain number of vortices? That the quattrocento shines out because the vortices of social power coincided with the vortices of creative intelligence? And that when these vortices do not coincide we have an age of "art in strange comers" and of great dullness among the quite rich? Is it that real democracy can only exist under feudal conditions, when no man fears to recognise creative skill in his neighbour? (150)

He would later find in the fascism of Mussolini a modern equivalent for the feudal conditions he thought might be required for real renaissance. Back in 1917, however, he turns his attention to the work of James Joyce, making a distinction that clearly anticipates Virginia Woolf's famous observation about human character changing in December 1910.[6] "Mr. Joyce's more rigorous selection of the presented detail marks him, I think, as belonging to my own generation, that is, to the 'nineteen-tens,' not to the decade between 'the 'nineties' and to-day" (160). Pound, it is worth pointing out, was never socially accepted in Bloomsbury as T. S. Eliot was, but his thought made an impact there nonetheless.[7]

Returning to his beloved troubadours in another essay, Pound directs attention to the prose "razzos" that sometimes prefaced work in the medieval manuscripts, seeing in their laconic comments about the troubadours "the seeds of literary criticism" (173). These quick turns from Dolmetsch and his early music instruments to Joyce, and back to the troubadours, are entirely typical of Pound. His comparative pedagogy asks that we consider these things together.

> My purpose in all this is to suggest to the casual reader that the Middle Ages did not exist in tapestry alone, nor in the 14th century romances, but that there was a life like our own, no mere sequence of cithern and citoles, nor a continuous stalking about

in sendal and diaspre. Men were pressed for money. There was unspeakable boredom in the castles. The chivalric singing was devised to lighten the boredom; and this very singing became itself in due time, in the manner of all things, an ennui. (176)

A philologist would make much of the citherns and citoles (loot-like musical instruments) and the sendal and diaspre (silks and ornamental fabrics) in setting off the fourteenth century from our own. We make of history what we can, basing our knowledge on events and artifacts of the age. In doing so, we think that the people of the time performed and re-performed our belated notions of their era. But, for Pound, they did not "continuously stalk" around in the garments we now have in our museums. Rather, they *lived*, much as we do today, their world closer to ours than our historicist, metonymic reductions can imagine. And, like us, they grew tired of the repetitions of their own time. Boredom was never very far from Pound's thought. He hated it and tried very hard to avoid it in his poetry and in his prose. And he recognized that any way of writing or mode of art (like teaching lessons) that went unchanged for a long period of time would become boring. His well-known advice to "make it new" stems from his pedagogical sense that failure to do this would lead to boredom, then cultural stagnation, thereby sapping all reason out of life.

Turning to earlier English literature, Pound makes a case for the value of translation: "A great age of literature is perhaps always a great age of translation; or follows it" (193), and he points to Edward Fitzgerald (translator of the *Rubatyat of Omar Khayyam*), Algernon Charles Swinburne, and Dante Gabriel Rossetti as Victorian translators of consequence, without saying directly that they paved the way for the poets of the "nineteen-tens." He was seriously committed to translation himself, as we know, but he also insists on the importance of the work of other English translators, going all the way back to Arthur Golding, whose sixteenth-century translation of Ovid he praises highly (we might jocularly call this "On first looking into Golding's Ovid"): "Can we, for our part, know our Ovid until we find him in Golding? Is there one of us so good at his latin, and so ready in imagination that Golding will not throw upon his mind shades and glamours inherent in the original text, which had for all that escaped him?" (197). Pound compares Golding favorably with his bête noir, John Milton, while claiming not to be arguing about poetical greatness, insisting that Golding is not only a good translator but a very good poet as well:

> I point out that Golding was endeavouring to convey the sense
> of the original to his readers. He names the thing of his orig-
> inal author, by the name most germane, familiar, homely, to
> his hearers. He is intent on conveying a meaning, and not on
> bemusing them with a rumble. And I hold that the real poet is
> sufficiently absorbed in his content to care more for the content
> than the rumble; and also that Chaucer and Golding are more
> like to find the mot juste (whether or no they held any theories
> there-anent) than were for some centuries their successors, saving
> the author of "Hamlet." (203–4)

One can see Pound's pedagogical temperament in the claim that Golding was "conveying a meaning," rather than rumbling. On the other hand, Milton, in Pound's view, cared more for the rumble. He represented everything Pound detested in poetry (though the latter can still find a few words of praise for the sonority of Milton's blank verse and admits that some of his short poems are not bad). Golding, on the other hand, reminds Pound of his studies of Ovid's *Metamorphoses* in college, where his professor brought to life the childish antics of Icarus, playing with the wax his father was using to make the wings that might help them fly out of imprisonment. Recalling that moment from his past as a student, Pound observes, "Yet if after sixteen years a professor's words came back to one, it is perhaps important that the classics should be humanly, rather than philologically taught, even in class-rooms." What is happening, however, as Pound sees it, is that the classics are being neglected by current education or deadened by philological methods of instruction, the kind of "education" he called the "onanism of the soul" (207). He was not against education. Far from it. But he thought it was often being done badly in those places where it was most important to get it right. Rather than produce new understanding—the natural course of education—philological learning was like Shakespeare's "expense of spirit in a waste of shame."

Perhaps the most significant single piece in this whole collection appears in the appendix. It was first published as a series of three articles called "The Serious Artist," provoked by *The New Freewoman*'s editor, Dora Marsden. Pound's articles appeared in that magazine late in 1913, though in *Pavannes and Divisions* it is erroneously attributed to the magazine's successor, *The Egoist*, which did not appear until 1914. Assuming that the note of attribution is Pound's own, he clearly thought of these two

publications as one magazine and probably preferred the Stirneresque title
of the final version to the feminist name of its predecessor.[8] He began the
series by complaining about having to defend poetry three centuries after
Sir Philip Sidney had done so quite adequately, but he nevertheless under-
takes to make the case again for the modern age after muttering that one
work of art—and there are different ways to understand this—was worth
"forty prefaces and as many apologiae" (219). Pound's case was based on
connecting poetry to science: "The arts, literature, poesy, are a science, just
as chemistry is a science. Their subject is man, mankind and the individual.
The subject of chemistry is matter considered as to its composition."[9] The
sentiment seems to contradict Pound's earlier words about the intangibility
of art ("The picture that suggests indefinite poems"), but Pound was a man
given to contradictions.

Having declared poetry a science, Pound then claims that it is a science that studies particularities, paradoxically reporting on the individualities
of human existence: "From the arts we learn that man is whimsical, that
one man differs from another. That men differ among themselves as leaves
upon trees differ. That they do not resemble each other as do buttons cut
by machine" (220). When Pound talks about the "science" of art, he does
not intend what semioticians and structuralists later meant by it. As he sees
it, the function of the arts as a kind of science is to provide what he calls
"data for ethics" (226), which include biological data, determined by quantitative observation, and artistic data, determined by the unique perceptions
of a gifted and trained individual: "The serious artist is scientific in that he
presents the image of his desire, of his hate, of his indifference as precisely
that, as precisely the image of his own desire, hate, or indifference. The
more precise his record the more lasting and unassailable his work of art"
(226). Pound's faith in the "gifted and talented individual" was in part a
faith in himself, but it would also eventually lead him down dangerous roads.

For now, Pound was content to contrast the artist with the "theorist,"
who generalizes from personal experience and then urges others to behave
as "he, the theorist, would like to behave," whereas "art never asks anybody
to do anything, or to think anything, or to be anything" (226–27). Pound's
motive here is honest, but his universalizing belief is problematic. Still, for
him, the serious artist and the scientist are set in opposition to the theorist
and the journalist, as individuals in search of the truth as opposed to others
who either mislead the public or simply tell it what it wants to hear. The
function of the arts, in this formulation, is to teach people about human
life—not to generalize about what it should be, but to describe what it

is. Such teaching, however, requires technical mastery of a medium, and it also requires passion. The verbal artist or poet must achieve "maximum efficiency of expression" but must also have discovered something—either about the world or about the medium itself (240–41). Those requirements explain why, for Pound, great art must always be different from the modes of expression that have become accepted and standardized in a culture.

In one of the concluding pieces in the appendix to the "Divisions," Pound makes a remark that takes us deep into his thinking about education and prepares the way for his next collection of articles, telling us that "[t]here is no culture that is not at least bilingual" (243). For him this is one explanation for the way that American artists whom he admires, like Whistler and Henry James, end up in exile, getting to London by way of Paris, absorbing foreign language and culture on the way. It is also, of course, his own pattern, and it points to his book of 1920, *Instigations*, which provoked an intelligent and sympathetic review in *The Dial*, with a title borrowed for our book: "SUPER SCHOOLMASTER" (Oct. 1920). This review was written by one of the editors, James Sibley Watson Jr., using the pen name of W. C. Blum. Watson quickly got to the heart of the matter: "An important point, however, about Mr Pound's critical writings, which has been generally neglected, is this: they do satisfy two very conspicuous demands of the American public; the demand for 'constructive criticism' and the demand for 'first rate school teaching'" (422). This is what has been lost in most glosses of Pound.

Watson seems to have gotten some things exactly right, noting that Pound's belief in good schoolteaching has led to his "doing his work in a schoolmasterly fashion," delivering a "correspondence course of lectures" to "a special public, a class of students," and "filling in the gaps in the curricula of his misguided but indispensable colleagues, the professors." Noting that Pound's work is insufficiently appreciated, Watson concludes by asking this question: "Is nobody aware that a contemporary writer is actually giving a course on the Comparative Literature of the Present, that a first rate literary man, a poet, with the rarest gift for translation is bothering to teach school?" (423). As an editor of *The Dial*, he knew quite a bit about Pound, who was a foreign advisor or editor and a regular contributor at that time. We, however, are still in the process of recognizing just how pedagogical Pound's work was, more than ninety years after Watson pointed it out for all to see.

The full title of Pound's book of 1920 was *Instigations of Ezra Pound*. The preposition "of" throws the author's name into the title, thereby—and this was not uncommon for this particular author—making Pound the instigator. Pound knew and took pride in his pedagogy of "instigation." He loved to goad or prod his readers, as we have already seen, and this book would be no different. The first section, called "A STUDY OF FRENCH POETS," runs for a hundred pages. It is a revised and expanded version of a collection of French poems presented by Pound in *The Little Review* in 1918. He had hoped, he tells us, to print the poems "interposing no comment of my own between author and reader; confining my criticism to selection. But that plan was not feasible" (3). That plan was not used for *Instigations* either, as Pound introduces the poets to his readers and explains the reasons behind his selections in what he calls "a qualitative analysis" (6), situating Théophile Gauthier as the main predecessor of the moderns and naming three poets as Gauthier's principal successors: Tristan Corbière, Arthur Rimbaud, and Jules Laforgue.[10] If Pound's project as foreign correspondent for numerous journals involved introducing incredibly fresh voices to the American public, then part of that pedagogy was in reintroducing older writers from other countries to the same unaware audience.

Pound clearly believes that such Parisian artists and writers gave France a civilization superior to that of Britain and the United States, and he thought that his native country badly needed some of that culture.[11] Discussing Rimbaud leads Pound to a personal observation that is quite interesting. After praising "Comédie en Trois Baisers" as a treatment of a subject older than Ovid with no silliness or vulgarity, the schoolmaster reflects, "How much I might have learned from the printed page that I have learned slowly from actualities. Or perhaps we never do learn from the page; but are only capable of recognizing the page after we have learned from actuality" (34). In the back and forth of life and art, of rereading and reexperiencing, this teacher is not afraid to let us see his human side. We are a long way from philology here. This moment is as memorable as Pound's own teacher's observation about the young Icarus was to him sixteen years later. He concludes his discussion of these three poets with praise of Rimbaud's "firmness of coloring" and "certitude" and then moves on to other French poets who worked in other modes of verse, starting with the symboliste Remy de Gourmont.

Speaking of de Gourmont's use of the litany, Pound observes that "[i]t was one of the great gifts of 'symbolisme,' of the doctrine that one should 'suggest' not 'present'; it is, in his hand, an effective indirectness."[12] We follow his guidance, then, through poet after poet, even as he gives his onetime antagonist Amy Lowell some credit for representing one of them adequately in her *Six French Poets* anthology. Pound offers a hint here, a prod there, shepherding us through this field of verse with bits of biographical information and interpretive guidance, embodying the words James Sibley Watson said about him, until he arrives at last at one of the most important figures in modern French literature, Jules Romains, and the movement called "Unanimism." Pound sees this movement as an attempt to deal with modern urban life as earlier cultures dealt with nature:

> Romains is not to be understood by extracts and fragments. He has felt this general replunge of mind into instinct, or this development of instinct to cope with a metropolis, and with metropolitan conditions; in so far as he has expressed the emotions of this consciousness he is poet; he has, aside from that, tried to formulate this new consciousness, and in so far as such formulation is dogmatic, debatable, intellectual, hypothetical, he is open to argument and dispute; that is to say he is philosopher, and his philosophy is definite and defined. (70–71)

We have encountered this distinction between poet and philosopher before in Pound's essays, but this is a refinement in that we find both figures supporting one another in the same writer's work. Pound compares Romains with Wyndham Lewis as writers who have captured some essential aspects of modern life, and he offers these lines from "Puissances de Paris" as an example of Romains's method:

> Je suis l'esclave heureux des hommes dont l'haleine
> Flotte ici. Leur vouloirs s'ecoule dans mes nerfs;
> Ce qui est moi commence a fondre. (72)

> [I am the happy slave of men whose breath
> Floats here. Their wishes flow through my nerves;
> That which is me begins to dissolve.]

Pound praises these lines for their simplicity, originality, and clarity, adding that Romains's style "has the freshness of grass, not of new furniture polish" (73). In this description, Pound's critical prose has risen to the occasion, and it is hard for any curious student to resist such praise.[13] The plainness with which Pound describes not the meaning but the *effect* of the poem reveals his eagerness for newness and draws on his enthusiasm for Ernest Fenollosa

(73). It is that simple and that difficult, a noun meeting a verb (something Pound's teachers would never think to say), which makes poetry happen.[14]

In the next section of *Instigations*, he moves to Henry James, using an article he wrote for a special *Little Review* number on James as the basis for his new version. He had, in fact, organized the tribute to James in the magazine and had driven himself to read through the many volumes of James's work to write the main article in that issue. The effort left him feeling rather overwhelmed, and his view of James remained complicated to the point of self-contradiction. Throughout this study, Pound will act not so much the literary critic as the teacher, assigning certain works and telling his students what to look for in them, situating James in his time and culture so as to make him more sympathetic and intelligible. He begins by warning his readers that "[t]his essay on James is a dull grind of an affair, a Baedecker to a continent" (107). It goes downhill from there, and up and down many times before its sixty pages are done. He is not sure whether James is less read than formerly or whether he ought to be more read than he is. He praises the novelist as a conversationalist and then says that only readers who have lived on both sides of the Atlantic are in a position to understand or appreciate his writings. While the novelist can be lauded for "making America intelligible," he also is mostly understood by those who can recognize their grandmother's friends in his characters (108). Pound himself, sure enough, had lived on both sides of the Atlantic and knew his grandmother's friends well enough, but he declines to present to his readers "a full volume of detailed criticism," offering some general claims instead.[15] He concludes his introduction to James's work by praising the author's mighty efforts to communicate, to educate his readers about human variety: "It is a recognition of differences, of the right of differences to exist, of interest in finding things different. Kultur is an abomination; philology is an abomination, all repressive uniforming education is an evil" (111). Pound was always thinking about the right and wrong sorts of education, and he saw James as on his side of those debates.

He also saw that James had limitations, such as an early ethical position, visible in his book on French writers, that was narrow and puritanical. In Pound's view, James worked his way out of this limited perspective by means of "his hatred of personal intimate tyrannies" and his persistent devotion to the art of fiction itself. The vast quantity of his work, though, made it impossible to generalize about its quality. The role that Pound saw for himself in dealing with James was to point readers to the best work and help them avoid the trivial and the boring, which were certainly there: "He is a very uneven author" (120). Pound tells us this over and over, sometimes branching out into criticism of specific limitations, such as James's "almost unpunctured ignorance of painting" (120), his poor taste in poetry, his obsession with furniture, his failure to appreciate Flaubert, and his ignorance of the classics, which left him "cobwebbed, fussed, blathered," and, like a philologist, "worried about minor mundanities" (129).[16]

Pound concludes with discussions of two posthumous works of James: *The Middle Years*, reminiscences to which James gave the name of one of his early short stories; and *The Ivory Tower*, an incomplete novel for which James left a set of notes that reveal much about his working methods.[17] Pound calls *The Middle Years* the most charming of the posthumous works and uses its return to James's youthful self as a way to look back at his own criticism of James. It is fitting, then, that he should revisit it at the end and consider the long process by which James grew out of that provincial attitude:

> Retaining the name of the author, any faithful reader of James, or at any rate the attentive student, finds a good deal of amusement in deciphering the young James, his temperament as mellowed by recollection and here recorded forty years later, and then in contrasting it with the young James as revealed or even "betrayed" in his own early criticisms, "French Poets and Novelists," a much cruder and more savagely puritanical and plainly New England product with, however, certain permanent traits of his character already in evidence, and with a critical faculty keen enough to hit on certain weaknesses in the authors analyzed, often with profundity, and with often a "rightness" in his mistakes. I mean that apparent errors are at times only an excess of zeal and over-shooting of his mark, which was to make for an improvement, by him, of certain defects. (166–67)

It is interesting to consider Pound's own revisionary process, in light of the comments he makes about James. Although Pound, more than most, seems to be set in his ways, he also rethinks a lot of things in his early years (as evidenced by the fluidity of his interests), staying away generally from a lassitude of thought and teaching. Throughout this study of James, Pound has no qualms about sharing personal contemplations, as in this remark about *The Middle Years* as a chronicle of the writer's "approach to the Metropolis": "Indeed, in reading these pages one can but despair over the inadequacy of one's own literary sensitization, one's so utterly inferior state of awareness;

even allowing for what the author himself allows; his not really, perhaps, having felt at twenty-six, all that at seventy he more or less read into the memory of his feeling" (157). Pound himself was only halfway to the age of seventy when he wrote these words, but he remembered keenly his own "approach to the London" at the age of twenty-three, and praises the quality of James's awareness as superior to anything to be found in English fiction before Joyce and Lewis. Then, having described the mind of Henry James, he turns, in the third chapter, to Remy de Gourmont, who, he tells us, "was less like the mind of Henry James than any contemporary mind I can think of" (168).

The first part of this chapter appeared originally in the Remy de Gourmont number of *The Little Review* in February/March 1919, and the second part of it had appeared in December 1917. By placing this section immediately after his long discussion of James, Pound clearly had a pedagogical purpose in mind. He wanted to situate James as a representative of the literary past in order to position de Gourmont as the modernist par excellence. This chapter serves as a transition from the past to the present, with writers like James, Hardy, Swinburne, and even Yeats being swept into that past, leaving de Gourmont as the lone representative of that era who could still be considered a contemporary.[18] Admitting that these views may be purely his own or even untrue, Pound insists that it would be impossible to find any other man born in the 1850s who was at home among the modernists (169). Comparing de Gourmont to James, Pound observes that the former "differentiates his characters by the modes of their sensibility, not by sub-degrees of their state of civilization," and he adds that de Gourmont "recognizes the right of individuals to *feel* differently" (170, emphasis in original). This theme, as we shall see in the next chapter, keeps coming up in Pound's thinking at this time, along with its opposite, the collective thought generated by the commercial press.

Catching himself summarizing de Gourmont's ideas, Pound observes that it is not just the ideas that are important, "the thing is that he held ideas, intuitions, perceptions in a certain personal exquisite manner" (174–75). For a moment, one might get the sense that Pound would have supported a thesis he disagreed with, so long as his pupil believed in the idea. And, as though he were still an enrolled student himself, Pound often gets lost in his complex and subtle thought. Stumbling through de Gourmont's works, Pound quotes extensively, forcing the reader to read the originals, before finally connecting de Gourmont to himself by reprinting a letter he received from the French author in June 1915.[19] Hearing that de Gourmont's thoughts echo

Pound's views on academic institutions, one can see why Pound got along so well with the writer. Pound can't help but print some of these letters as he goes on to discuss the senseless things said by journalists about literary artists from John Keats to T. S. Eliot. His own support of Wyndham Lewis and Gaudier-Brzeska, he says, has cost him dearly, and he ironically warns young people desirous of finding "smooth berths and elderly consolations" to behave more circumspectly than he has himself (195).

The fourth section of *Instigations*, called "in the Vortex," uses a quotation from de Gourmont (translated here) as a transition to a discussion of modernist writers: "The only books are those in which a writer tells of himself while speaking of the customs of his contemporaries—their dreams, their vanities, their loves, and their follies" (196). Agreeing that this is true for all prose, Pound, in his teacherly mode, wonders whether it works for poetry as well. He turns to the works of T. S. Eliot, which were not very extensive at that time, but which Pound clearly admired, and almost wishes he were a French critic, "skilled in their elaborate art of writing books about books," so that he might point out Eliot's method of "conveying a whole situation and half a character by three words of a quoted phrase." But he is reluctant to reduce Eliot to a formula that some lesser poet might try to imitate, satisfying himself by saying that Eliot is more interesting than any other poet currently writing in English (198). Next, Pound praises James Joyce for his "swift alternation of subjective beauty and external shabbiness, squalor, and sordidness," insisting that Joyce's scope is well beyond that of his contemporaries: "there is nothing in life so beautiful that Joyce cannot touch it without profanation—without, above all, the profanation of sentiment and sentimentality—and there is nothing so sordid that he cannot treat it with his metallic exactitude" (206). He also offers measured praise of Joyce's stories in *Dubliners* and verse as well before moving on to *Ulysses*, which was still unfinished but had been largely serialized, at Pound's instigation, in *The Little Review*.[20] In these years, Pound acted as a sort of agent for Eliot, Joyce, and Wyndham Lewis, bringing attention to their work, helping them place or sell it, and praising it in print at every opportunity. He assumed the role of the former teacher, if you will, writing recommendations to editors on behalf of a literature he unreservedly believed in. While he could be dogmatic and impulsive about his positions, his support was untiring.[21]

At this point, it is hard to escape the feeling that Pound—like a teacher who needs to fill a lecture—is just throwing in everything he has at hand from his recent work in the magazines, including a review of the *Others Anthology*, in which he singles out Marianne Moore and Mina Loy for praise. He discusses recent poems by Eliot and William Carlos Williams, along with a diatribe contrasting the poet with the journalist, and he reprints the American law against obscenity, with mocking commentary by himself and a judge's opinion suggesting that "classics" might escape the judgment of obscenity because they have the sanction of age and fame, and "appeal to a comparatively limited number of readers." Pound's comment on this begins with these paragraphs:

> The gentle reader will picture to himself the state of America IF the classics were widely read; IF these books which in the beginning lifted mankind from savagery, and which from A. D. 1400 onward have gradually redeemed us from the darkness of medievalism, should be read by the millions who now consume Mr. Hearst and the Ladies' Home Journal! ! ! ! ! !
>
> Also there are to be no additions. No living man is to contribute or to attempt to contribute to the classics. Obviously even though he acquire fame before publishing, he can not have the sanction of "age." (249)

After this outburst of exclamation marks and serious critique of the anti-quatedness of how we are to understand literary instruction, Pound calms down and concludes the section with some verses lamenting the failure of the United States to read the classics.[22] We are indeed in the realm of comparative literature, as James Watson told the readers of *The Dial* in 1920. In the last sections of the book, Pound covers Provençal poetry, Greek translators, and Chinese characters, offering his own version of an essay by Ernest Fenollosa for the final selection.[23]

In the part on Greek translators, Pound laments the current state of classical education ("The classics have more and more become a baton exclusively for the cudgelling of schoolboys, and less and less a diversion for the mature" [321]), and proceeds to show his readers what they are missing by looking at a range of translations of ancient Greek not only into English but into Latin and French as well. Although Pound's learning is on display, he is personally engaging, as he refuses to sink into philological distance from his readers. He tells us, for example, of his own deficient training in Greek, which he has clearly taken some pains to remedy, and, in demonstrating the difficulty of translating personal names from one language to another, he points out that James Joyce's children, who speak Italian, know him as "Signore Sterlina" as in the pound sterling, the official currency of England. He also says that the phonetic translation of his name into Japanese means something like "This picture of a phallus costs ten yen" (335). (This is questionable.) He shows us a long Latin translation of a passage in Homer and then offers his own slightly abbreviated version of it from Canto Three. What he emphasizes, again and again, is what is lost in translation—or what is added that does not belong there. He will pause on a single word in the Greek and compare various Latin versions, for example. He is a teacher whose own interest in language itself is so visibly present that it is infectious.

After Homer, Pound moves to Aeschylus and critiques Browning's translation of the *Agamemnon*. Taking on Browning's claim that he may have missed the music but has captured the ideas of the poet, Pound argues that ideas without emotion are poor stuff, pointing out that even Rossetti does a better job of capturing the emotion of Aeschylus than does Browning. Admitting, though, that he has been "extremely harsh" in dealing with a certain passage in the translation, Pound writes, "I have read Browning off and on for seventeen years with no small pleasure and admiration, and am one of the few people who know anything about his Sordello, and have never read his Agamemnon, have not even now when it falls into a special study been able to get through his Agamemnon" (349). What is at stake for Pound is a "disagreeabilizing of the classics," whether through bad pedagogy or translations that fail to capture the emotional power of the originals. And he sees the loss of the classics as leading to sloppy thought and feeling. This is an assumption, for him, an article of faith, not something he can really prove or demonstrate, but it is certainly the driving force behind this long discussion of the difficulties of translation. It is also a problem—this simplified sense of "right" and "wrong"—and it will become exacerbated before long.

It is a relief to turn from such unfounded negatives to the positive emphasis of the concluding part of this book, which is Ernest Fenollosa's essay "The Chinese Written Character as a Medium for Poetry," simply edited by Pound, as he says, to "remove a few repetitions and shape a few sentences" (357). In Fenollosa, Pound discovered a teacher's teacher, whose lectures resonated with his own thoughts in astonishing ways. Introducing the essay with a few paragraphs, Pound points out how modern Fenollosa's work was and how, before his death in 1908, he had developed a view of poetry so prescient that "[t]he later movements in art have corroborated his theories" (357). Writing very consciously as an American, Fenollosa—like Pound—was prodding or goading his fellows toward a clearer understanding and appreciation of the cultures of China and Japan: "We need their best

ideals to supplement our own—ideals enshrined in their art, in their literature and in the tragedies of their lives. We have already seen proof of the
vitality and practical value of oriental painting for ourselves and as a key
to the eastern soul. It may be worth while to approach their literature, the
intensest part of it, their poetry, even in an imperfect manner" (358). The
word "imperfect" is an astonishing concession. Unlike many of his college
teachers, Pound could see the value in nomadically exploring unfamiliar
literary territory without needing to possess a mastery over the minutest
details in the subject. He, too, felt that poetry was the most intense part
of any culture's literature and that the study of alien cultures was crucial
to the improvement of one's own vision and craft. Pound also found in
Fenollosa and hence in Chinese poetry the type of dynamism he had so
desired to find in social life, in cultural life, and—perhaps most of all—in
the university. For Fenollosa, "[a] true noun, an isolated thing, does not
exist in nature. Things are only the terminal points, or rather the meeting
points, of actions, cross-sections cut through actions, snap shots. Neither can
a pure verb, an abstract motion, be possible in nature. The eye sees noun
and verb as one: things in motion, motion in things . . ." (364). Pound
scholars seem relatively split on Pound's actual knowledge of the Chinese
language.[24] Feng Lan writes, "Pound never achieved a proficient mastery of
Chinese, notwithstanding his efforts to learn this language from the mid
1930s, but his reading knowledge of classical Chinese with the assistance of
dictionaries was stronger than has been recognized by contemporary scholars"
("Confucius" 327). Perhaps the most important thing to note here is that
Pound's engagement with Fenollosa was an aesthetic jumping-off point. He
never claimed total knowledge of the subject. In fact, in a letter to his father
(September 1928), Pound wrote, "No I am not a sinologue. Dont spread
the idea that I read it a zeasy as a yourapean langwidg" (qtd. in Qian 17).

  Fenollosa's approach was personal; he was a student of beauty, who
found himself moved by the poetry of China and Japan, and wanted to
share what he had learned. So he traveled the country lecturing and teaching,
leaving at his death a rich set of notes and transcripts, which his widow
shared with Pound because she had read and liked his poetry. Pound used
this material for some work on Noh plays and for the poems in his *Cathay*
volume of versions of Chinese verse, which became one of his notable early
successes.[25] His antipathy toward philologists is echoed by Fenollosa's toward
"professional grammarians" (365), who refuse to recognize that the structures
of the Chinese language are based on "the universal form of action in nature."
(They're not.) But for Fenollosa, "this brings language close to *things*, and
in its strong reliance upon verbs it erects all speech into a kind of dramatic

poetry." The case that Fenollosa was making for this language as especially suited for poetry has been disputed by later linguists, but Pound embraced it, supporting with his own footnotes Fenollosa's contention that "Nature herself has no grammar" (371) and that poetry must be concrete rather than abstract, using "material images to suggest immaterial relations" (376).

Such romanticizing notwithstanding, Fenollosa, like Pound, connected poetry to science, and contrasted it with classifying logic, arguing that evolutionary thought *"could not make its way until it was prepared to destroy the inveterate logic of classification* [emphasis in the original], and insisting that "Science fought until she got at the things. . . . Poetry agrees with science and not with logic" (382). (In these words, we might hear echoes of Agassiz's method, the one that so enchanted Pound.) Praising Shakespeare for his "persistent, natural, and magnificent use of hundreds of transitive verbs," Fenollosa connects him with the "wealth of transitive verbs" (384) in the Chinese language. The case he made for the poetical qualities of the images in Chinese writing anticipates very well the case Pound and his associates made for Imagism. No wonder that Pound felt that he and Fenollosa were part of the vortex of modern culture, teaching the masses new possibilities for the future. We return, in a few pages, to an older Pound engaging with Chinese culture and comparative methods, but first we wanted to write a little about another book of his that was really meant for student audiences.

A decade after *Instigations*, Pound published *How to Read*. Although neither man would appreciate or endorse the comparison, the purpose and more of the import of Pound's book (though not the tone and trimmings) anticipate such later primers as Harold Bloom's *How to Read and Why*, a defense of "great" works also intended for public consumption.[26] Unlike Bloom's (however much one might disagree with his list or politics), Pound's text lacks, as Ruthven not inaccurately puts it, "the patience of a first-rate expositor," making "Pound's *How to Read* . . . really a book about how to read Pound" (26, 21).[27] Still, the work is informative and pedagogically useful, not only for those who wish to learn about the idiosyncrasies of its author. The following statement comes early in Pound's text and situates it nicely:

> The general contempt of "scholarship," especially any part of it connected with subjects in university "Arts" courses; the shrinking of people in general from any book supposed to be "good"; and, in another mode, the flamboyant advertisements telling "how to seem to know it when you don't," might long since have indicated to the sensitive that there is something defective in the contemporary methods of purveying letters. (5–6)

Published in 1931, *How to Read* is the first of Pound's books that locates the audience at a very elementary level, with the author poised some distance above the readers. He would return to the topic a few years later with what he termed "fuller and simpler explanations" (*ABC of Reading* 11) of his method. The first explanation of this method, however, took only fifty small pages with large print, making it look very elementary indeed. "To tranquilize the low-brow reader, let me say at once that I do not wish to muddle him by making him read more books, but to allow him to read fewer with greater result" (*How* 8). This way of teaching is clearly a pedagogical version of the "luminous detail" method of Pound's "New Philology," which he has kept in mind for almost twenty years. In this new version, as in his articles of 1911, he wastes no time before attacking his old enemy, philology:

> Let us by all means glance at "philology" and the "germanic system." Speaking as an historian, "we" may say that this system was designed to inhibit thought. It was necessary to curtail this pernicious activity, the thinkists were given a china egg labelled scholarship, and were gradually unfitted for active life, or for any contact with life in general. Literature was permitted as a subject of study. And its study was so designed as to draw the mind of the student away from literature into insanity. (14–15)

Pound goes on to point out that both American and British universities adopted the philological method in the later nineteenth century and kept it in place in the early twentieth because it was supposed to have "a refining influence on the student" (15). It was a (not so effective) version of what Louis Althusser would later call an "Ideological State Apparatus."[28]

From his first lectures at the London Polytechnic, Pound had been proposing something different in the way of literary instruction, something recognizable as comparative literature. He notes early in this little book that " 'Comparative Literature' sometimes figures in university curricula, but very few people know what they mean by the term, or approach it with a considered conscious method" (8).[29] For Pound, comparative literature meant reading the very best works from different cultures, preferably in the original languages, because literature existed to "incite humanity to continue living" (16) and to keep the tools of language—unlike the ideological language found in most periodicals—clean. In words that resonated with later academics such as F. R. and Q. D. Leavis, Pound argued that "the individual cannot think and communicate his thought, the governor and legislator cannot act effectively or frame his laws, without words, and the solidity and validity of these words is in the care of the damned and despised *literati*" (17). Here, as elsewhere, Pound situated literature as the exact use of words, against what he called "rhetoric" or "loose expression" (18). He illustrated what he meant by a historical example. Greek culture arose from the literary works of Homer and endured, he claimed, while Macedonia rose from the rhetoric of the Sophists and quickly fell again. Good literature leads to good government and cultural achievement; rhetoric, which is never good, leads to hollow and fleeting victories.

It is worth noting that Pound found the same process at work later, as the Italian Renaissance followed the great literary achievements of Dante, while the disastrous regime of Cromwell in Britain was accompanied by what Pound saw as "the abominable dog biscuit of Milton's rhetoric" (*Literary Essays* 201).[30] Pound's gross simplifications notwithstanding, his case for the importance of literature follows versions made by Sidney and P. B. Shelley, and he knew that. He had been making the case for years in works like "The Serious Artist," which we have already considered. George Orwell was to make a similar case a few years later in "Politics and the English Language."[31] Even so, this case remains unproven. But the equations (poetry=truth and rhetoric=lies) are too simplistic, and the idea that good literature causes good government, though sincere, is unfortunately not always supported by historical reality. When Pound says that literature makes life more bearable, he is very close to the nucleus of it all, but when he says that it leads to good government, he is on much shakier ground. In later years, he would argue that good economics makes good government, which, in general, is a much more persuasive position, whether or not we would honor Pound's personal sense of "good economics."

When he moves from the political impact of literature to the inner workings of poetry, as he does very soon in this book, he is on much firmer ground. Here, the schoolmaster offers concepts that can help any student perceive more clearly what is actually going on in different kinds of poetry, however obscure his vocabulary may be. He directs the reader's attention to three processes (still imparted by many teachers to this day) that can be discerned in poetic texts: Melopoeia (the musical sense of words), Phanopoeia (imagistic sense of words), and Logopoeia (connotative, ironical, or other play with verbal meanings). After some nice illustrations, he proceeds to offer a relatively short reading list of works in which these properties may be found, from the ancient Greeks to the eighteenth century, at which point, he argues, the modern novel began to rival poetry in importance. He recommends some of the novelists of the eighteenth and nineteenth centuries, especially those who wrote in French and English. But he argues that there is no "point in studying the 'History of English Literature' as taught," partly because "some of the best books in English are translations" (43).

Pound really believed that the only way to learn about literature was the way he had really wanted to learn (even if it meant being self-taught)—by studying comparatively, despite resistance of the English faculty at Penn to that program. While he allowed that his readers might need translations to get a sense of the literature he was recommending, he also believed strongly in the importance of learning at least one language beyond one's native tongue: "I don't in the least admit or imply that any man in our time can think with only one language. . . . No one language is complete" (47). He is not impractical about this, admitting that it is possible to learn a bit of a language and gain something by studying carefully a few poems in that tongue. Finally, he offers a compressed version of a curriculum in comparative literature from Confucius to Corbière that would equip the student with dependable "axes of reference" (46). Even this, though it stresses only a dozen authors and a few collections like "A Provençal Song Book," is a bit daunting, but it is not wildly impractical. He concludes his lesson by urging instructors and lay readers to challenge the ideas he has put forth. Pound proposes

> a definite curriculum in place of the present *émiettements*, of breaking the subject up into crumbs quickly dryable. A curriculum for instructors, for obstreperous students who wish to annoy dull instructors, for men who haven't had time for systematized college courses. Call it the minimum basis for a sound and liberal education in letters. . . . (50)

His list of texts "is the result of twenty-seven years' thought on the subject and a resumé of conclusions" (52), and the pedagogical intention behind his "minimum basis" is not entirely unlike that of people such as E. D. Hirsch (if one could forgive the comparison).[32] Though he is firm in his own literary values, Pound is still careful not to conflate those values entirely with pedagogical effectiveness. Conceding that different books might work better for different students and teachers in different circumstances, Pound writes of his list: "Swallowed whole it is useless. For practical class work the instructor should try, and incite his students to try, to pry out some element that I have included and to substitute for it something more valid"

(52). One gets the sense that this is not something Pound's teachers at Penn would have allowed.

The poet's next attempt at an introductory textbook comes a few years later in the more comprehensive yet outwardly unsystematic *ABC of Reading*. The difference between the two primers is glaring, as the prejudices of Pound's growing fascistic leanings have invaded what ought to have been a wonderful celebration of literature. But, by 1934, the two for Pound could never be set apart. If only he had heeded his own warning in *How to Read* about authors who "stuff expandable and compressible objects into rubber-bag categories . . . limit[ing] their reference and interest by supposing that the pedagogic follies which they have themselves encountered, constitute an error universally distributed, and encountered by every one else" (7). We do not discuss this book at length here (it is discussed in our first Preface and much of what Pound otherwise has to offer regarding teaching has been covered elsewhere), but we do want to touch on a few moments where the "Super Schoolmaster" is still at his best.

The most well-known line from *ABC of Reading* is Pound's loose definition of poetic writing: "*DICHTEN = CONDENSARE*" (92). Here, in keeping with his earlier Imagistic sense of poetic economy, Pound puns on the German *dichten* "to write (poetry)" and *dicht* "tight" or "heavy with." To write poetry is to condense language, to get rid of the excess (and perhaps also—as some of Pound's readers take the line—to condescend). Faced with stacks upon stacks of paper, most teachers today would endorse such a view. Joking aside, though, we might see how Pound the teacher really wants his students to get at the essence, at what's important. Such a lesson is now inseparable, for Pound, from what he takes to be the Chinese ideogram, which "does not try to be the picture of a sound, or to be a written sign recalling a sound. . . . It *means* the thing or the action or the situation, or quality germane to the several things that it pictures" (21). One of the more elemental moments, as we have tried to make the case in our book, typical not only of Pound's scholarship but moreover of his pedagogical method, comes when he turns to chemistry to explain his comparative approach: "You can't judge any chemical's action merely by putting it with more of itself. To know it, you have got to know its limits, both what it is and what it is not. What substances are harder or softer, what more resilient, what more compact" (60). When applied to the classroom, this comparative method provides students an educational model based upon a positive sense of self-determination. Education is no longer about the scholar-professor presenting

Truths to be memorized and repeated, but rather about discovering how to read the world through difference.[33] To this end, Pound advocates more for a paratactical approach, forsaking explication and directing students to consider texts on their own. His pared-down approach "would be to give the quotations WITHOUT any comment whatever" (95). We might call it "comparative learning."

During the 1920s and 1930s, Pound's thoughts easily moved from Fenollosa to Confucius and Mencius (Confucius's most important student). Feng Lan finds an easy harmony for Pound's "theory of 'precise' language, which he postulated by appropriating the Confucian doctrines of *zheng ming* (to rectify names) and *cheng yi* (to make thought sincere)" (11).[34] As Pound knew, Confucius had a proper regard for education. Confucious understood the mentoring role of the teacher, one who would be able to pass along what was so valuable about tradition. Also important for Pound was Confucius's patience and his understanding the right balance between learning and critical reflection. Pound found in Confucius a connection between learning and life, a sense of natural order derived from right-naming, a model for ideal teacher-student relationships based on student-driven inquiry, and the general sense that education had an ethical purpose. Learning, philosophy, poetry, history, and economics—everything we had and continue to cut up into individualized disciplines—was swiftly coming together for Pound, offering him a harmonious glimpse of a possible future humanity.[35]

Once again, Pound was ahead of his time here, and his disappointment with the backward thinking of the American educational system in this regard would continually erupt. For instance, in a later letter to Achilles Fang (October 1957), he points out how "[t]he hatred of the Chinese Classics boils thru most of our Universities . . . and at least one of their degraded stooges and brain-washers has plainly said that they are NOT trying to interest pupils in the great literature" (qtd. in Qian 158). Importantly for Pound—and American universities were quite slow at catching up to him on this point—great literature did not stop at the imaginary cultural borders of Europe. For decades, Pound would write to friends, congressmen, and even Mussolini about an "immediate need of Confucius" (Moody II 247).

This "Chinese paideuma" of Pound—as L. S. Dembo calls it—was not only about philosophical coherence.[36] It was an ethical and pedagogical project too, about how one ought to live one's life fully and virtuously.[37] Lan turns to Pound's (idiosyncratic) translation of Confucius: "What heaven has disposed and sealed is called the inborn nature. The realization of this nature is called process. The clarification of this process . . . is called education" (157; quoting

Pound, *Confucius* 99). He writes that *jiao* [教]—the ideogram for education, to teach)—"refers to the passing down of knowledge from one generation to the next, it also suggests that what is passed down must concentrate on human concerns" (157). As we have seen with what the schoolmaster was willing and unwilling to do in *ABC of Reading*, education worked best when it was self-motivated. Like his handbooks, Pound's anthologies, both formal and informal, all had this in common: they directed the student to the great works themselves, which were then to be explored and understood on their own terms. The anthologist's work, therefore, involved, as he put it early on in *The Spirit of Romance*, "selection rather than in presentation of opinion" (7). John G. Nichols observes how Pound's anthologies "invite[d] a comparative reading practice": "Pound radically reimagined the anthology format, whether mainstream or coterie, to insert readers within the flux of literary tradition and selection. Pound argued for anthologies that 'worked' or made bold statements in their selection of poets, ideally forcing students into literary debates, but still condemning any anthology that 'does ALL their work for 'em'" (68, 67; embedded quotation from a letter to Laughlin). Looking at how Confucian thought intersected with both Pound's economical philosophy of language and his attitude toward editing, Ruthven notes that Pound "came to regard Confucius as the supreme example of the critic-as-anthologist, the man who . . . had eliminated superfluities from a collection of three thousand odes by preserving the 'best' three hundred" (Ruthven 138; Canto 53). Contrary to Pound's (and other early scholars') understanding, Confucius was not actually an "editor" of the three-hundred-plus odes, but such, shall we say, "un-luminous" details were really beside the point. The model of a living, dynamic Confucius, one able to teach through self-restraint, was already established in Pound's mind.

Moving a bit past some of Pound's personal, political, and pedagogical recklessness (to which we return in our final chapter), we conclude this chapter by moving to the 1950s and St. Elizabeths. There, Pound was approached by a young English teacher named Marcella Spann, who would, for a time, become a friend, a muse, and a collaborator. Facing the daunting task of teaching her own class, she had gone to Pound for help (her former teacher was a disciple of Pound's). Pound, who in Spann's words, "taught like a kind father" (qtd. in Moody III 393), helped with lesson plans, paper grading, and even suggested devising an anthology, which would at least give Spann suitable material with which to work. Nicknamed the "Spannthology," the collection would become known to various teachers (some of whom still use the text today) as *Confucius to Cummings*.

While it might feel challenging, looking back from a very different multicultural space today, to acknowledge the diversity of Pound and Spann's anthology, it is hard also not to recognize the sheer breadth of the work. Writers from Confucius through Sappho through Li Po through Saint Teresa de Ávila appear beside the familiar names of Shakespeare and Dante. Pound's favorites, such as Cavalcanti, mingle beside his former collaborators and those very different twentieth-century voices he championed: Lewis, Williams, Doolittle, Moore, Eliot, Bunting, and Cummings, which close out the collection. For his own part, Pound added two of his early poems, a much softer voice than that of his previous decade. The work was assembled with an eye and, perhaps more importantly, an ear for the classroom. And the editors maintained Pound's "Confucian" model. Pound tells his reader not to worry about finding what looks like a "jumble of fragments" because they would lead to "sorts of fact the poets of earlier time chose to sing" (ix). As a teacher, here, Pound does not overstep; he allows his students to discover the answers on their own: "As any schoolchild would be insulted if one suggested that it had not intelligence enough to solve a puzzle or pruzzle, we assume that any reader who has been able to get into a junior college will be able to put our mosaic together to her, or to his, satisfaction" (x). Most important, for Pound, is establishing the spark of curiosity, so that the student would return again and again to the pleasure of the great works. He writes, "I cannot too greatly emphasize a statement in one of the prefaces that this book is intended as start, that is mainly to arouse curiosity, but also to alert the pupil to the extent and variety of the fields where she or he can browse later with enjoyment" (322).[38]

The editors also incorporate some interesting appendices, including a syllabus for a poetry course taught by Spann's former teacher Vincent Miller, who reminds his students that "Pound is set against talking like a professor" (333).[39] Finally, knowing that there would be a classroom need to have questions accompanying the textbook, Pound, in his economical way, gets right to the essence: "I therefore suggest that the teacher start by asking himself, and then asking the pupils, the following: Why is the poem included in the anthology? What moved the author to write it? What does it tell the reader? These three lines of inquiry will, or at any rate should, keep both teacher and pupil from divagating into consideration of their own personal bellyaches" (335). The Confucian Anthology had truly become, for Pound, "the basis of an education" (321). Moody makes the point (rightly so) that, although a collaboration, "Pound made the project very much his own" (III 394). Readers familiar with Pound will no doubt recognize as much, but it would not be something that the cover of the book would immediately suggest. This manner of mentorship was typical of Pound's career—never more so than in his advocacy for contemporary writers in his dealings with modernist periodicals.

CHAPTER 4

Periodical Studies

"TO HELL WITH HARPER'S AND THE MAGAZINE TOUCH"!

—Pound to Harriet Monroe (qtd. in Paige 11)

Contributor, promoter, scout, critic, correspondent, collaborator, and editor—these are all academic hats Ezra Pound wore as he situated himself at the center of modernist periodical culture. He was a friend and antagonist—often at the same time—to editors and writers alike. Acting in these various capacities, Pound was relatively able to shape his own discourse of modern culture, creating what the great modernist scholar Hugh Kenner would call "The Pound Era."[1] More relevant to our study here, Pound's work on periodicals was importantly part of his pedagogical strategy. His instructive essays continued to promote his comparative method, and they publicized a lot of contemporary literature that was being ignored by both universities and popular presses. While most of these publications did not provide Pound the forum he ideally sought, he was able to encourage, mentor, and advocate for writers—acting as a teacher, in a sense—whose views on literature and literary history would, in a few short decades, dominate the rhetoric of English departments. Pound's interactions in these years also illuminate what are sometimes unfortunate aspects of teaching in higher education: the ego, the itinerant intellectual lifestyle, the desire for control. Finally, we see once more Pound's ambivalence about his audience—those who would or would not occupy the seats of his theoretical lecture hall. He was shrewd enough to know what a public wanted, and he was sometimes able to deliver as much. Most of the time, though, he refused to compromise with the public flavor, steadfast as he was in his judgment. This was not just sour grapes and not just a matter of personal taste. In the explosion of popular culture—culture that was clichéd, repetitive, and ideological—Pound saw a danger to individual liberty, and he made it his goal to teach against this.

This chapter is composed of two parts. The first part details some of Pound's frustrating and frustrated experiences with various journals, and the second part follows Pound when he later decided to write critically about such journals. Let us begin with a few related comments of his, which themselves span a couple decades:

> I am doing a series of satires on English Magazines, and it is a fairly amusing lark, I don't know whether the solemn quarterlies or the "popular" weeklies are the more ludicrous. (*Pound/Joyce*, 128)

> I had intended to provide the book derisively with an appendix, vermiform. Papa Flaubert compiled a sottisier, I also compiled a sottisier. I do not yield a jot in my belief that such compilations are useful, I concede that there may be no need of reprinting mine at this moment. At any rate the snippets are there on file. You can't know an era merely by knowing its best. (*Make It New*, 16)

> Later in London I did a *sottisier*, trying to make a few people see why the printed matter on sale in that city would finally kill off the inhabitants; witness Dunkirk. (*Speaking*, 91)

> Never yet got any attention to "Studies in Contemporary Mentality" (yu prob/ bombadeering at time) anyhow tellin the goddam Brits wot was pizin'em via print on noose-stands. Even the O. M. [T. S. Eliot] cdnt see the utility, when I tried for a reprint in volumette, and now lookat their goddam hempire. (*Pound/Lewis*, 263)

Ezra Pound was involved in "periodical studies" before such codified criticism existed.[2] He read periodicals and submitted stories, articles, and poems to them from a very early age. He also interacted with their editors, sometimes assuming editorial duties himself. And, finally, he studied periodicals and sought to teach others about their vices and virtues, publishing such studies—in periodicals.

The four quotations above are from different moments in Ezra Pound's career, but they all refer to the same one of those published studies of periodicals. In the first, he was writing to James Joyce, in September 1917, about a series of twenty articles called "Studies in Contemporary Mentality" that appeared in *The New Age*, running through January 1918. In the second, he was writing about the same series, as Forrest Read noted years ago in connecting the two quotations (*Pound/Joyce*, 128 n.4). Here, in the introductory section of *Make It New*, Pound was acknowledging, somewhat cryptically, that he had accepted advice to leave the series out of the book, where he had intended it to appear as an appendix. He was also, however, defending its usefulness. (The "snippets," clipped from pages of *The New Age*, must have been sent to Faber with the other materials for the book, which was mainly a collection of things previously published in various magazines.) The third quotation is from one of his radio broadcasts during the war, in which he blamed the periodical culture of Britain and the United States for what he saw as their downfalls. The fourth quotation confirms that it was T. S. Eliot who, while working at Faber and Faber, was responsible for eliminating "Studies in Contemporary Mentality" from *Make It New* in 1934, perhaps repaying Pound for the cuts he had made in Eliot's *The Waste Land* a decade or so earlier.

In any case, it is clear that, even as late as 1950, Pound still was thinking of his earlier series and regretting that it had not been republished. A *sottisier* is a collection of stupidities, such as those in Flaubert's *Bouvard et Pécuchet*, or the "Current Cant" section of *The New Age*, which regularly quoted stupidities collected from various sources. But Pound's was not just a collection of amusing banalities; he intended them as teaching lessons. In 1950, he told Lewis that, back in 1917, he had attempted to explain to his British readers how they were being poisoned by the printed material they got from newsstands (or "noose-stands," as he later called them). These printed stupidities were making the whole nation stupid, in Pound's view. There were other magazines, of course, including the one he was writing for (*The New Age*), that Pound thought were not purveying cultural poison, and his elaborate involvement with them is part of the whole story of Pound educating the masses through the periodical.

Schoolmaster Ezra makes an important point in the last line of the second quotation: "You can't know an era merely by knowing its best." These words have special weight because, as we have seen, no one championed the best more fiercely than Pound. But for him, the periodical world ran to both extremes, with the worst too often winning the battle and distorting public perceptions or reinforcing what he thought were stupid beliefs. To truly understand culture, students would need to study work in popular forums too. Printed periodicals were the dominant medium of Pound's day—

especially the early decades of the twentieth century, when radio and then television had not yet gained control of the public mind. Before he switched to radio in 1940, his engagement with such periodicals was enduring and persistent, and it began in his early years. A photograph of him lounging in his tower studio or "den" as a boy (Moody I, after 144) shows a number of interesting objects on the wall behind him, including some fencing foils and a poster for *Scribner's Magazine*. As he was setting out as a writer, he sent his work to magazines, and he often fenced, intellectually, with their editors. He was sending poems to *The Bibelot* as early as 1905, when he was twenty years old, and one of his first published poems appeared in the large-circulation monthly *Munsey's* in 1906.

Students of modernism know something about Pound's involvement in what he called "Small Magazines," though few of us are aware of the full extent of his involvement with them and with the other magazines of modernism. Drawing on the information in Donald Gallup's *Bibliography*, we can find an interesting pattern in Pound's contributions to magazines if we follow the number of contributions per year from the time he was twenty until just after he reached the age of forty and moved to Rapallo.

Table 4.1. Pound's Contributions to Magazines, 1905–1926

Year	Number of Magazine Contributions
1905	1
1906	4
1907	0
1908	5
1909	6
1910	8
1911	7
1912	37
1913	53
1914	47
1915	46
1916	31
1917	71
1918	117
1919	89
1920	89
1921	23
1922	16
1923	6
1924	24
1925	11
1926	3

We find in these raw numbers that his peak years of contribution occurred when he was in London. He arrived there in 1908, but it took him a few years to make connections and establish himself. He left in 1920, and from 1912 through 1920 he averaged around one magazine publication per week. We can get a good idea of just what he was publishing—and where—if we look at the distribution of his work for the year in which his periodical contributions first jumped to well over one per week: 1917. Of his seventy-one contributions to magazines that year, he had ten in *Poetry*, fourteen in *The Egoist*, nineteen in *The Little Review*, twenty-six in *The New Age*, and just a handful in other publications. Furthermore, though some of these publications were original poems, they were mainly critical or pedagogical essays, which were often collected later in various volumes. For example, for several years Pound wrote art criticism in *The New Age* under the name of "B. H. Dias"; he wrote music criticism there as well under the name "William Atheling"; and, most interestingly for our purposes, he wrote a series of critiques under his own name. These publications extended into 1918 and ultimately ran to twenty articles—the *sottisier* or "series of satires on English Magazines" called "Studies in Contemporary Mentality."[3]

Gallup's bibliography lists more than seventeen hundred contributions to periodicals by Pound starting in 1902, when he was seven years old, and ending with his arrest for treason in May 1945. In 1908, while he was on his way to London, he wrote his parents from Venice, sending them stories he was writing, and asking that they send them around to magazines: "Try first on 'Outlook' then if not accepted Everybodies, McClure, Cosmopolitan, Book News in order" (*EPtP* 110). *Book News Monthly* was a local Philadelphia journal that had been publishing Pound for several years, but he clearly wanted to get his work in the large circulation magazines if possible. He wrote again in a few days with more stories, suggesting that his mother "try first on Smart Set & afterwards, if rejected, where you like" (111). In July, still in Venice, where he had his first book of poetry printed at his own expense, he wrote again, urging his parents to get publicity for him as "Sometime Fellow in U. Penn. a promising magazine writer, etc." (121). He also sent a list of people he expected his parents to notify about his book, including specific editors at *Book News* and *Munsey's*, and then, from London in August, he urged his father to send copies of his book of poems to *Scribner's* and *McClure's* (129). In December 1910 he wrote his father about a meeting he had had the previous summer with an editor from *Everybody's* magazine, boasting, "I shall get them subdued if given time" (210). On or about this time, Pound's human character changed. Only a few years later, he would write in a satirical poem about "That canting rag called *Everybody's Magazine*" and complain in an article that "the modern poet is expected to holloa his verses down a speaking tube to the editors of cheap magazines—S. S. McClure, or some one of that sort" (*Pavannes* 37, 102).

This shift in attitude came about as Pound got deeper into the publishing world, becoming directly involved with certain magazines of different sorts, in varying capacities, official and unofficial.

Table 4.2. Pound's Editorial Involvement with Magazines, 1909–1932

Years of Pound's Involvement	Editors	Journals
1909–1910	F. M. Hueffer	*The English Review*
1910–1920	A. R. Orage	*The New Age*
1912–1921	Harriet Monroe	*Poetry*
1912–1916	W. H. Wright, H. L. Mencken	*The Smart Set*
1913–1914	Dora Marsden	*The New Freewoman*
1914–1919	Dora Marsden, Harriet Weaver	*The Egoist*
1914–1915	Wyndham Lewis	*Blast*
1916–1919	Margaret Anderson	*The Little Review*
1920–1920	J. Middleton Murry	*The Athenaeum*
1920–1923	Scofield Thayer, James Sibley Watson, Jr.	*The Dial*
1927–1928	Ezra Pound	*The Exile*
1930–1932	Samuel Putnam	*The New Review*

Pound's thinnest connection in the above list is probably with *The Smart Set*. His name never appeared on its masthead, but he had some rapport with its editors—first W. H. Wright and then H. L. Mencken—and he described himself to James Joyce as an unofficial editor who could send them things to consider (*Pound/Joyce* 18). He did indeed send in three of Joyce's *Dubliners* stories, and *The Smart Set* published two of them. His own work also appeared in the magazine on nine occasions from 1912 to 1916. Also included in this list is *The English Review*, though Pound's association with it was informal and very brief. As we described in our first chapter, Pound socialized with its first editor, Ford Madox Hueffer, and, though they played tennis together frequently and remained friends for quite a while, Pound was never directly involved in the editorial work of the magazine. In the cases where his involvement was more direct, he often followed a pattern of withdrawing—to put it mildly—when he disagreed with the editor(s) and then returning in a less official capacity.[4] This happened with *Poetry*, with *The Little Review*, and with *The New Age*. In the case of *The Athenaeum*, he had no editorial connection, but he wrote as a paid drama critic under the name of "T.J.V." from March 1920 until he was fired in July of that year (Moody I 389, 398).

He frequently disagreed with A. R. Orage, the editor of *The New Age*, but became one of the few paid contributors to the journal Orage sometimes called the "no wage."[5] They split over Vorticism, but Pound returned to the magazine with a vengeance after his nemesis, Beatrice Hastings, left it, and he gradually moved closer to Orage's views on economic matters, though they never agreed about poetry. That did not stop Pound from covering both art and music for the magazine for several years during which time, though he did not have an editorial say, he published more frequently in *The New Age* than in any other periodical. It did not hurt, either, that Orage and Pound had similar critiques of the compartmentalization of knowledge, sometimes even using the same metaphors. Here, for example, is Orage complaining about readership and Pound complaining about university teaching: "Not the least of the revolutionary journal's troubles is the difficulty to drive into the minds of its readers that life is not composed of water-tight compartments" (Orage 415); "Does any good mind ever 'get a kick' out of studying stuff that has been put into water-tight compartments and hermetically sealed?" (*Guide to Kulchur* 32).[6] It is also significant that both Hueffer and Orage were men with strong views who neither needed nor accepted outside help, though both enjoyed Pound's company. Hueffer, of course, was a terrible businessman and lost control of his journal shortly after its first year of operation. Orage, on the other hand, managed to keep *The New Age* going from 1907 until he resigned in 1922. Though none of these ten journals had a vast circulation, three of them do not quite fit the category of "little magazines." *The New Age* was a political weekly that took a serious interest in literature and the arts; *The English Review* was in the format of the big monthly reviews like *Blackwood's*, though it was far less conservative, and it was meant to pay its way over the years as those magazines did; and *The Smart Set* had a wide circulation—which did not prevent Hoffman, Allen, and Ulrich from listing it as "little."[7] Pound interacted with all these editors, but he never had control over what they published.

What he wanted, however, was just that: control. And he achieved it—in varying ways and to varying degrees—with most of the other magazines on this list. In the case of *Poetry*, he was one of a number of poets contacted in 1912 by the founding editor, Harriet Monroe, and invited to contribute. Monroe was herself a poet, living in Chicago, where she had social and economic connections. In 1911, she began collecting subscribers who would pledge $50 a year for five years to help her start a magazine that would contribute to the cultural prestige of Chicago in the same manner as the Art Institute and the Symphony. This funding would enable her to pay contributors decently. The first issue of her magazine appeared in October 1912, and by November she was naming Pound "Foreign Correspondent." He was encouraged to submit work he found abroad, by himself and others, but he never had full control of even a section of the magazine. Monroe, who was twenty-five years older than Pound, valued his work and his advice, but she ran her own magazine, with the help, in particular, of Alice Corbin Henderson, a younger poet, who screened all the submissions and wrote shrewd critical essays as well as poems (with the poems appearing under her maiden name, Alice Corbin) until her health forced her out in 1916.

Pound and Monroe agreed about the value of poetry, but Monroe's impulses were more democratic. She put some words of Walt Whitman's on her masthead and never wavered in her commitment to them: "To have great poets there must be great audiences too." She saw the creation of such an audience as the mission of her magazine. Pound, on the other hand, hated that motto and muttered against it for years—sometimes in print, in *Poetry* and other magazines—insisting that "[t]he artist is *not* dependent upon his audience" (*Poetry* 5:1.29). He was an elitist, and his deep immersion in the European renaissance left him thinking that artists required the support of aristocratic patrons like the Medici if art were to flourish in the modern world. Monroe's hundred subscribers were too many for him, and too undistinguished. But he persisted, "discovering" T. S. Eliot and sending "The Love Song of J. Alfred Prufrock" to Monroe, who found it depressing and hesitated for months before printing it. Pound considered Alice Corbin Henderson to have a better ear than Monroe, so he directed more of his foreign correspondence through her and included her poetry as well as Monroe's in the *Catholic Anthology* he edited in 1915.[8] Monroe and Henderson wanted their magazine to be American with international connections. Pound wanted the magazine to be international, with American poets included when they reached an international standard.[9]

He sent in the work of Robert Frost, whose first book had appeared in England, and of Ford Madox Hueffer, H. D., and poems by James Joyce as well. He had a real eye for literary talent, but he also had his blind spots. He never noticed Emily Dickinson and rarely mentioned Wallace Stevens in his whole career as a promoter of poetry, being interested, mainly, in writers and artists he had discovered himself. He was supportive though frequently of two minds about William Carlos Williams, a friend from his youth, and his view of other writers often changed dramatically. He urged Monroe to publish only poetry of the highest quality, shrinking the pages devoted to verse and increasing the criticism if necessary. Though his tutorials were often unsolicited, he had no trouble acting the teacher. "Yrs. ever pedagogically," he signed off on a letter to Monroe in 1913 (Paige 23). And here he is writing to her as though she were a first-year college student and not a poet herself: "Poetry must be *as well written as prose*. Its language must be a fine language, departing in no way from speech save by a heightened intensity" (Paige 48).[10] Monroe saw a continuum of poetry, extending from Native American chants and cowboy songs to the highest level of literary achievement, and she felt that an American audience could be created by means of that continuum. She resisted elements in Pound's work that she thought would insult or offend that audience, asking him to change some of his nastier poetic expressions and refusing to print some of his poems altogether. They were two strong people who were devoted to the cause of poetry but saw it in very different ways. Monroe was consistent and eloquent in her praise of Wallace Stevens, for example, and she found new poets like Glenway Wescott and Yvor Winters, barely noticed by Pound. As a result of these differences, Pound's connection with the magazine fluctuated from 1912 to 1920, but never quite ended until the war years.[11]

In the meantime across the Atlantic, Pound continued to work with the formidable Wyndham Lewis, whose visual and literary work he admired. Together they developed the theory of "Vorticism" in the arts, borrowing some ideas from their unofficial teacher T. E. Hulme, and started the magazine *Blast* in 1914, which was full to the brim with manifestos and shocking literary and visual texts, including the first chapter of what would become Hueffer's *The Good Soldier*, and a crafty story by Rebecca West.[12] When the magazine appeared, however, only Lewis was named as an editor, with Pound remaining in the background. Vorticism was a name for the kinds of modernism that Pound and Lewis approved of, to the exclusion of those they considered passé (like Imagisme) or wrong-headed (like Futurism and

Cubism) or just ignored (like the wealth of culture across the globe that is still being recovered). The magazine was a shocker, but it was eclipsed by the larger shock of the Great War that followed close on its heels. *Blast* managed a second issue but then disappeared, ending in 1915.[13]

Pound's relationship with the British magazine *The Egoist* was as complicated as that with the American magazine *Poetry*. For a while, he saw the two as branches of a transatlantic literary enterprise over which he had some control. Before *The Egoist* was *The Egoist*, it was called *The New Freewoman*. Rebecca West, the assistant editor there, invited Pound to help edit the literary section of the magazine. The editor, Dora Marsden, wrote the social and philosophical section but did not give her full attention to the literary part of the magazine, which began to grow when West started working there. Pound had met West through Hueffer and Hueffer's companion, Violet Hunt. He had also found a financial backer in the poet John Gould Fletcher, which allowed him to offer to pay contributors to the literary section out of funds Fletcher provided, but he insisted on total control over that part of the paper—control that quickly grew from a few columns to a third of every issue. Dora Marsden remained firmly in charge of the journal, provoking Pound into writing the important series of articles on "The Serious Artist," which he later reprinted in *Pavannes and Divisions*. What Pound wanted, as he explained eloquently to various people, was a place to publish work by himself and a few other writers he chose. By this time, he had "discovered" Joyce, Eliot, and Lewis, whose works he sponsored in the magazine, as its title changed from *The New Freewoman* to *The Egoist*. This change in title suited both Pound and Marsden, who was influenced by the egoistic philosophy set forth in Max Stirner's *The Ego and His Own*, which had appeared in Germany in 1845 but was first translated into English in 1907 by Steven Byington, who was a regular contributor to *The New Freewoman*. The date of this translation made it a part of the modernist movement in the English-speaking world. And in 1909, James Huneker's *Egoists: A Book of Supermen* linked Stirner and Friedrich Nietzsche to writers like Marie-Henri Stendhal, Charles Baudelaire, and Gustave Flaubert, making explicit the connection between modernism and the ego—something implicit in all of Pound's magazine work.

Pound had made it explicit enough in a letter of September 1913. He was writing to the American literary critic Milton Bronner, suggesting that male editors wanted to run things themselves but female editors might be more pliable (Moody I 219). As it happened, however, he kept running into exceptions. Harriet Monroe resisted his attempts to control *Poetry*, and Dora Marsden appointed Richard Aldington literary editor of *The New Freewoman* when Rebecca West left, ending Pound's dominance of that literary section, even though Joyce's *Portrait* would soon appear in the revamped journal. When Harriet Shaw Weaver (who had been financing *The New Freewoman*) began editing *The Egoist*, she shared Pound's admiration of Joyce's work and became for Joyce a patron along the lines of Pound's beloved Sigismondo Malatesta. Her editorship, though, remained her own. Pound's very ugly tendency toward misogyny broke loose in some letters to John Quinn, in which he proposed a "male review" that would not allow any contributions from women because "most of the ills of american magazines (the rot of medieval literature before them for that matter) are (or were) due to women" (*Pound/Quinn*, 54).[14] He allowed that there might be "six women writers whose work I should regret losing but the ultimate gain . . . in vigor—in everything—might be worth it" (54). Thankfully (with a slight exception to be discussed in a moment), the "male review" never quite materialized, and it is hard to say just how serious Pound was in proposing it. He did, however, finally find an accommodating female editor in Margaret Anderson and *The Little Review* in 1916.[15]

Margaret Anderson started *The Little Review* on a shoe string in Chicago in 1914. In its early years it looked much like its neighbor *Poetry* and shared a number of contributors with it, but it was anarchistic in spirit and embodied, perhaps more than any other journal, the quintessence of the "little magazine"—as the word "Little" in its title proclaimed. Pound himself referred to it as "the Small Review" in a letter to Harriet Monroe in 1914, leading one to believe that he was offended by the cuteness of the word he avoided in the title of his own article on such magazines. But he did not make a direct connection to Margaret Anderson's magazine until 1916—a year in which the magazine moved to California briefly, back to Chicago, and then on to New York. It is also the year Anderson met Jane Heap, who helped her as editor for some time. One issue they published famously had the first thirteen pages blank, as they thumbed their noses at the literary establishment, complaining they had not received enough work of quality to fill the pages. Pound, who began contributing that year, obviously found this educational gesture sympathetic, and in April 1917 he joined the magazine officially as its foreign editor, essentially deserting *Poetry* to do so, though he continued publishing in *Poetry* for some years. He explained his reasons for this move in a manifesto opening the May issue of *The Little*

Review, taking the occasion to attack Monroe for what he considered her excessive deference to old fogies and the Christian religion. (The charge, as was often the case with Pound, was more than unfair. Monroe thought of herself as "a quite untroubled heathen" [Monroe, 449], and she made her own editorial decisions.)

He persuaded *The Little Review* to adopt a motto in deliberate contrast to that of *Poetry*: "MAKING NO COMPROMISE WITH THE PUBLIC TASTE." In response to a query from a reader about that motto, Jane Heap replied sardonically, "I should like to write you a long heart-felt letter about that slogan. It has been one of my compromises for the past three years. It came to us, among many other precious things, from Ezra Pound" (*LR* 7.2:33). Pound wanted to educate the public, but he often despaired of being able to do so. The writer who had hoped to appear in the large-circulation magazines found that his work, and the work of the writers he chose to promote, was welcome only in the more specialized journals with smaller audiences. So he decided to make the maximum use of those small magazines, educating the part of the public that would not be put off by such a motto. Pound continued to publish in both *The Little Review* and *The Dial* for some years; his major achievements for these two journals were the publication of *Ulysses* in one and *The Waste Land* in the other. While he was often wrong about writers he dismissed, he was rarely wrong about the ones for whom he advocated. Pound's formal affiliation with *The Little Review* lasted only until 1920, when he shifted allegiance to *The Dial*, where he received a salary as Paris Correspondent until a dispute with the unbalanced editor, Scofield Thayer, ended his time there.

His next-to-last direct experience with a journal was the most complete, as he was the editor. He oversaw *The Exile* through four issues over two years, 1927–28, before abandoning it. It was a difficult process, partly because he was working from Rapallo and most of his contributors were far away, but there were other problems as well. He had an American collaborator, a journalist named John Price, who advised him about expenses and also looked for American contributors, but Pound was the only one given editorial credit on the masthead. To keep publishing costs down, Pound decided to have the magazine printed in Dijon and then shipped to the United States to ensure American copyright of the contents. But American customs insisted on treating it as a book and charging more than a magazine would have cost—another example of the sort of American bureaucracy that Pound despised. The result was that the first issue was the only one printed in Europe. The second and third were handled by a Chicago printer who moved to New York for the fourth and final issue.

The contents of the magazine consisted of work by Pound; by some of his protegées, old and new—like Richard Aldington, John Rodker, Robert McAlmon, and Ernest Hemingway, who had a one-line poem in one issue—by recent discoveries like Louis Zukovsky; and old friends like W. B. Yeats. Pound's contributions ranged from bits of *The Cantos* to diatribes about American bureaucracy and information about his work on various periodicals. The magazine sold only a few hundred copies per issue, and the publisher simply abandoned it in 1928, saying he could no longer afford to publish (Monk, 352). If we compare an issue of this journal to one of the better-known magazines Pound helped edit, such as *The Little Review*, the loss of energy and excitement is palpable. It is important to note that, for a brief moment, Pound achieved his long-sought magazine for men only. (This was likely part of its downfall.)[16] The only piece in it with a woman's name attached, "Stella Breen," was actually written by George S. Seymour. Though Pound's interests were shifting to social and economic issues at this time, and he was isolated in Rapallo, the lack of excitement in 1927–28 is not entirely Pound's fault. It was also the case that the energy that had turned Pound's brand of early modernism into a kind of vortex was simply no longer present in Euro-American culture, and patrons who supported such work were also disappearing.

Pound did return to the editorial side of the periodical world one more time, however, when he joined Samuel Putnam's Parisian magazine, *The New Review*, in 1930 as associate editor, serving for four of the five issues published during the two-year run of the journal. Putnam later described him as "more or less of a nonfunctioning though by no means silent editor" (155). Pound wasn't silent in print either, writing for them articles on artistic and cultural matters that Putnam later described as moving toward "a pre-fascist mentality" (152). Putnam's memories were no doubt affected by the fact that his memoir was written while Pound was in danger of being tried for treason and executed. He had little or no appreciation for Pound's early critical and scholarly work, though surprisingly he admired *The Cantos* without reservation. The Pound he describes is cranky and humorless—quite unlike the "Super Schoolmaster" we have been considering. To the extent that it may be accurate, it reads like a caricature, catching a Pound in transition toward that figure seesawing somewhere between madness and treason. Pound's last experience on the editorial side of the periodical world could not have been a pleasant one.

~

Pound's practical experience with these journals and his many attempts to penetrate the world of the large-circulation magazines left him with strong feelings about the role of periodicals in the modern world. And, with the practical college courses for which he advocated in mind, he needed to teach people about these real-world contexts. He found direct expression on four occasions: his "Studies in Contemporary Mentality" in *The New Age* in 1917–18; an article called "Data" in his magazine *The Exile*, No. 4 (Autumn 1928); a fuller treatment of what he had written in "Data" in a new article, "Small Magazines," published in the American academic periodical *The English Journal* (College Edition) in 1930; and an article he wrote for Orage's *New English Weekly* in 1934 called "Murkn Magzeens" ("Murkn" means both "American" and "murky" or obscuring realities in Pound's idiom). These articles tend to fall into one of two patterns: either measured praise of the noncommercial journals or sharp criticism of popular magazines. (He also muttered about popular magazines occasionally in his radio broadcasts.) It is clear that he saw his "Studies in Contemporary Mentality" as a *sottisier*, or collection of stupidities, which he enjoyed presenting to the readership of *The New Age*. His motivation for writing about the small magazines in an American academic publication a dozen years after "Studies in Contemporary Mentality" is clarified by a remark he made in *The Exile*, introducing his annotated list of small magazines and presses:

> . . . as institutions which would never have fed any of the men who did the work are now ready to feed almost anyone who will write anodyne monographs about the matter, one may as well set down a few dates, and give a list of the periodicals where the struggle took place. (*The Exile* 4:104)

Those "institutions" that would not support artists but will now support those who comment on their work must be the colleges and universities of the United States, which Pound would address directly in his 1930 article on "Small Magazines" for the College Edition of *The English Journal*. Back in 1917, however, he had turned his attention directly to the popular magazines of Britain in his twenty articles on Contemporary Mentality.

Table 4.3 gives a fair idea of the range Pound covered in this series of articles, but it doesn't convey the pedagogical attitude and tone that he takes in them. Wyndham Lewis, writing Pound about these articles from France, told him, "They are certainly the best things the New Age has

Table 4.3. "Studies in Contemporary Mentality" as it appeared in
The New Age from August 1917 through January 1918

Date	Volume: Issue	Title	Notes
1917-08-16	21:16	I.—"The Hibbert"	
1917-08-23	21:17	II.—"Blackwoods"	
1917-08-30	21:18	III.—On Quarterly Publications	Quarterly Review; Church Review; Edinburgh Review
1917-09-06	21:19	IV.—"The Spectator"	
1917-09-13	21:20	V.—"The Strand," or How the Thing May Be Done	
1917-09-20	21:21	VI. "The Sphere," and Reflections on Letter-Press	
1917-09-27	21:22	VII. Far from the Expensive Veal Cutlet	The Quiver
1917-10-11	21:24	VIII. The Beating Heart of the Magazine	The Quiver
1917-10-18	21:25	IX.—Further Heart Throbs	The Family Herald and Punch
1917-10-25	21:26	X.—The Backbone of the Empire	Chambers' Journal
1917-11-01	22:01	XI.—Bright and Snappy	Answers
1917-11-08	22:02	XI.(12)—Hash and Rehash	(Misnumbered from this point on); Answers
1917-11-15	22:03	XII.(13)—The Emblematic	Old Moore's Almanac
1917-11-22	22:04	XIII.(14)—The Celestial	The Christian Herald
1917-11-29	22:05	XIV.(15)—Progress, Social and Christian	The British Weekly
1917-12-13	22:07	XV.(16)—A Nice Paper	Forget-Me-Not
1917-12-20	22:08	XVI.(17)—Aphrodite Popularis	Nash's Magazine
1917-12-27	22:09	XVII.(18)—The Slightly Shop-worn	Sixpenny weeklies; The Bookman; The English Review; The Church Times
1918-01-03	22:10	XVIII.(19)—Nubians	The Church Times
1918-01-10	22:11	XIX.(20)—? Versus Camouflage	Conclusions

contained for many a day" (*Pound/Lewis*, 114), and Pound replied that "Orage hopes to get the Contemporary Mentality published as a book" (115). Although that did not happen, the articles still serve as an excellent example of the "Super Schoolmaster" at work. (The numbering of the series went wrong, with two articles numbered "XI." In referring to articles after the first of these number elevens, we use the corrected numbers provided in parentheses in the table.)

As a scholar and teacher investigating periodicals, Pound begins by tackling the complex problem of dividing them into useful categories. He recognizes the complexity of the problem but insists that his work is not meant to be definitive. He begins his attempt at categorizing magazine genres by saying that he will work not as a "theologian interpreting the Divine Will" but "as a simple-hearted anthropologist putting specimens into different large boxes—merely for present convenience—tumbling things apparently similar into the same large box until a more scientific and accurate and mature arrangement is feasible" (#6; *NA* 21.21:446). As we shall see, his criteria are a combination of goal and audience, with a specific eye toward what can be learned about these forms of popular culture. Here are the five categories he generates, in his own words:

1. Those designed to keep thought in safe channels; to prevent acrimonious discussion in old gentlemen's clubs. e.g., respectable quarterlies, "The Spectator," [and all that sort].

2. Periodicals designed to inculcate useful and mercantile virtues in the middle and lower middle classes or strata, e.g., "The Strand," and "Cocoa" in general.

3. Trade journals, such as "The Bookman," "The Tailor and Cutter," "Colour," etc.

4. Crank papers. Possibly one should include here as a subheading "religious periodicals," but I do not wish to press this classification; I do not feel the need of two categories, and my general term will cover a number of crank papers which are not definitely religious, though often based on "superstition," i.e., left-overs of religions and taboos.

5. Papers and parts of papers designed to stop thought altogether.

(#6; *NA* 21.21:446)

Pound's categories might not make much taxonomic sense, but they are characteristically his. One might expect a sixth category—"that from a long way off look like flies." Kidding aside, because this is really no joking matter, Pound wanted to teach others about the dangerous relationship between culture and politics, even if he cannot seem to see his own biases. By "contemporary mentality," he means what we would now probably call ideology. In his introduction to *Make It New*, he referred to his method as an examination of "symptoms which the visiting anthropologist or student of Kulturmorphologie would have noticed as 'customs of the tribus Britannicus'" (17). He is using an ordering system that investigates the ways in which one medium, the magazine, regularly promotes a particular ideology—an ideology that hides, or, as he says, "camouflages," certain realities. This means that when he looks at a magazine, he not only attends to the "content" but examines the advertising as well, exploring, as a periodical studies scholar would today, the relationship between the two.[17] For example, he sees most Christian Churches as corporations:

> "The Church Times". . . .but why go on with this camouflage? Christ Himself, His brilliant remarks, His attractive personality, His profound intuitions, being now scarcely more than a bit of camouflage draped over a corporate body, or, rather, several corporate bodies styling itself and themselves, "His Church." These corporations are useful to various people and participants; so effective is the camouflage that only now has someone in America let out the egregious cat that Lincoln once consorted with freethinkers, read Payne and Voltaire, wrote an essay in accord with their beliefs, and that this did not ruin his character. (#19; *NA* 22.10:193)

He connects the promises of advertisers (in this case, specifically of corsets) to those promises made by certain Christian writers:

> As the paradisiacal promise, such as that concerning the corsets, has always been used as a lure, so this wheeze about the horror of nothingness, the end of the world, the day of judgment, etc., has been used as a shake-up, as an hysteria-producer to weaken the will, and it has even masqueraded as an argument for believing or accepting or tolerating all sorts and conditions of doctrines. (#11; *NA* 22.01:11)

Calling attention to how easily some exploit the line between preaching and teaching, he continues this discussion by noting that "to judge from our periodicals the vast majority of our neighbours do not know enough science to keep their bowels open. I think there is not one paper of all those I have looked at which does not proclaim some cathartic." The point here is that the advertisers and the marketers of religious nostrums share an interest in concealing certain things from the people they address. Pound discusses both kinds of propaganda regularly. Some of the magazines he considers are specifically religious, and others most definitely are not, but they share, as Pound sees them, in the process of ideological distortion or camouflage.

Pound's treatment of the magazines is more anecdotal than systematic. He is witty, biting, and lively. He is something like contemporary bloggers, discussing what comes to hand, taking up a new project each week. One of his more interesting finds is an article he cites as "My Girls and the New Times, a frank talk, by a middle-aged mother" from a magazine called *The Quiver* (#7; *NA* 21.22:465). Founded in Victorian times, *The Quiver* was an illustrated eight-penny magazine with a religious bent that had become known for publishing serial fiction. According to Pound, it was popular with servants and especially women. He mentions this article in his seventh piece, and then in the eighth he begins by saying, "I return with interest undiminished to the 'frank' and middle-aged mother—my periscope for surveying the no-man's land of the unexplored popular heart" (#8; *NA* 21.24:505). He begins with style, inventing a new term for a certain kind of formulaic writing:

> "Those days of peace which now seem so remote were not altogether happy for parents." I take this sentence from near her beginning. For the word "peace" substitute almost any other temporal designation, for "parents" substitute any other noun indicating any other group of humanity, the sense of the statement will remain, I think, unimpaired. "Cliché," as generally used, has meant a set phrase; we have here something slightly different; it may be called the "gapped linotype." (#8; *NA* 21.24:505)

In the passage above, we see the reverse side of Pound's enthusiasm for Jules Romains. Discussing Romains, you will remember, Pound talked about "nouns meet[ing] their verbs for the first time." Here, on the other hand, Pound is chastising the clichéd prose—nouns and verbs that are old friends. He is considering not a semantic formula, but a syntactic one, a grammar of sentimentality—what he marvelously phrases a "gapped linotype," rather than a phrase locked in type (cliché). Beyond the evident misogyny (though the resentment is widespread) it is as though these authors he is reading were working from almost basic writing exercises, which certainly, in his view, are not "literature." For Pound, this signifies the substitution of formula for thought, and he returns to the concept a number of times in discussing the article. The frank mother is concerned with daughters who have grown discontented and have sought new lives of their own because of what the mother calls a "restless wavering temperament that seeks escape from home." We have another name for this temperament—we call it "modernism" and see it as a response to the conditions of modernity. This is quite explicit in the mother's discourse: her girls "would discuss Shaw and Nietzsche, but they would not discuss a leak in a gas-pipe, or the making of a simple soup."

Pound is a bit daunted by this. To reach the popular mind, his periscope needs to "go further. We must find some family where they did not read Shaw and Nietzsche. However, let us keep on with this stratum" (#8; *NA* 21.24:505). The need to get beyond, or, more precisely, below the level at which Shaw and Nietzsche are read becomes a refrain in these articles. There is plenty to study at this level, and he dissects the mother's discourse in considerable detail—too much for us to follow here—but his conclusions from this investigation resonate:

> Note the ground tone. The ground tone not only of this little "frank talk," but of all this sort of writing. Whether the talk is "frank" makes little difference; if it is not the talk of a mother, or of someone expressing her own personal and typical mentality, but merely the tour de force of someone writing for a given audience, it is at least a successful tour de force. It represents the mentality of the not innumerous readers who accept it. This sort of didacticism proceeds by general statement, it is specifically ignorant of individual differences, it takes no count of the divergence of personalities and of temperaments. Before its swish and sweep the individual has no existence. There are but two conclusions: 1. That these people do not perceive individuality as existing; 2. That individual differences in this stratum are so faint as to be imperceptible. (506–7)

Beneath the aesthetic reinvestment in the individual ego for which Pound is constantly lobbying lies an important critique of methodic storytelling. One is almost reminded of Vladimir Propp's folktale morphology here, though he and Pound are coming to their subjects from vastly different angles. The less systematic, more politically engaged Pound noted (and critiqued) narrative similarities across the various journals, distinguishing between the common and the literary. Pound finds the obliteration of the individual under the pressure to conform to be one of the major effects of the kind of journalism he is investigating—and he finds it detestable. As we have seen, his arguments on behalf of poetry and the other arts all have to do with the expression of individuality by persons who have earned the right to do that by some combination of the quality of their vision and their mastery of the technical features of their art. In the print media, this sets the truth of poetry in direct opposition to what Pound sees as the lies of journalism, which is why it is imperative for the schoolmaster to teach us about both sides of this opposition.

In the ninth article, we find Pound noting that, "[i]n the hope of getting below the Shaw-Nietzsche zone I purchased the 'Family Herald'" (#9; *NA* 21.25:527). He knew he had reached that underground zone when he found in the magazine an advertisement for Rankin's Head Ointment. In explaining this choice, he goes on to observe that "[t]his paper I had often heard mentioned. Whenever a stylist wishes to damn a contemporary, especially a contemporary novelist, he suggests that said novelist is specifically fit to 'write for the "Family Herald"'" (527). The *Family Herald* was a one-penny weekly, subheaded "The Household Magazine of Useful Information and Entertainment." The Rankin's ad for the treatment of lice gave Pound a way of ranking *The Family Herald* in the order of popular magazines he was trying to generate:

> As an indication of stratum note that the "Family Herald" is the first paper in which I have found ads. relative to "nits and vermin in the hair," and the ad. beginning "IF YOUR CHILD has nits or head pests." It is arguable, by these portents, that the "Family Herald" reaches, or at least approaches, the verminous level, but still it is a cut above "Punch." The "family physician" is useful, and "Punch's" book reviews are of no use whatever, though they be camouflaged by Punch's "pleasantry." (528)

A more patient teacher, perhaps, might have been a little slower to dismiss things outright, but that was not Pound's way. Though nearly all of it was laughable to him, we have a teacher exposing his students to all kinds of writing, comparing texts that were not, at the time, often thought to be linked as different sides of the same historical discourse. Pound was certainly looking for stupidity in this series, but he was also looking for flashes of intelligence or sanity in unexpected places. His work was to be not just a *sottisier*, but something more complex and, finally, more interesting, though in his later thoughts about popular magazines these nuances tend to disappear, and his teaching on this topic becomes less interesting as a result.

In addition to looking at the articles and the advertisements, Pound turns his attention to the more "literary" texts in the journals he is studying. With the verse, he is usually content with a mocking phrase or a quotation, but he gives the fiction more extended attention. Part of this involves noting who appears where—and with whom. He can hardly control his glee at the combination of authors he finds in the popular monthly *Nash's Magazine*:

> In this life we find certain perfect adjustments. Who, for example, could have dreamed of finding a poem by E.W. Wilcox, a serial by Miss Corelli, a poem by Chas. Hanson Towne, a tale by Gouverneur Morris, another by Robt. W. Chambers, another by Stephen Leacock, and "Beyond" by John Galsworthy, together with sundry actresses' limbs, all, all assembled in the one set of covers, all surrendered to one for 8d.? Christian and Social Progress has found no more happy equation; for what, in Zeus' name, could be more Christian than Miss Marie Corelli, or more social than Mr. John Galsworthy? And how united the tone, how beautifully, how almost transcendentally all these people "belong"; what utter and super-trinitarian unity thus binds them together in Nash's! (#17; *NA* 22.08:148–49)

Although Pound is clearly poking fun here, he is onto something that would take scholars generations to realize (and something Pound himself would never accept)—that modernism isn't a small collection of Joyce, Eliot, and Lewis, but a vast muddle of diverse voices, each in its own way bound to its historical condition. As Pound concedes facetiously, "All these people belong." Whether or not this is a "good" thing is another matter.

From his elitist position, Pound feels no need to discuss the "actual works of Corelli, Chambers, Galsworthy and Co." because they are already familiar to himself and his readers, but he enjoys situating them among the ads in the magazine:

Your hair; Macassar Oil; Eyes Men Idolize; The Kind of beauty that men admire; Add a pleasure to life; Protective Knickers; Author's Manuscripts; Somebody's Darling; A sweet little set, beautifully hand-made and picot edged; Irresistible; What does your brain earn; Good Pianist; Asthma; Daisy; don't let pain spoil your good looks; Why People Marry; King of Hearts; Autumn Beauty; Neptune's Daughter; Beauty pictures; Soap; Safety-filler; the cure of self-consciousness; Lovely Eyelashes; Add to your income; Power: Scientific concentration; Height increased; Healthy Women; Esperanto; Makes straight hair wavy and lustrous; YOU can PLAY the PIANO. (#17; *NA* 22.08:149)

This mélange, then, is the background for the assemblage of writers Pound noted but will not discuss. Instead, he teaches us about the commercialism of culture, and, while the contemptuous attitude feels unscholarly and uninformative—not to mention unnecessarily vicious toward a public that, too, might want to learn how to "play the piano"—he is not incorrect in linking the fiction he reads to this new sociocultural concoction.

In another article, in the enormously popular *Strand* magazine, he will give one writer seriously mocking attention: Arthur Conan Doyle. He begins by noting, grudgingly, that Doyle, who has "never stooped to literature," has "done it," contributed something to the culture: "Sherlock has held us all spellbound" (#5; *NA* 21.20:426). Pound sees this as a sort of conjuring trick, which he proceeds to expose in the present instance. After discussing the improbabilities in the story in which Holmes defeats a German spy, Pound concludes:

Sherlock is unique, but mankind remains amazingly unaltered and unalterable. He likes a relief from reality, he likes fairy stories, he likes stories of giants, he likes genii from bottles. Sherlock with his superhuman strength, his marvellous acumen, his deductive reasoning (which is certainly not shared with the reader), has all the charms of the giant. He is also a moral Titan: right is never too right. The logical end of these likes is, or was, God. The first clever Semite who went out for monotheism made a corner in giantness. He got a giant "really" bigger than all other possible giants. Whenever art gets beyond itself, and laps up too great a public it at once degenerates into religion. Sherlock is

> on the way to religion, a modern worship of efficiency, acumen, inhumanity. Only a man on familiar terms with his public as Sir Arthur, as habituated to writing for that public, would dare "lay it on so thick." (#5 *NA* 21.20:426)

As with advertising, Pound connects the Holmes stories to religion, and suspiciously, in this case, to a modern faith infused with "efficiency, acumen, inhumanity."[18] Pound understands popular desire and knows that as one form of worship fades another will rise—here, a celebrity culture tied to an economic marketplace and a national sense of exceptionalism.[19] As the twentieth and twenty-first centuries made clear, such is the "giant" that is "really' bigger than all other possible giants." Pound, himself, as we discuss in the next chapter, would fall into his own trap in this regard. If only this teacher were able to see how prescient his own words were about an art that "gets beyond itself" and "degenerates into religion."

Pound is much gentler with a serialized romance we might expect him to despise, which he finds in *Forget-Me-Not*:

> The paper is printed for people who prefer keeping their hands clean. It is religious and moral, i.e., it is religious in providing a paradise, sic: a country house, a picture gallery, etc.; it is moral in that virtue is rewarded. It has even some literary merit, I mean solely that part of the complete novelette which forms the number before me must be well told, even though it is not well written. (#16 *NA* 22.07:129)

Lurking in the phrasal difference of "well told" and "well written," we might finally see the schoolmaster's distinction between rhetoric and literature. Popular readers liked stories that were "well told," stories that—for Pound—carried an ideological message. He thought (incorrectly) that "well written" works could free themselves from such political and economic interference. Pound goes on to point out some ways in which the tale is not well written, adding that to its audience this can make no difference at all: "I feel about these dainty little romances very much as the landed class feel about religion: 'Why destroy it, why attack it, what are you going to put in its place? It keeps so many people contented.' This feeling is, of course, in the present case, sheer sentimentality. The reader would be neither more nor less happy if the flaws were removed" (129).[20] Only a terribly misinformed reader would align Pound with the Marxist thinker Theodor Adorno, but (with apologies to both) Pound's critique here is not unlike much of Adorno's understanding of popular culture as insidiously ideological.[21] Both can (rightfully) be called elitist, but their thinking—right or wrong—originates with a desire to unshackle the masses from an oppressive economic regime that has ceaselessly invaded the cultural sphere. Where they differ is in the end, with Adorno seeing art that isn't easily consumable as reawakening the collective and Pound the "free" individual.

Taken together, Pound's articles are lively, shrewd, opinionated, and unlike anything else being written at that time, because their author was really an original, a teacher—for better and worse—like no other. But the common critical thread that holds these pieces together is Pound's view that a mentality of camouflage is being spread through this medium—in its religion, in its advertising, and in its fiction. As a result, individual differences—those that embody great art—are suppressed by the religiosity, nationalism, and corporate capitalism purveyed in these popular journals. It is a powerful indictment, fueled by Pound's belief that literature should tell the world the truth about itself and enable individuality to flourish. Thirteen years later, writing for the College Edition of *The English Journal* (the predecessor of *College English*, the foremost publication of the National Council of Teachers of English), Pound examined the other side of the question, looking at the achievements of what he called "Small Magazines." Teaching college teachers about this branch of periodicals, Pound began with an indictment of the larger American magazines that had failed to support modern writing: "During the ten or twenty years preceding 1912 the then-called 'better magazines' had failed lamentably and even offensively to maintain intellectual life" (689). Very importantly for Pound, "intellectual life" was not the mere passing on of older ideas (ideas Pound generally valued immensely), but rather encouraging participation in an intellectual and artistic tradition. As nearly all of Pound's instruction makes clear, ideas die when they lose their edge. This failure of the "better magazines," in Pound's view, resulted in the "active phase of the small magazine in America," starting in 1911 with Harriet Monroe's founding of *Poetry*. He described the process in an eloquent paragraph:

> The elder magazines, the *Atlantic*, *Harper's*, *Scribner's*, *Century*, had even in their original titles more or less and in varying degrees abjured the pretentions of the London "Reviews," i.e., to serious and consecutive criticism of literature. They had grown increasingly somnolent, reminiscences of General Grant being

about their maximum effort toward contemporaneity. About the beginning of this century there was a new and livelier current in the trade. The methods of Armour's meat business were introduced into distribution. A commercial talent blossomed in the great firm of Condé Nast. A bright young man observed a leakage in efficiency. The advertising men had to collect such ads as the contents could attract. In the new system the contents were selected rigorously on the basis of how much expensive advertising they would carry. ("Small Magazines" 690)[22]

Pound's disparate lectures about individual publications really come together in this later essay. The literary works, he astutely realized, were no longer of primary importance to most of the editors; they were chosen predominantly on the basis of the advertising revenue they would draw. A century of popular print, radio, television, and now online media has only confirmed Pound's suspicion. It is clear that Pound understood the history of American periodicals very well in 1930. Later studies like Theodore Peterson's *Magazines in the Twentieth Century* have endorsed and elaborated many of his views.[23] And the first major academic book on the topic—*The Little Magazine* by Hoffman, Allen, and Ulrich—emerged directly from Pound's article, simply extending and codifying what he sketched out. After explaining the need for small magazines like *Poetry*, Pound gave a brief history of his engagement with that magazine, including his differences with the editor, and then went on to discuss the other journals to which he had been connected, with special praise for Hueffer's *The English Review* and for *The Smart Set*, observing that the editor W. H. Wright, who tried to emulate *The English Review*, "knocked his circulation from 70,000 to 40,000 in, if I remember rightly, the first six months" and then resigned. Here we might once more see Pound's endorsement of the slogan "MAKING NO COMPROMISE WITH THE PUBLIC TASTE."

Pound is a bit less certain, on this occasion, about the early history of the small magazine, suggesting that *The English Review* had "Continental inspiration." We know that he had corresponded with the editor of the Belgian journal *La Wallonie* and mentioned the *Mercure de France* in an article about Remy de Gourmont in 1915. After mentioning this uncertainty, he returns to the magazines he knows from experience, discussing *Blast*, *The Little Review*, and *The Dial*, and offers well-informed opinions about their work before moving on to describe Eliot's *Criterion* as cautious and to praise Hueffer's (now "Ford's") current project, the *transatlantic review*. He then discusses the way certain small magazines turned into small publishers and printed experimental books, before summing up his thoughts on the subject with these four conclusions:

1. The last twenty years have seen the principle of the free magazine or the impractical or fugitive magazine definitely established. It has attained its recognized right to exist by reason of work performed.

2. The commercial magazines have been content and are still more than content to take derivative products ten or twenty years after the germ has appeared in the free magazines. There is nothing new about this.

3. Work is acceptable to the public when its underlying ideas have been accepted. The heavier the "overhead" in a publishing business the less that business can afford to deal in experiment. This purely sordid and eminently practical consideration will obviously affect all magazines save those that are either subsidized (as chemical research is subsidized) or else very cheaply produced (as the penniless inventor produces in his barn or his attic).

4. Literature evolves via a mixture of these two methods. ("Small Magazines" 702)

Functioning as a teacher of teachers, Pound, for once, clearly and calmly shares information that he had gathered through years of practical experience with the journals he discusses. In the face of mass distributers, he is able to advocate for the importance of the small publishers, almost anticipating their proliferation in the second half of the twentieth century. Pound had the faith that great individual publications would eventually create their own audiences. We see this today in the numerous websites devoted to the arts, sites that command small but dedicated audiences and that are often tied to classroom learning.[24] While the arts have not garnered as much private or public support as he would have wished, and while that support often comes with political considerations attached, Pound's words about independent presses remain of great consequence. His thinking and rhetoric here contrast sharply with the mode of his discourse just four years later, when he wrote "Murkn Magzeens" for Orage's *New English Weekly*, using his old art critic pen name, B. H. Dias. This change may be due in part to the different audience he assumes, but it may also be due to internal changes that are turning the super schoolmaster into a proud pontificator. When he wrote "Studies in Contemporary Mentality" for Orage's previous weekly, *The New Age*, he was harsh, but also lucid and witty, and he presented himself as an investigator looking at the behavior of a strange tribe of popular periodicals. He approved of individualism and truthfulness, criticized the journalistic deceit he called "camouflage," and condemned all attempts to suppress individual differences.

In "Murkn Magzeens," on the other hand, he offers from on high opinions about everything from the Roosevelt administration to the history of Russia. He proposes to ignore what he calls the dead but unburied journals and to offer the reader instead a list of living ones: "I am making the main division between the live magazine and the hoary pimps of antiquity" (235). His annotated list includes literary journals like *Hound and Horn*, political and economic journals like *New Democracy*, and " 'Red' or sunset magazines" in which "[t]he proletaires are expected to dictate with NO KNOWLEDGE of economics or of whatsodamnelse whatsoever." In the course of making his list he offers his usual faint praise of Harriet Monroe, whose *Poetry* is still alive, with an assistant editor, "young [Morton] Zabel," "shaking up the critical section": "However the editress has done her damndest in an ungrateful soil, and has put up with a great deal of writing she herself presumably dislikes very much." Pound also takes a moment to attack the British and American academic worlds along with the old magazines, lumping them together as enemies of modern art and literature. Such outright dismissals are sometimes voiced among students and pundits today more sympathetic to immediate revenue than education: "No literate person under forty has any respect for the old-line publications and the so-called academy is a pure or impure joke" (236).[25] By 1934, the pedagogical Pound was not aging well himself.

CHAPTER 5

The Instructor as Propagandist

Said Mr Adams, of the education,
Teach? at Harvard?
Teach? It cannot be done.

—Pound, "Canto 74"

So wrote Ezra Pound from his cage outside Pisa as he was awaiting what he thought might be his execution for treason.

A day after the Germans in Italy surrendered and a week before the war in Europe ended, Pound tried unsuccessfully to surrender to American troops, but they did not know who he was. (He had been charged *in absentia* with treason two years earlier, following his Radio Rome broadcasts.) The next day, two Italian partisans briefly arrested him before letting him go. Worried for his safety, Pound was finally able to surrender to the Americans in Genoa. It was May 1945. A few weeks later, he was transferred to the "DTC"—the Disciplinary Training Center—where he would stay alongside rapists and murderers in a six-by-six-and-a-half foot cage, "the line of cages inside the punishment area, labeled 'DEATH CELLS.'"[1] His belt and shoelaces were removed, and he was left in the open, with a blanket covering the wet, concrete floor. As Carpenter chronicles, "there was a can in the corner of the cage, which they would not remove until it was completely full and stinking. A guard stood outside the cage, watching him all through the night, and bright lights shone continuously on him" (659).[2] "It was no place," Moody writes, "for an intensely individual civilian not subject to the disciplines of war" (II 117). Pound remained there for three weeks until it was medically necessary to move him. Finally out of the cage but still in detention, he was given a typewriter, composing most of his "Pisan Cantos" from memory. Six months later he was transferred back to the United States to stand trial. He underwent a series of psychiatric examinations and judicial hearings. A few minutes after the judge's charge, the jury returned with the verdict that Pound was of "unsound mind" to stand trial. He was committed to St Elizabeths Federal Hospital for the Insane in Washington, DC, remaining there for a dozen years, before heading back to Italy upon his release. He was seventy-two.[3]

This chapter considers the middle and later years of Pound, when his teaching ceases to be a healthy model of an educational method. He was never what one would call a "disinterested" scholar, but, during this time, malicious interests—if one will excuse the phrase—overtook his teaching. He was no longer driven by inquiry; he believed he knew the shape of the puzzle, and everything simply fit into his model. "[I]t is evident," Leon Surette writes, "that [Pound's] devotion to economic reform was based on a genuine desire to reduce human suffering and want and to restore a social order in which the artist held a place of honor. But it all went terribly wrong. Unable to understand the great events unfolding around him and unable to admit—even to himself—his incomprehension, he could only denounce those he could not persuade" (*Pound in Purgatory* 97).[4] After a reading of a few passages from Canto 74 (the Canto has been much discussed, but some of the lines focused on haven't been as chewed over in the context of the poem or Pound's guise as a teacher), we go back to Pound's early encounters with C. H. Douglas and economic theory before briefly touching on his treasonous radio broadcasts, his time at St. Elizabeths, and his final years.

However one feels about Pound as a person or as a poet, and however one chooses or does not choose to read Pound, it is hard not to admit that, before him, there was nothing on Earth like "Canto 74." Written partly on a piece of toilet paper, it begins:

> The enormous tragedy of the dream in the peasant's bent
>   shoulders
>   Manes! Manes was tanned and stuffed,
>   Thus Ben and la Clara *a Milano*
>   by the heels at Milano
> That maggots shd/ eat the dead bullock
> DIGONOS, Δίγονος, but the twice crucified
>   where in history will you find it? (445)

Calling this opening "a requiem for Italian fascism," Richard Sieburth sees Pound's thoughts on the death of Mussolini evoking "the sacrificial slaying of twice-born Dionysos in the form of a bull . . . here devoured by the maggotlike *partigiani* responsible for his murder" (xxxvi). Like the Persian philosopher Mani (or Manes), the founder of Manicheanism who was killed twice (flayed and filled with grass for his teachings), and like the god Dionysus who was born twice (the second time from Zeus after one of Hera's fits), Mussolini—as Pound describes him here—was "twice crucified" (beaten and then hanged "by the heels").[5] The "tragedy" is entire—the realities of fascism itself, the end of the dream, and perhaps Pound's belief in both. "Pound at a single stroke," writes Sieburth, "transforms a poem of elegy . . . into one that must bear witness to 'the enormous tragedy' of Italy's Fascist dream—a burden of tragic vision hardly supported by the body of the text, whose open and Odyssean form now undergoes a final and truculent political closure" (xxxvi).[6] "Where in history will you find it?" Pound asks himself as well as a reader he could only dream up at the moment, and he begins to answer this question: "OÝ ΤΙΣ, OÝ ΤΙΣ? Odysseus / the name of my family" (445). The paper Pound initially wrote this on had the heading "Nekuia," linking his own middle way of Canto 74 with the title of Canto 1, drafted in 1917, in what would have to have seemed almost a lifetime ago.[7] The Nekuia is the episode of the *Odyssey* where Odysseus travels to Hades to seek the advice of Tiresias on how to get home. If such a myth could conjure the first sails of what would become the enormity of Pound's lifetime achievement, then they almost certainly would have been an apt allusion here: Pound in his own Hades, trying to get back home; he was, in every sense of the phrase, "a man on whom the sun has gone down . . ." (450). Offering his name as OÝ ΤΙΣ or "No Man," Odysseus tricked the Cyclops. In detention, Pound, similarly without a name ("I am noman, my name is noman"), connects the tale of Odysseus to Wanjina, of Australian mythology, who created the world by naming things. Wanjina, though, erred in the eyes of those in power, as did Pound, by naming too much, and his father sealed his mouth:

> but Wanjina is, shall we say, Ouan Jin
> or the man with an education
> and whose mouth was removed by his father
>   because he made too many *things*. (446–47)

Wanjina evokes the Chinese Ouan Jin, who was also a threat, because he was "the man with an education." Perhaps the best way to describe Canto

74 is with a term Pound borrows from Confucius—"the process" ("Tao," often translated as "the way"). The Canto follows Pound's meandering thoughts from Mussolini and Dionysus to Odysseus and Dante to political and economic diatribes to past memories of deceased friends and places he could not imagine revisiting, save in his mind:

> yet say this to the Possum: a bang, not a whimper,
> > with a bang not with a whimper,
> To build the city of Dioce whose terraces are the colour of stars.
> The suave eyes, quiet, not scornful,
> > > rain also is of the process.

The "Possum" is Pound's old friend and sometimes collaborator T. S. Eliot, who had kept up correspondence with Pound during the war and had helped him personally and professionally during his confinement, even as they had grown apart philosophically and temperamentally.[8] Eliot's "The Hollow Men," published two decades earlier, after the First World War concluded, closes with the lines "This is the way the world ends / Not with a bang but with a whimper" (80). Inverting these lines, Pound—awaiting the bang of his own possible execution and witness to the devastation of Italy—seems to be staking a less modest end for what he believed were the early noble intentions of fascism and the dream of his paradise, "the city of Dioce whose terraces are the colour of stars."

Pound rails against Churchill and British monetary policy, which devastated Indian peasants, forcing them "to pay two bushels of grain in taxes and interest which a short time before [they] had been able to pay with only one" (Terrell 365). He sarcastically notes how "the total interest sweated out of the Indian farmers / rose in Churchillian grandeur," aligning English policy with the "usurers" of his invectives, before offering a broadside against the presumptions of liberal democracy and his own incarceration: "Oh my England / that free speech without free radio speech is as zero . . ." (446). Pound warns the United States, too, of a "militarism progressing westward . . . / and the Constitution in jeopardy" (446). Minus the immediate context (and that is a big "minus" here), Pound's concern about militarism is not unlike that of President Eisenhower's warning, in his farewell address, of the growing "military industrial complex." (Pound, in his willful blindness, could not see the same problem with the rise of fascism.) Beneath the tireless diatribes, both in print and on the radio, one can see that Pound was not as such "anti-American." He believed in the principles of John Adams and Thomas Jefferson but thought that people like Roosevelt were betraying those values. Pound's earlier misguided text *Jefferson and/or Mussolini* (1935) offers as much: "The challenge of Mussolini to America is simply: *Do the driving ideas of Jefferson, Quincy Adams, Van Buren, or whoever else there is in the credible pages of our history, FUNCTION actually in the America of this decade to the extent that they function in Italy under the DUCE?* The writer's opinion is that they DON'T" (104).[9] Of particular interest for our book (and we return to this question after preliminaries) is Pound's sense here of the relationship between politics and teaching, especially regarding his own role as a writer who wanted to enlighten. "Jefferson participated in one revolution," Pound writes, "he 'informed it' both in the sense of shaping it from the inside and of educating it" (14).

A curious thing about this Canto: whether he is denouncing "Churchill's backers," King David ("the prime s.o.b."), or "Meyer Anselm / That old H." (Mayer Amschel Rothschild, the patriarch of the Rothschild family), Pound can find moments where the Old Testament runs concurrently with his own beliefs, regarding what Jean-Michel Rabaté calls the "Jewish ideogram of justice" (190).[10] (Along with his own copy of Confucius, a US Army–issued Bible was one of the few books Pound was allowed to keep at the DTC, and he read and reread it.) As Stephen Sicari understands this illogicality, "It was [Pound's] genius to find congenial passages in a book he was not prepared to find congenial to his purposes, passages that allowed him to continue his poem's journey and elevate the destiny of his wandering hero . . ." (213). At these times, Pound can incongruously see himself in the sandals of biblical prophets sent to tell the Israelites of their false ways. The redemption Pound sought in his own failed paradise echoed in the story of Isaiah, who hoped "to redeem Zion with justice" ("Canto 74" 449).[11] This line particularly hits Pound at his new home:

> 4 giants at the 4 corners
>> three young men at the door
> and they digged a ditch round about me
>> lest the damp gnaw thru my bones
>>> to redeem Zion with justice
> sd/ Isaiah. . . . (449)

Amid the four guard towers and army sentries, cast as "giants," sits Pound. While many of his Cantos had moved seemingly indiscriminately between a mythological or cultural history and the accidents of his own present life, things feel very different now, as the epic voice has been taken to a whole other lyric space, "private and memorious in character" (Surette, *A Light* 178). "The wartime Italian writings," for Ronald Bush, "stress the power of monuments to consolidate what is sometimes called collective or cultural memory" ("Pisa" 261).[12] Michael Alexander notes that "the dream collides with public life in an unforeseen and tragic guise that must compel the attention of anyone who reflects upon the modern fate of poetry" (193). This intrusion from the "real world" makes one rethink the very possibilities of lyric form:

> and gun sales lead to more gun sales
> > they do not clutter the market for gunnery
> > > there is no saturation
> > Pisa, in the 23rd year of the effort in sight of the tower
> and Till was hung yesterday
> for murder and rape with trimmings . . .
> > > Hey Snag wots in the bibl'?
> > > wot are the books ov the bible?
> > > Name 'em, don't bullshit ME. 莫 OÝ TIΣ. (449–50)

The horrible aftereffects of domestic and global arms dealing disturb the natural balance between economic supply and demand. An overabundance of the supply just creates more and more demand, with the suppliers—as Pound notes often—providing munitions to opposing sides. There is no saturation.[13] The tower of which Pound speaks is that where Ugolino della Gherardesca, a thirteenth-century count, was locked up with his sons and starved. Dante memorializes their story, describing how the sons offered themselves as food so their father would not grow hungry. In this context, it is difficult to not also see the tower more metaphorically as the fascist project (Pound, here using his new calendar dating from Mussolini's March on Rome), which had for a moment been within "sight." In this very real space, though, symbolic heights lead not to paradise but to an executioner's rope, as Pound tells the story of his new companions.[14] Pound, not surprisingly, won't really let himself go to the story of the "Two Thieves" (one of whom was unnamed), but the echo is there. There are also the echoes of sound—something Pound's initial work with the visuality of the ideogram tended to overlook[15]—in the anagrammatic and associative echoes of "me": "Na**me** 'em, don't bullshit **ME**."[16] This exhortation to "name" or to find the right name leads the poet back to Odysseus, and then, a page later, to the names of his onetime friends and collaborators: Basil Bunting (the "struggler in the desert" and one of the dedicatees of Pound's *Guide to Kulchur*) and E. E. Cummings—both imprisoned for their objections to war.

Then, the "Nekuia" brings Pound to the names of the dead:

> Lordly men are to earth o'ergiven
> > these the companions:
> Fordie that wrote of giants
> > and William who dreamed of nobility
> > > and Jim the comedian singing:
> > > > " Blarrney castle me darlin'
> > > > you're nothing now but a StOWne "
> and Plarr talking of mathematics
> > or Jepson lover of Jade. . . . (452–53)

Ford Madox Ford ("Fordie") and W. B. Yeats ("William") both died in 1939, and James Joyce ("Jim the comedian") died two years after. The English writers Victor Plarr (a member of Yeats's "Rhymers' Club") and Edgar Jepson had also passed. After going through a few more names, Pound—now an Odysseus without a crew—mentions a still-living personal hero, "Uncle George" Holden Tinkham—a Republican senator from Massachusetts who opposed Roosevelt's entry into the war—and a few restaurants from around the globe.[17]

He then offers the words that serve as the epigraph of this chapter and can be understood as a luminous detail, connecting education to the history and literature and politics we have been discussing:

> Said Mr Adams, of the education,
> > Teach? at Harvard?
> > Teach? It cannot be done. (453)

It is not the first time in the *Cantos* that Pound would meditate on teaching. The pages are filled with the poet's bitter memories and various thoughts on improving educational institutions, whether he is reproving "dry professorial talk" (26), declaring that "the teacher's job is not / just filling paper with detours / nor in dull float" (719), or lamenting that "They (congress) wd. do nothing for / the education of boys but to make soldiers, they / wd. not endow a university (in 1826)" (168–69). And, though the years, he would return again to these thoughts from almost any related topic.[18] Why, we must ask, following memories of deceased friends and in the midst of the physical shock of the DTC and the dread of an unknown future, would Pound suddenly turn to Henry Adams and his own deep-rooted concerns about higher education? Published early in the twentieth century, *The Education of Henry Adams* details how the self-taught author did not learn anything important from his formal schooling, which could not engage sensibly with the actual changing world. "What he could gain at Harvard College he did not know," Adams writes, "but in any case it was nothing he wanted" (294). Like Pound, Adams bemoaned the state of institutionalized education. According to both, there were many things Harvard could boast, but actually teaching was not one of them. One should also be reminded here that in 1932, as Pound was comfortably settled in fascist Italy, T. S. Eliot was appointed the Charles Eliot Norton Professor at Harvard. As Pound wrote in a letter to Harriet Monroe at the time, "With Possum Eliot apptd. To Hawvud, he won't bring the glad polyanna yawp, but the ignorance of the Stork-Auslander-Mabie-Canby period can't continue" (December 27, 1931; Paige 238).

More germane, perhaps, is an encounter between Pound and the philosopher George Santayana in Venice in 1939 and a subsequent letter Pound wrote to the philosopher, asking him if he "would consider and on what terms [he] would consider, etc., a desperate attempt to save further generations from the horrors of past education. All of which arises from my transmission to Eliot of your little story of Henry Adams 'It can not be done'" (February 6, 1940; Paige 338).[19] The exact remark Pound uses for Canto 74 comes not from Adams's book, but from Santayana's recollection of a conversation with Adams published (years after Pound's canto) in Santayana's autobiography.[20] The possible collaborative project among Santayana, Pound, and Eliot would have involved "setting down either a method or a curriculum or both" and it would have elaborated "on the Ideal University, or the Proper Curriculum, or how it would be possible to educate and/ or (mostly *or*) civilize the university stewd-dent (and, inter-lineas, how to kill off bureaucratism and professoriality)" (338–39). Noting how Pound's "ideas seem to invite some sort of pluralism," Martin Coleman finds many points of overlap between the pedagogic Pound and the educator in Santayana (13). "The points of contact between Pound and Santayana regarding education," he writes, "can be taken as cues to self-knowledge, cues to ask, What are we doing as teachers? What determines successes? What conventions of professorial life block these inquiries?" (13). In initiating contact with Santayana, Pound, for his part, wanted to invite these discussions, and he used Santayana's quip about Adams as his way of doing so. "The Henry Adams anecdote is above price," he wrote to the philosopher: "it is your story and ought to be in the opening pages if not the opening paragraph. Anyhow, the idea arose from it" (339). Santayana modestly declined Pound's collaborative offer.

All of these things were circulating around Pound's head as he waited in his cage with only the library of his mind. Whatever one wants to make of these lines—are they remorseful, stubborn, bitter?—it is a testament to the importance with which Pound held educational systems that such a reference would arise in this miserable context. The "Pisan Cantos" would go on to win the first-ever awarded Bollingen Prize (called by Pound the "Bubble-Gum" prize), and not without controversy. The judges for the award included some of the most important poets of the day: Conrad Aiken, W. H. Auden, Louise Bogan, T. S. Eliot, Robert Lowell, Karl Shapiro, Allen Tate, and Katherine Garrison Chapin (who happened to be married to the attorney general who indicted Pound for treason). After some back-and-forth regarding the appropriateness of giving Pound the award, he finally won out, beating William Carlos Williams's *Patterson* (Book II). Pound's *Pisan Cantos* "represent[ed] the highest achievement of American poetry" for the year and, in the committee's view, to deny him the award because of his politics "would in principle deny the validity of that objective perception on which any civilized society must rest" (qtd. in Carpenter 792; see Moody III 277–88). The American public was divided about the incident; the government was not happy. A decade later, the man responsible for the "highest achievement of American poetry" would be released from St Elizabeths.

Hearing him speak in 1914, none of Pound's friends, family members, or teachers would have been able to envision that he would have ended up here, but, in retrospect, one can connect the dots.[21] Before Pound was of "unsound mind," before he was indicted for treason, before he was a champion of fascism and a vicious anti-Semite, Pound had found an unusual calling in the writings of the British engineer and economic theorist C. H. Douglas. "What [Pound] really wanted," A. David Moody writes, "was a society of and for the genuine individuals, a civilization which would transcend nations and collective cults and corporations, and from which enlightenment would spread and prevail" (I 371). Pound was not a defender of the masses, but he believed in preaching a brand of humanism, which would educate talented individuals. Though there are overlaps early on in Pound's poetry and prose, it really wasn't until he met Douglas in the *New*

Age offices of A. R. Orage that Pound's cultural pedagogy began in earnest to line up with economic philosophy. In 1919, Orage serialized what, a year later, would become Douglas's first book on his theory of "social credit," called *Economic Democracy*. After hitting it off personally and intellectually with Douglas, Pound published a few enthusiastic reviews of the amateur economist, who became, in Pound's eyes, a defender of individual liberty. Culture and economics would never be separate for Pound again, and his teachings would reflect that, mostly not for the better.

While working as an engineer, Douglas noticed an unhealthy gap between prices of goods and the purchasing power of the consumer.[22] "Douglas's remedy for the flaw he had perceived in the economy," as Carpenter explains it, "was that 'the State should lend, not borrow': that there should be Government intervention in the form of 'Social Credit,' a new 'money,' the closely controlled circulation of which would enable manufacturers to lower their prices, and allow consumers to buy freely. This would dispense with bank loans, destroy the power of the money-lenders, and inaugurate a new era of personal freedom and prosperity" (Carpenter 358).[23] Douglas's vision called for something akin to what we sometimes see today in a tax rebate, but one that would be continual, wouldn't be able to be loaned out for interest, and would eventually expire if not spent. The economics does not actually work in the real world, as many economists have noted (though they, including such luminaries as John Maynard Keynes, took Douglas's suggestions regarding what is today called "underconsumptionism" seriously), because, among many other reasons, it would result in continual inflation, which a "Just Price" could not counter. Pound, unschooled in economics, would not concede this point (and some Pound enthusiasts still follow suit).[24] The problem remained for him that when private banks issued credit (what ought to have been, for Douglas and Pound, a national undertaking), those banks would only do so for interest, sometimes exorbitantly so, creating consumer debt rather than actual purchasing power. And Pound saw usury, taxation, and feudal tributes as effectively the same thing—all "destroyer[s] of civilizations."[25] Neither Douglas's nor Pound's critique of capitalism was the same as the socialists' critique, which stressed collectivity where Pound stressed personal greatness. His critique charged the usurious foundation of capitalism with hollowing out the individual and, accordingly, hollowing out all cultural institutions. As he later wrote in Canto 45, it was "CONTRA NATURAM" (230).[26] Subsequent articles in the *New Age* from 1919–1920 carried some of the initial Poundian attacks on usury—on what was for him (and sadly many others) the metonymic Jew.

Noel Stock quotes from a *New York Herald* interview with Pound, in which the poet calls Douglas's work "the one contribution to creative thought which has been made in five years" (309).[27] And Moody quotes Pound as confessing that "[i]f it weren't for Douglas, I should have remained ignorant" (I 372). Just how much Pound *initially* had faith in the theories is unclear. Although both the ferocity and the quantity of his words propounding Douglas speak volumes, Pound might have also been excited by having another unexposed academic field to dig his teeth into. Speaking of the zeal in Pound's newfound mission, Carpenter writes, "It might be supposed from this that he had lost his sense of proportion; yet he was only behaving in character. The fervor he now devoted to questions of economics and government was the same with which he has pushed himself into the London literary world . . ." (493).

Pound knew art. Pound knew more than his teachers about the possibilities of art. Pound did not know economics and, despite his own beliefs, he was not a "super schoolmaster" in that field. Lack of knowledge, though, never did deter him, and he also began railing against college professors who were, as he believed, ignoring this real cause of all world events.[28] After moving to Rapallo in 1924, Pound continued his work in many interrelated spheres, but all of them would now include his thoughts on economics. He was publishing and promoting writers in various literary journals and writing introductory books meant for the student unfamiliar with the world. He had hoped that some of these books would be adopted by school systems, but also knew of his limited audience there. A year before completing his *ABC of Reading*, Pound published his *ABC of Economics*, wherein he would advocate, following Douglas, for "[c]ounting money as a certificate of work done" (29). So much of the *ABC of Economics* is simply wrong, with especially revealing moments such as when Pound issues universal pronouncements like: "It is empiric opinion," "It is nevertheless undeniable," or that he found a "Scientific solution."[29] Pound's aim was to instruct the populace about "the fundamentals of economics so simply and clearly that even people of different economic schools and factions [would] be able to understand each other when they discuss them" (7). He failed at that; ("The foregoing is perhaps very confusing" [51]). Even calling the text a "very rudimentary treatise" (55), as Pound does, does not accurately reflect its content, which reads more like a conversation with an incompetent economist about an obscure area of his field and less like an introductory textbook. Suffice it to say, even in fascist Italy, Pound's book would not be adopted by the universities.

And yet, beyond the lack of expertise, beyond the inexcusable vituperative claims, lies a real understanding of the connections among history, economics, and culture, and a sympathetic (albeit naive and terribly misguided) vision. "There are enough goods," Pound argues, "there is superabundant capacity to produce goods in superabundance. Why should anyone starve?" (15).[30] As to the nature of men asking for work before asking for food, he writes, "If this statement indicates a great naïve trust in humanity I am willing to stand the charge" (34). Some of the things Pound espouses, such as the "shortening of the working day" (46), made sense, and still might make sense a few generations hence if the supply of labor does end up greatly outpacing available jobs—as even Keynes predicted.[31] Other things he describes, though exaggerated to inconceivable ends, were eerily prescient: "The practice of governments has been to neglect internal economy; to commit every conceivable villainy, devilry and idiocy and to employ foreign affairs, conquests, dumpings, exploitations as a means of distracting attention from conditions at home . . ." (37).[32] At the heart of the brochure is Pound's self-assumed professorial role. He writes that "we are so little taught economics (a dry, dull and damned subject)," and he wanted to "go on writing because . . . no thoughtful man can in our time avoid trying to arrange those things in his own mind in an orderly fashion, or shirk coming to conclusions about them" (20, 44).

During this time, Pound opened a college of sorts. Dubbed the "Ezuversity," the lessons were, in James Laughlin's words, "simply Pound's continuous and fascinating monologue" on topics as diverse as those which could occupy Pound's mind (qtd. in MacNiven 71). Pound would correspond often with younger writers seeking advice.[33] In addition, he would open his home to those able to visit, even going so far as to pay for some of the visits, such as for the Jewish poet Louis Zukofsky. Zukofsky, Laughlin, Robert Duncan, and others would call on Pound in Rapallo, seeking help and guidance with their own writing; in a sense, they were seeking a super schoolmaster to give them direction.[34] Laughlin—who, in the words of his recent biographer Ian MacNiven, "more than any person of the twentieth century, directed the course of American writing and crested the waves of American passions and preoccupations" (3)—had written to Pound out of the blue in August 1933:

Dear Ezra Pound—

Could you and would you care to see me in Rapallo between August 27–31? I am American, now at Harvard, said to be clever. . . . Specifically, I want 1) advice about bombarding shits . . . ; 2) sufficient elucidation of certain basic phrases of the CANTOS to be able to preach them intelligently; 3) to know why Zukofsky has your support. I presume to disturb you, because I am in a position (editor Harvard Advocate and Harkness Hoot) to reach the few men in the two universities who are worth bothering about, and could do a better job of it with your help. (qtd. in Gordon 3)

Seeing as how teaching at Harvard "cannot be done," Pound invited ("visibility high") Laughlin to visit (qtd. in Gordon 3). In a poem published years later in the *Paris Review*, Laughlin wrote, "And you accepted me into your 'Ezuversity,' / Where there was no tuition, the best beanery since Bologna, / And the classes were held at meals in the dining room. . . ."[35] MacNiven writes that "[o]n fine afternoons, the lecture might continue on a walk up a *salita* weaving steeply through olive groves and terraced vegetable plots" (72). Whatever was on Pound's mind—"the failure of universities to educate the young, or the need to rescue Vivaldi's unpublished musical scores from dusty archives, or the desperate lack of good government in most countries" (73)—would become the unofficial lecture for the day, with his recent books such as *ABC of Reading* and recent obsession—economics—becoming the often revisited topics. "He would dive in" to the water, Laughlin remembered, and, after rising back up for air, Pound "would say something like, 'Victor Hugo was an absolute nut, y'know'" (qtd. in MacNiven 75). "Laughlin adored Pound immediately," Greg Barnhisel writes, "calling him 'this marvelous, dynamic eccentric, a most hospitable man, a born teacher, a person who loved to talk to young people, carrying on fantastic pedagogical monologues" (51). After leaving the Ezuversity, Laughlin returned to Harvard, and he would soon begin publishing his anthology *New Directions in Prose and Poetry* (which would eventually become his famous imprint *New Directions*), including writers then ignored (and unbelievably so) by many mainstream presses. These writers included William Carlos Williams, Gertrude Stein, Marianne Moore, E. E. Cummings, Elizabeth Bishop, Henry Miller, and, of course, Pound. A decade later, Laughlin would publish, as Pound waited in limbo, the *Pisan Cantos*.

In an earlier letter to Pound, the now-graduate of the Ezuversity James Laughlin admitted, "For a great deal of intellectual, amical, and actual B&B I am as grateful as is possible . . . Old prof. whiskers' course in civilizations and cultured cussin' is worth any 16 Haavud and Jerusalombia can put together" (77). One might sense in the portmanteau "Jerusalombia" Laughlin's socially fashionable anti-Semitism, even though Columbia University in New York City was still not at the time hospitable to Jews in academia. Laughlin's anti-Semitic pose would soon fade, and he would even try (fruitlessly) to pull back Pound from the nether regions of his. Pound kept impressing upon his "students" his more and more compulsive thoughts on global finance conspiracies, moving from C. H. Douglas to the economist Silvio Gesell (who advocated for stamp scrip), before finally arriving at the fascist movements overtaking Europe—what he believed could possibly spell out a new sociocultural Paradise. In Pound's eyes, Mussolini's fascism would be able to defeat both the socialists and capitalists, and Pound hoped that his new hero would adopt the economic policies of Douglas and Gesell ("never mind that," according to Alec Marsh, "neither Major Douglas nor Pound's Gesellite correspondents could see any point of agreement" [96]), leading to cultural support and a new artistic renaissance.

This is not the place for an extended discussion of Pound's anti-Semitism.[36] There is a predictably unfortunate critical game of piecing together bits of quotations and anecdotes to prove either way whether Pound was or was not an anti-Semite. We do not do that here. Unequivocally, Pound was an anti-Semite. (Anti-Semites are often polite to their Jewish neighbors.) None of Pound's friendships (Louis Zukofsky[37]), admirers (Allen Ginsberg[38]), denials ("My last antithesis sprang from no anti-Semitism"[39]), diffusions ("the pinch-penny aryio-kikes . . . with none of the Jews' moments of pity, excitement, or need of opulent display"[40]), qualifications ("Usurers have no race"[41]), or mannerly words ("redeem Zion with justice") excuse him. Pound was not just "critical" of the Jew (Cookson 14), his actions were not just "regrettable" (Brooke-Rose 250), he was not just "lapsing occasionally" (Stock 479), and he was not a specialist whose social "diagnosis . . . decreased anti-Semitism" (Kenner 465). "Although Pound said many critical things about the Jews and particularly the Jewish religion, it is false to label him an anti-Semite," writes Cookson in a shakier moment. No defense of Pound as a poet, teacher, or human ought to have a syntax of this sort that begins "Although. . . ." People who are not anti-Semites do not say and believe things like "Until a man purges himself of this [Jewish] poison he will never achieve understanding."[42] Pound's anti-Semitism was malicious, it was fanatical, and it was relentless.

Suffice it to say that, before the 1930s, Pound was a casual anti-Semite, typical of many Americans of his class (and others) at the time.[43] And, like many of the modernists, Pound conflated myth and modern reality. However, unlike many of his companions with initial fascist sentiments who would eventually return from the brink, Pound accelerated off the cliff.[44] By the 1930s, the early writings on Douglas, which were peppered with derogatory comments about Jews controlling finance, became widespread sentiments, and his lectures began to take on dangerous new proportions:

> Among the worse than Jewspapers we must list the hired pro-
> fessors who misteach new generations of young, who lie for hire
> and who continue to lie from sheer sloth and inertia and from
> dog-like contempt for the well-being of all mankind. . . . USURY
> is the cancer of the world, which only the surgeon's knife of
> Fascism can cut out of the life of nations. ("What Is Money
> For?" [1939], *Selected Prose* 299–300)

The critique of the "Jewish media" and the left-leaning academia ("hired professors") sounds frighteningly recognizable today in certain conspiratorial circles—including those that hope to undo the ethical commitments of higher education. Generations after one believed that such dangerous rhetoric was a symptom of another historical era, one finds it normalized in media outlets again. How easy it is to use rhetoric and new phraseologies to insinuate such repugnant thought into the popular consciousness and uncritically reduce sociopolitical complexities into easily targetable populations. Pound, at his best—but certainly not in the passage quoted above—understands the perilousness of language. "It is not only a question of rhetoric, of loose expression," he writes in 1931, early on in *How to Read*, "but also of the loose use of individual words" (18). In contrast to such rhetoric, Pound admired the exactness of first the "image" and then the "ideogram," which were socially responsible precisely because they were unyielding to the whims of a new age. But Pound, too, would find the razor-sharp exactness he was searching for in the "surgeon's knife of Fascism." A few paragraphs before this thought, Pound had inquired: "Has literature a function in the state, in the aggregation of humans, in the republic, in the *res publica*, which ought to mean the public convenience (despite the slime of bureaucracy, and the execrable taste of the populace in selecting its rulers)? It has" (17). And then, as if he were not aware of his own darkest sides, he added, "[a]nd this function is *not* the coercing or emotionally persuading, or bullying or suppressing people into the acceptance of any one set or any six sets of opinions as opposed to any other set or half-dozen sets of opinion" (17).

Well Pound could be a bully, and his critiques of "hired professors"— very different from his earlier denunciations of professors in the philological mold—would henceforth be inseparable from his criticisms of world Jewry. Ironically, Pound himself had by now, in a manner of speaking, finally received the institutional recognition and sanctioning that he had earlier coveted. As K. K. Ruthven writes, "on 12 June 1939, [Pound] had accepted the honorary degree of Doctor of Letters offered him not by Penn but by Hamilton College. In possession at last of that long-desired qualification, he broadcast from Radio Rome during the Second World War as 'Dr' Pound, under a dictatorship which treated 'free expression of opinion' as something not granted as of right but available only to 'those who are qualified to hold it'" (16). With Italy and the United States at war, Pound's 1942 radio broadcasts were heralded with "Rome Radio, acting in accordance with the Fascist policy of intellectual freedom and free expression of opinion by those who are qualified to hold it, has offered Dr. Ezra Pound the use of the microphone twice a week" (Stock 507).[45]

It is not our intention here to go through the very hateful radio speeches a salaried Pound broadcast during the war, but we want to take a moment to juxtapose a few of them. After beginning his October 26, 1941, speech with the claim that Winston Churchill's "gang, whether kike, gentile, or hybrid is not fit to govern" (Doob 7), Pound eventually winds his way into a sermon on higher education:

> In fact it warn't no bed of roses fer author and painters. Though my generation allus thought we ought to plant something or other, and try to git a new crop of somethin' or other. The idea of the Returnin' Native was prevalent, except possibly to Thomas S. Eliot who saw from the start that you folks weren't episcopal enough to suit his episcopal temperament, and he somewhat looked down on my pagan and evangelical tendencies. Waaal, frankly, I allus though it would be a good thing to come back and put some sort of a college or university into shape to teach the young something. Not merely the god damn saw dust and substitutes for learnin' and literature they git handed. (Doob 9–10)

Pound's "paganism" was his contemporary, comparative method, which paid fidelity neither to an organized religion nor to an antiquated academic creed. While one motive (support for artists) remained the same, the type of college Pound now had in mind was vastly different from the one he had dreamed up decades earlier. Recalling his 1914 "Preliminary Announcement of the College of Arts" (detailed in chapter 1), which he published in the pages of *The Egoist*, we find that the curriculum there included sculpture, painting, music, comparative poetry, Russian novelists, Russian contemporary thought, dramatic criticism, photography, crafts, and dance. Now, in his mind, any viable institution would have to teach everything from the vantage point of global economics, and not just any economics, but a hateful, conspiratorial one, which reduced individual people in the world to false propagandist mythologies:

> Just WHICH of you is free from JEW influence? Just which political and business groups are free from JEW influence, or, bujayzus, from JEW control? Who holds the mortgage? Who is a dominating director? Just which Jew has asked what Jew to nominate which assemblyman who is in debt to WHOM? . . . Just which college or university will distinguish itself by adding to its history courses a course in the study of chewisch history . . . and the effects of Jewsury and of usury on the history of Europe during the past thousand years? (Doob 254; March 19, 1943)

When Pound challenges colleges to add "a course in the study of chewisch [Jewish] history," he is not warmly anticipating the rise of Jewish studies programs in the United States. He means that history departments ought to begin teaching how the paths of history were all based on Jewish plots to control world finance. A lecture from "Dr." Pound might now include how England "let in the Jew and the Jew rotted your empire, and you yourselves out-Jewed the Jew. . . . And the big Jew has rotted EVERY nation he has wormed into" (Doob 59; March 15, 1942).

Shreds of the "comparative method" are still there in his many speeches, but the method has been perverted by an anti-Semitic mania.[46] Calling his new teaching "a little healthy inquiry" (Doob 115; April 30, 1942), Pound would jump from topic to topic, nothing very far from his mind. His April 30, 1942, speech, for example, could run in a few minutes from anti-Semitic vitriol to Goethe to the philological pedagogical method he had contested so many years ago:

> Don't start a pogrom. That is, not an old style killing of small Jews. That system is no good whatsoever. Of course if some man had a stroke of genius and could start a pogrom UP AT THE top, there might be something to say for it. But on the whole legal measures are preferable. The sixty Kikes who started this war

might be sent to St. Helena as a measure of world prophylaxis. And some hyper-kike, or non-Jewish kikes along with 'em. I shall be content if I contribute my buffalo nickel to arouse a little sane CURIOSITY, a little healthy inquiry as to what causes the whichness. Goethe was gittin' at something when he wrote his play "Faust." I can't do ALL the researchin' but thaaar, as I see it or feel it, is a field for proficuous research. The error of philology in the XIX century was to split everything up into slivers, get a man concentrated on a small enough microscopic area, and mebbe you can prevent him seeing what it has to do with the next field, or with the national income, or with the health of the nation. (Doob 115)

Pound was right to note that everything connected, but he was horribly wrong in how his jigsaw puzzle of social history came together. He is also quite aware that questioning political authority held the same dangers, albeit on a larger scope, as questioning academic authority. Such awareness might have been a remnant of his earlier confrontations with university sanctioning. Pound speaks of a "Boy named Mac":

he shows a couple of REAL questions to a professor and the professor shows blank incomprehension. Don't shoot the pore beggar. Most of your professors were up against what you are up against. Those favored few who GOT the cushy jobs got there for a reason. They didn't annoy their precursors. And the ones that RISE were those who showed no EXCESSIVE curiosity. Don't matter whether it is literary merit, which is largely precision, or history. . . . (Doob 180; June 25, 1942)

The rhetoric sounds familiar: professors (especially in the humanities) are not experts. They were sycophant-students who were granted entry into a secret cabal, and they now pass along what the powers-that-be want them to disseminate. Any questioning of their authority would be labeled treasonous (the student, in the future, still "may want to pass an examination").[47] Although not in Pound's lifetime, the last few generations of doctoral candidates seeking jobs in the humanities have regularly sought to do the opposite—question their intellectual precursors and adopt an excessive curiosity that might actually end up (in a healthy, self-critical way) upsetting powerful social institutions. Ironically, the "new modernist studies," in which modernism has been reimagined as operating away from those mostly white, male, European giants codified into critical monuments, might be a case in point.[48]

Following the radio broadcasts, the detention center, and the aborted trial in the United States, Pound was sent to the psychiatric ward of St. Elizabeths. It was a sad irony that the man who wanted his nation to support the production of writers now had his room and board subsidized. The experiences and significances of Pound's time here, like much of his life, are debated among literary critics, popular writers, opinion columnists, and psychiatrists. Even with the shock of detention, Pound remained able to act the schoolmaster, publishing books and new Cantos, helping others publish some journals, and offering new translations. Pound was still "concerned . . . about the world's ignorance and the task of education that still confronted him," and the "Ezuversity" was now replaced by what Noel Stock calls the "Pound Centre" (541, 547). There, Pound took on individual apprenticeships. Along with his wife, who visited almost daily, he received poets—older ones looking for conversation, and younger ones looking for guidance, looking for a teacher. Visitors included E. E. Cummings, Archibald MacLeish, William Carlos Williams, Charles Olson, T. S. Eliot, Marianne Moore, Conrad Aiken, Robert Lowell, Thornton Wilder, Allen Tate, Louis Zukofsky, H. L. Mencken, Stephen Spender, Elizabeth Bishop, James Dickey, Katherine Anne Porter, Al Alvarez, and Huntington Cairns of the National Gallery of Art in Washington.[49] According to E. Fuller Torrey, who wrote a much-contested book on his time with Pound at the hospital, St. Elizabeths Hospital "had become a sacrarium for savants" (219).

After advocating early in his career for contemporary writers to be studied, Pound now found himself as one of those writers. He received professors and graduate students interested in his work, among them Hugh Kenner, Malcolm Bradbury, and Marshall McLuhan. As the years go by and scholarly work becomes its own sort of monument, we should be reminded that it is no coincidence that teachers' views of art are shaped primarily by the writers they come across. And oddly, for an institution that wanted nothing to do with the student Pound, the poet Pound would soon begin to be *studied* in colleges across the country. A conference at Columbia University in September 1953 on his *Cantos* would be followed by others and by course syllabuses that would include Pound and the modernist writers he championed. "No sooner did a disciple or group of followers fall away, or a magazine or journal he was trying to capture, prove unwilling, than he was busy gathering new followers, forming new groups, helping to establish or capture other publications" (Stock 569).

Not all of Pound's admirers, however, were poets or friends with altruistic intentions. Alex Houen offers an important corrective to the sense that Pound's anti-Semitism ended after the war. Speaking of Pound's affiliation with American discrimination and the fight against desegregation, Houen writes that Pound's "racism takes on such proportions that it pervades the dynamic of his writing more generally" (392). In this regard, Pound's persistent desire to teach the world about economics and his insistence on individual rights of free speech led some very dangerous people, like the anti-Semitic conspiracy theorist author Eustace Mullins, to St. Elizabeths.[50] John Kasper, who "had just graduated from Columbia and intended to work for a doctorate in English and philosophy" (Carpenter 799), was another. If there is any question about the type of graduate advisor Pound might have been, we might take another look at how Pound, meeting Kasper, "had instantly persuaded him to turn aside from 'fugg of am/ universities' to 'basic stuff'—the dissemination of such writers as he currently considered important" (Carpenter 800). Kasper opened a bookshop, promoting writers Pound encouraged alongside other fascist and Nazi literature. After *Brown v. Board of Education of Topeka* (1954), which desegregated schools nationally, Kasper lectured to racist organizations, working with the Ku Klux Klan and other neo-fascist groups. In and out of jail for years, Kasper finally received a long federal sentence after a school bombing in Nashville. A *New York Herald Tribune* headline read: "Segregationist Kasper is Ezra Pound Disciple" (Carpenter 828). It is unclear whether Pound believed most of Kasper's doctrine (this is unlikely) or whether he just stubbornly relished the attention. Still, a letter from the schoolmaster instructed Kasper to "[s]tick to the main points when possible . . . Antisemitism is a card in the enemy program, don't play it. they RELY on your playing it" (qtd. in Carpenter 829). Pound would become smarter about his teachings, if not remorseful.[51] A letter from St. Elizabeths related that "A dirty jew has just sent me Jim's [James Joyce's] letters edited by his Obesity S. Gilbert, the impertinence of the kike lying in the assumption that I wd be DEElighted to review the book for a parsimonious fee/ etc" (qtd. in Carpenter 828). Such opinions remained, but the vigor with which he expressed them was generally more private, more muted.

Pound's final real project at St Elizabeths was the anthology we previously discussed, *Confucius to Cummings*. The anthology, for Kenner, shows how Pound "persisted in his overestimation of classrooms" (509). One gathers that Kenner means not that Pound overestimated the importance of the classroom—something neither Pound nor we can ever do—but that Pound overestimated his own sense of acceptance in a national curriculum, which did not seem to want to listen to what he had to say. After Pound was released from the hospital, he sailed to Naples. When asked, on board, about his time in an insane asylum, he replied that all of the United States was an insane asylum. He then stood for a few photographs, his hand outstretched, offering the Fascist salute (Moody III 447). His last decade and a half, spent in Italy, found him mired in depression. He still received visitors but, for the most part, engaged them silently. Anyone who knew him fifty years earlier would not have believed he could be so uncommunicative, but anyone who followed the course of his life could hardly have been surprised. He died in Venice on November 1, 1972.

It feels coarse, now, to return to a romantic sense of the poet or of the function of poetry. But that is what Pound himself did, as he needed to do, while waiting to hear his fate at the DTC:

> Hast 'ou seen the rose in the steel dust
> (or swansdown ever?)
> so light is the urging, so ordered the dark petals of iron
> we who have passed over Lethe. (469)

Echoing the opening of Canto 74, Pound returns to the Lethe river. How else could one possibly end this Canto, which is in its own Hades, but with a trip over the river of forgetfulness? Just before, Pound describes a rose of steel dust, conjured by magnets, and Ben Jonson's line about "swan's down"—the poem and the feathers so very far away.[52] "Beauty in art," Pound had written more than thirty years earlier, "reminds one what is worth while" (*Literary Essays* 45). Canto 74 and its contexts also remind one what is worthwhile, however ugly each is and however much Pound did not intend them that way. The schoolmaster could hardly be called "super" anymore, but we should still listen to his words, if only judiciously to rebel against his later teachings, for he was truly one of the very few people of his time who had passed over the Lethe.

Afterword

Schools of Fish

The most damnable and idiotic reply I ever received in my life was from my old professor, Schelling, when I was trying to persuade him to admit some men of literary ability (proved ability) to the benefits of the literary scholarships of his dept. He wrote me: "The University is not here for the unusual man."

    . . . The whole of our literature suffers from ignorance; and the American parody of German philology is often, most often, *not* a symptom of enlightenment but a conspiracy to prevent the student from learning more than his teacher.

    . . . The only way to make a civilization is to exploit to the full those individuals who happen to be given by nature the aptitudes, exceptional aptitudes, for particular jobs. By exploit I mean that they must be allowed to do the few things which they and no one else can.

—Pound to Simon Guggenheim, February 24, 1925
(qtd. in Paige 196)

It is a system that privileges the eye, the gaze, and assumes the power of an innocent eye: no names, no studying, no learning—the eye engendering the world. [The student] knows something about a dead and decomposing creature, but he does not know and cannot (in Roland Barthes's phrase) "speak the fish." He can, however, now speak and write Agassizese, for this is what he has really learned: to produce the sort of writing his teacher wants.

—Robert Scholes, *Textual Power*, 131

The two quotations above are each similarly critical—ironically so, it turns out—of a problem with academic culture. Both writers are speaking specifically about American higher education, and both call attention to the uneasy power relationship between teacher and student. The first writer sees the instructional system as "a conspiracy to prevent the student from learning more than his teacher," while the second writer charges the system with rewarding those who either cleverly or thoughtlessly become parrots of their instructors. Although one is more bitter than the next, each of these indictments of higher learning calls attention to the knowledge-system (what poststructuralist theorists would call "discourse"), with the caution that such a system stifles real creative opportunities—not just in a value-free aesthetic sense but moreover for unknown possibilities of knowledge itself.

That is where the similarity ends. One writer is confident about a subjectivity that can grasp objectivity, and the other writer cautions against such a supposedly "disinterested" conceptual space. One writer knows all the answers, and the other writer knows his own limitations. The first writer, of course, is Ezra Pound; here (in 1925), he is writing privately to the philanthropist and recent poetry patron John Simon Guggenheim (the brother of Solomon Guggenheim). The author of the second epigraph above follows Pound by sixty years. He is my coauthor (and teacher) Robert Scholes, critiquing in a scholarly-sanctioned venue (Yale University Press) what had evolved from "Imagist" minimalism to later become Pound's didactic pedagogical stance. Scholes's public monograph on literary theory and teaching, we might add, was made possible in part by the efforts of Pound (and many, many others) who advocated in the first part of the century for the social importance of literature and engaged critique. Where Pound is certain, Scholes is demure; where Pound is speaking out against a highbrow establishment that he feels had slighted him in the past, Scholes is turning to "a parable about the relationship between words and things" (129) to look to the future to try to improve a communal institution that had treated him very well.

Pound can castigate his professorial antagonist Felix Emmanuel Schelling by stating that the latter thinks the "University is not here for the unusual man." Pound wants these unusual men—those "who happen to be given by nature the aptitudes . . . to do the few things which they and no one else can"—to populate the institution as teachers, rather than the "mediocre minds" who are currently there. By "unusual," he means the exceptional, creative man who is not mired by the tedious particulars of turn-of-the-century philology; by "unusual," he means the man who does not miss the literary forest for its barren leaves; by "unusual," he means himself.

As we explored in our first chapter, Pound's animosity against institutions of higher learning is deep-seated. His letter of 1925 testified to an anger he still held toward the University of Pennsylvania and its faculty, which not only refused to grant him an advanced degree but moreover, in his mind, did not even seem to understand its own subject matter. After Wabash College, he would never formally teach again, but, as we have maintained throughout this book, the rest of his life could be seen, for better and worse, as one great body of instruction. Still, he would resentfully return to his time at the University of Pennsylvania and the faculty there who deprived him of his rightful chair by their side. On one hand, we might view the diatribe in Pound's letter as yet another moment of arrogance, the still-bitter memories of a teenager who could not be bothered to do the work his teacher—right or wrong—asked of him, because he (the teenager) had already figured out the secrets of the world. On the other hand, we might view Pound standing by his earlier critique of academia as filled with "ivory-tower" scholars who knew little of the current art world and even littler of why it ought to matter.

Wary of Pound's certitude, Robert Scholes (in the second epigraph I quoted) rebukes the poet for confusing *a* mode of artistic representation with *the* mode. Pound's system "privileges the eye, the gaze, and assumes the power of an innocent eye: no names, no studying, no learning—the eye engendering the world," as Scholes argues earlier (*Textual Power* 131) and again in his Foreword here. Derived from Louis Agassiz and described by Pound in the *ABC of Reading*, the method has two steps: 1) "Let the pupil write the description of a tree"; 2) "Of a tree without mentioning the name of the tree (larch, pine, etc.) so that the reader will not mistake it for the description of some other kind of tree" (66).[1] What troubles Scholes is not that Pound's Imagistic method is aesthetically misplaced but that the "how-to" educational model shuts out all other angles, other ways of "speaking the fish." Rather than trawling through numerous possibilities, the student is snared, merely able now "to produce the sort of writing his teacher wants" and nothing more (Scholes 131). The objectivity that Pound sought in capturing his fish does not, naturally, belie his comparative method. "AFTER the era of 'Agassiz and the fish,'" Pound writes, ". . . general education is in position to profit by the parallels of biological study based on EXAMINATION and COMPARISON of particular specimens" ("The Teacher's Mission" 60).[2] Neither does such fishing contradict Pound's general advice to study his catch in a roundabout way: "It doesn't, in our contemporary world, so much matter where you begin the examination of a subject, so long as you keep on until you get round again to your starting-point . . . keep on until you have seen it from all sides" (*ABC of Reading* 29).[3] All these "open" intentions notwithstanding, and though Pound could often claim that "[i]t is not the teacher's place to enforce an opinion" (*ABC of Reading* 173), he does seem fairly rigid in his pronouncements—specifically, here, that the direct encounter with the object is paramount to knowing it. This is the enforced opinion against which Scholes protests in this moment, even if he will significantly return to Pound's general instruction later on. The poststructuralist influence on Scholes suddenly becomes apparent, as the relationship between knowledge and power structures is interrogated further.[4] Scholes writes that the student "seems to be reporting about a real and solid world in a perfectly transparent language, but actually he is learning how to produce a specific kind of discourse, controlled by a particular scientific paradigm, which requires him to be constituted as the subject of that discourse in a particular way and to speak through that discourse of a world made visible by the same controlling paradigm" (132).[5]

Scholes returns to Pound's now-infamous example "again and again until it stinks in all our nostrils" (133). Rather than giving the student a fish or teaching the student how to fish, the teacher, according to Scholes, ought to open up all the possibilities of fishing: "what the student needs from the teacher," he writes,

> is help in seeing discourse structures themselves in all their fullness and their power. The way to see the fish and to write the fish is first to see how one's discourse writes the fish. And the way to see one discourse is to see more than one. To write the fish in many modes is finally to see that one will never catch *the* fish in any one discourse. As teachers of writing we have a special responsibility to help our students gain awareness of discourse structures and the ways in which they both enable and constrain our vision. And the only way to do this is to read and write in a range of discursive modes. (144)

Returning one more time to Pound, still a student and not yet twenty years old, we find, in a letter to his mother, an enthusiasm for schoolwork yet to be done: "Charming evening with Bill. have gathered stuff to start my studies in Provencal & extended work in Old French & learned what books I must gather from the four corners of the earth" (*EPtP* 48). Pound knew the enormous task ahead of him and was set to gather all the books he needed from the "four corners of the earth." And he would soon come to understand that phrase more faithfully than many of the other modernists. While he had his own prejudices and blind spots, learning, for him, did not stop at the borders of Europe.

It is hard to reconcile the promise of the young Pound with the monstrous teacher he would become during the war years and the decade leading up to it. And it is even harder to reconcile the personal generosity of the man with some of the sweeping words that came out of his mouth. We approached our book with the belief that Pound—even his darker side—is better off not ignored, especially for future generations of teachers and students. And we mean this not only in a scholarly or poetic way but moreover in terms of what he has to offer the contemporary classroom. Even before he set off for Europe, Pound had a good sense of what was not working with higher education, and yet he was a firm believer in its importance and future potential. He was a good teacher of literature and the arts and saw their relationship to social culture ("the grisly roots of ideas that are in action"), and he imagined them all in ways that none of his teachers could fathom. Had he not lost himself in that dark wood without a guide to see him out, he would have been an important voice defending the humanities for generations.

It feels as though almost every journal, newspaper, and book publisher today, as well as television channel, radio program, and internet blogger, wants to get in on the question *what's wrong with higher education?*[6] A generation ago, the blame was laid at the feet of "tenured radicals" and "multiculturalists" who dared to reread new texts and previously ignored texts other than the classics, while venturing new understandings of those classics through fundamental hermeneutic frames (politics, gender, race, sexuality) that had previously been discounted. Pound, most likely, would have also been upset about many of the changes to university reading lists as well as the execution (not the principle) of its interdisciplinary turn, however much he railed against the curriculum at the time. It feels almost ridiculous to make the claim, but Pound's sense of "great art" overlaps quite readily with that of many of his fiercest detractors, incongruously including people like Harold Bloom.[7]

Today, the discussions of higher education have moved mostly away from the "culture wars" rhetoric to the business of academia, and things feel even bleaker for those in the humanities, those who have the unenviable task of carrying forth the very cultural and intellectual histories they are continually reassessing. Pound understood the value of the humanities, and he was one of its greatest advocates. He was able to push publishers to publish works that otherwise would have been ignored for decades, and he was even able to secure—mostly because of his personally engaging lectures—a lot of private funding for the arts. But without such voices, submerged as we are in our quantitative models today, how are we to measure and advertise the slow societal and individual effects of a humanistic education? Would it not take ten, twenty, thirty years to understand the effect of a day spent considering Aristotle on friendship or George Eliot on nineteenth-century social life or Chinua Achebe on the effect of a colonial system? I have no way to assess any of this, but I know it is important—important for individuals who either naively believe that they will always make a difference in our world or naively believe that they won't.

Pundits who lay claim to answering all the problems (beware anyone who can offer a solution in a one-page op-ed or a ten-minute interview!) write more and more opinion pieces declaiming the institutions of higher education. One usually receives two very different types of answers. From policy "think tanks" and many journalistic outposts, one hears of the unpalatable rising cost of tuition and of students who leave college in debt, without a job, and without any real career preparation. They received a mediocre education in an obsolete field because tenured professors are lazy and too political instead of enthusiastic, objective, and practical. On the other side, one hears from faculty members (and some in administration) of the dangerous influx of business interests on learning. Faculty will complain about the hollowing out of standards and a necessary curriculum, of students not learning fundamentals of humanity, and of online courses that are often merely recycled Wikipedia pages or outdated lectures, with the result that colleges reinforce class division rather than offer opportunities for advancement. Students at great colleges will be afforded time and care, and they will have access to the wonders of cultural histories in remarkable ways, while most students will be expected to treat their education as if it were merely a hindrance on the way to the nine-to-five job. While recent work by Rachel Sagner Buurma and Laura Heffernan offers a corrective to both the historical accuracy of the vocational/liberal arts split and its present-day manifestation, the future threats to institutionalized learning remain.[8] Through this dangerous possible future frame, students would receive a mediocre education because of administrative cutbacks on teaching lines, which would leave adjunct laborers—those often without a say in governance—underpaid, overworked, overwhelmed, and disconnected from academic decisions and affairs. As I wrote earlier, things feel even more dire in the humanities, where the perception is that anyone can teach the material—even via a lecture uploaded to a website—because, contra Pound, learning is about a one-way transmission of ideas from teacher/text to the student-consumer.

We are given opposing studies skewed in one direction or another, leaving teenagers (or their parents) making life decisions based on anecdotal and often individualized stories caught in twenty-first-century celebrity ideology ("Bill Gates didn't have to finish college"). Oversimplified solutions (use more media, use less media, have more testing, have less testing) assume that, in this simplified, quantifiable game, individual students will always fit a model. Such is the danger of an educational system, as Pound at his best understood, that can only trawl for a school of fish in one pond. Yao and Coyle see in Pound one who "anticipated some of the concerns that we ought now to share in light of recent efforts to quantify results in education and to take certifying authority away from the academy itself, where it has remained pristine for nearly two centuries now" (Yao/Coyle xviii). While Pound was not very keen on keeping that authority in the hands of academics who exhibited "mental LAZINESS, lack of curiosity, [and a] desire to be undisturbed" ("The Teacher's Mission" 59), he would have been more appalled by the precipitous rise of "outside" pecuniary interests, especially as they have begun, to the detriment of the humanities, to stress measures of quantity over quality. And this is not to say that Pound was blind to the predicaments of students regarding future employment. "Education," he could write, "that does not bear on LIFE and on the most vital and immediate problems of the day is not education but merely suffocation and sabotage" ("The Teacher's Mission" 62), and he could warn that an " 'education' in 1938 which does not fit the student for life between 1940 and 1960 is a sham and an infamy" (*Guide to Kulchur* 56). He therefore saw the immediate relevance of academia to actual life, so long as the university courses showed how everything fit together.

Biased as I am, I have a faith in individual faculty, even in spite of those teachers who sometimes forget their ways. When Ronald Reagan wanted to end the welfare system, he found one woman in a Cadillac. Similarly, and without wanting to fall into a Pound-esque conspiracy theory, I think it is safe to say that when certain business interests wanted to get their cut of a multi-billion dollar industry, or certain politicians wanted to get a hold of an ideological apparatus—the university system—they found their "narrative" in a few lazy or, to their eyes, overly political tenured professors who would become rhetorical scapegoats, masking the political and economic aspirations of others. Pound himself would critique the "beaneries" along these lines, but he was also quick to note that professors who "desired to get and retain job" also "wrote under a terror . . . forced to maintain a pretense of omniscience" (*Guide to Kulchur* 70). But, thinking again about Pound's letter to his mother, we might also ask, why did the young Pound want to head off to "the four corners of the earth" to search for books he hadn't read and things he didn't know? "Charming evening with Bill," he confessed. It was all because his professor of romance languages and literature at Hamilton College, William Shepard, had taken an evening out of his life to spend with a student who couldn't quite fit in.[9]

I have been fortunate in my own career to have had great mentors, to have met super schoolmasters who have been welcoming outside the classroom, offering to discuss life matters unrelated to dissertation footnotes . . . even though everything was, in the end, related. I am personally thankful that one of those schoolmasters was Professor Scholes.[10] But I am also thankful that both Scholes and I have had Pound indirectly as a teacher, seeing the good things he has suggested and being warned away from the more dangerous paths, ones that anyone can start down and get lost in. Bob Scholes is no Ezra Pound, but they do overlap in more than one important pedagogical way. Pound welcomed attention and gratitude, but he did not need to see his name on each of his collaborations. Moreover, he sometimes seemed to like his students more when they sent him belligerent letters in response. To my knowledge, I have never sent Bob a belligerent letter, but I have benefited in countless ways from intellectual collaboration with him. He was the first person to ask me how my first day of teaching went. (It went badly, but he assured me it hadn't gone as badly as I had thought.) This book—now "our" book—was a collaborative effort, like so many of Pound's earliest projects. Slight disagreements (such as how to situate the importance and worthiness of Pound not only in modernist studies but also in studies of pedagogy) gave way, I believe in a positive manner, to nuanced engagement, the type that Pound would promote: "And this function is *not* the coercing or emotionally persuading, or bullying or suppressing people into the acceptance of any one set or any six sets of opinions as opposed to any other set or half-dozen sets of opinion" (*How to Read* 17).

Answering an interview question about how the semiotics program (now the Department of Modern Culture and Media) at Brown University came about, Scholes relates that

> it didn't arise in a programmatic way. It wasn't the case that, aha, here's semiotics: how can we publicize it, how can we dramatize

it, how can we spread the gospel of semiotics. It really came about in another way, trying to devise a program that answered certain student needs and student desires for particular kinds of study. . . . The needs are needs for serious ways to come to terms with contemporary media, with film, with video, with various mass and pop forms of discourse. There's a need to understand how one is situated among all these things. (qtd. in Bagwell 15)

There's a need, in Poundian terminology, to understand the Paideuma: "What we do in the semiotics program is to look at texts and try to generate a theory of how these texts communicate and also how the people who utter texts, emit texts, have themselves been shaped by the institutions which enable them to utter those texts" (qtd. in Bagwell 15). There are echoes, here, although not in terms of haughtiness, of Pound's claim that he could tell you about the social-economics of a period just by looking at its art. The relationships among the pieces are important to understand because they determine the world around us, and it matters how we are taught to read that world. "I've been accused of being a closet moralist," Scholes concedes, adding that "I suppose to some extent I have to plead guilty to that. My approach to literary texts is anchored in pedagogy. I'm a teacher first and a critic or interpreter or semiotician or whatever second" (18–19).[11] Importantly, for Scholes, the teacher and the student are in it together, each hoping to grasp the world just a little closer.

Turning, for a moment, to some serious levity, I wish to propose an academic formula. Moviegoers joke about a game called "Six Degrees of Kevin Bacon," modeled on John Guare's play *Six Degrees of Separation*, which posits that everyone on earth is linked to everyone else through at most six levels of separation (someone knows someone who knows someone else, and so on). The game for movie buffs involves tying any given actor or actress to the prolific actor Kevin Bacon in only six connections or fewer (by way of costarring in movies). A mathematician friend of mine recently informed me that mathematicians play a similar game with the prolific (forgive me) polymath Paul Erdős.[12] Having an "Erdős number" of 1 would mean having collaborated with him on a publication; having an "Erdős number" of 2 would mean having collaborated with someone who collaborated directly with him, and so on. With the assumption that my coauthor would not approve of this reflexive spotlight, I offer a new game called "The Girandoles of Robert Scholes" to designate those who have collaborated with him or with his collaborators. A very, very cursory list would include Nancy R. Comley (*Hemingway's Genders*, etc.), Mark Gaipa and Sean Latham (*The Little Review "Ulysses"*), David Hamilton and Nancy Sommers (*Fields of Writing*), Richard Kain (*Workshop of Daedalus*), Robert L. Kellogg and James Phelan (*The Nature of Narrative*), Carl H. Klaus (*Elements of Writing*, etc.), Janice Peritz (*Practice of Writing*), Eric S. Rabkin (*Science Fiction*), Michael Silverman (*Elements of Literature*), George E. Slusser (*Coordinates: Placing Science Fiction and Fantasy*), Rosemary Sullivan (*Elements of Fiction*), Gregory L. Ulmer (*Text Book*), and Clifford Wulfman (*Modernism in the Magazines*). And, if we were to believe Amazon.com's author page, we would have to add "James Joyce" to the list. Furthermore, if we were to include journal articles, recent work in the digital humanities, and edited collections of which he was a part (as we should), the number would increase more than tenfold. Scholes himself would have a Scholes number zero, but even that is not quite right, as he was always rethinking, rewriting, struggling with his earlier viewpoints and—to borrow a metaphor from his rethinking of Agassiz—not casting the same rod into the same waters to catch the same fish.

Games can be silly, but the pedagogical importance of collaboration is genuine, especially, as Pound understood, at a level of engagement between teacher and student. "There is no man who knows so much about, let us say, a passage between lines 100 to 200 of the sixth book of the Odyssey that he can't learn something by re-reading it WITH his students, not merely TO his students," Pound wrote and then added: "I believe the ideal teacher would approach any masterpiece that he was presenting to his class *almost* as if he had never seen it before" (*ABC of Reading* 85–86). I can't say that I have ever seen a more worthy statement about teaching. Collaboration—whether as a process with students or a partnership among colleagues—is more common in the sciences and social sciences, but it ought to become more widespread in the humanities. Collaboration allows individuals to get out of their own heads; it allows educators in very different areas to share knowledge in unforeseen ways; it allows teachers to become inquiring students again, connecting the cultural dots they might otherwise miss. "I have been unable," writes Pound in 1957 in a letter to the mid-century American literary critic Van Wyck Brooks, "to get one single professor to indicate another live mind on his OWN campus. The departments do not communicate with one another." A year later, Pound could write to him again, professing that a "little collaboration, or at least communication between half a dozen literates COULD get some sanity into curricula" (qtd. in McDonald 109). New ponds with bright centers and dark corners, flickering images and deep spaces yet to be explored—this was Pound's great pedagogical anchor, and (the politics of college curriculum committees notwithstanding) it ought to be pursued as much as possible.

"We do not know whether the Erdős span can be traced further back into the early 1800s," the mathematicians Rodrigo de Castro and Jerrold W. Grossman write, but "[w]hat we can be sure of is that the Erdős connection will extend forever into the future" (63). Robert Scholes christened his sailboat the Lookfar, a name he borrowed from a boat in an Ursula K. Le Guin novel. The ability, while fishing, to look far, to see the as-yet unrealized rivulets of humanity—now isn't that the mark of a super schoolmaster?

David Ben-Merre

Notes

Prefaces

1. *Ezra Pound to His Parents: Letters 1895–1929* is cited parenthetically throughout as *EPtP*.

2. For years he lived off money sent to him by his parents, supplemented by his earnings from journalism and poetry, with occasional support by one patron or another. In fact, he explains at the very beginning of *ABC of Economics* that he has written a "brief formal treatise" to protect himself "against charges of unsystematized, uncorrelated, dilettantism, idle eclecticism" (13).

3. Following Cooper's views on the relationship between literature and biology, Pound saw this as an example of the way poetry should be taught. Give the student examples and make them really look at them until they see what is there. As I argued almost thirty years ago, however, that is not what was really going on in Agassiz's laboratory, nor is it really the way Pound himself taught. Agassiz, who was a resolute denier of the theory of evolution, just couldn't see evidence for the validity of that theory, no matter how many specimens he looked at. What his students were learning was a discourse, a way of speaking about living creatures that Agassiz approved of and used himself. He had written a book on the classification of animals, and at least one of the students who had been forced to look at fish and report to his professor had actually read Agassiz's *Essay on Classification*. Pound, of course, keeps telling his students to look at the poems, but he also gives them ways of seeing what they are looking at. He gives them a discourse, with critical terminology like "phanopoeia," "melopoeia," and "logopoeia," which helps them look for certain kinds poetical effects, along with evaluative terms like "inventors," "masters," "diluters," "good writers," and "writers of belles-lettres," with definitions and examples. Armed with this discourse, they are encouraged to compare works and evaluate them.

4. In English literature, Pound is consistently unfair to John Milton, and I think this is partly because of the subject matter of Milton's great epic poem,

which comes out of the Book of Genesis. Pound's view of Genesis was colored by his translation of Voltaire's critical examination of that text. My view of it is close to that of Voltaire and Pound, but that does not prevent me from admiring much of Milton's work in *Paradise Lost*. As we have seen throughout this book, Pound sometimes praised the writing of authors whose values matched his own, while claiming to be concerned only with the quality of their work.

In *ABC of Reading* he claims to be critical of Milton because Milton used an excessively Latinized English, but, if he had looked, he could have found many places in Milton's work where English is used delicately or gorgeously. His shabby treatment of Milton is just one of the problems in this book, however. There are many more. Some of these result from his attempt to expand *How to Read* into something more like a textbook with an anthology of sample works in English. The book is supposed to have two distinct parts, a discussion section followed by a collection of sample literary texts, but Pound can't resist adding discussions to the literary section, which results in a good deal of repetition. And the pressure to deal with literature in English leads him into areas where his knowledge is thin or spotty. For example, he discusses English fiction of the eighteenth century without ever mentioning Samuel Richardson, whose treatment of the human psyche opened the way for much later fiction in both English and French. And his main example of nineteenth-century English realism is Anthony Trollope rather than George Eliot, who is the great English realist of that period. He has nothing to say about Charles Dickens and William Makepeace Thackeray, either, and he ignores the great American novelists of that period: Nathaniel Hawthorne, Herman Melville, and Mark Twain.

While privileging translations into English, like those earlier ones of Arthur Golding and Gavin Douglas, Pound ignores the most influential translation of the English Renaissance: the King James Bible. He does not like that text, and he did not himself read Hebrew, as Milton did. These are explanations rather than justifications for his failure to deal with this enormously significant text. He got a lot of mileage, himself, out of his "Ballad of the Goodly Fere," but his interest and sympathy for biblical texts stopped with Jesus himself. As I have said, I agree with Pound's position to some extent, but must acknowledge the verbal power of the texts Pound ignored, including the prose of the Pauline Epistles, in which Greek is used economically and effectively, and the narratives of the Old Testament, which I have read only in translations, having no more Hebrew than Pound himself. But the biblical texts in English translation have a place in any discussion of the history of English literature, which is part of what Pound claims to be presenting to his student readers in this book.

He does not claim to be an expert in the novel—which does not stop him from pontificating about it at times—but he does claim expert status in poetry. This book, I am afraid, does something to dismantle that claim. His treatment of Milton is not the only problem. He writes with such confidence about English poetry that his readers may not realize that his knowledge of it is really rather thin, as if he had gotten most of it by reading a few anthologies—like *The Oxford Book of Verse*, which he mentions—and knew only the poets and poems that appeared in them. He is good on Chaucer, whom he likes, and he has clearly read around in the work. But he seems never to have heard of *Sir Gawain and the Green Knight*, a poem contemporaneous with Chaucer and of comparable quality. In the English Renaissance, his praise of Shakespeare is weak, and he does not do justice to Ben Jonson. In the Exhibits section of *ABC of Reading*, he gives us an awful lot of Gavin Douglas. He seems to know well one poem by John Donne, whom he praises as the best of the metaphysical poets, but he does not go deeply into Donne's verse or consider his extraordinary prose, which he should have admired. He calls Golding's translation of Ovid "the most beautiful book in the language" (127), which is an extraordinary claim. He trivializes Robert Herrick, exalts John Wilmot Earl of Rochester, and damns Alexander Pope with faint praise, while situating George Crabbe as Pope's equal. In looking at the English nineteenth century, Pound is right, I believe, to praise Fitzgerald's *Rubaiyat*, and his views of English poetry become more persuasive as they approach his own time.

5. Personal accounts of Robert Scholes as a teacher, scholar, and colleague are recounted in Geoffrey Green, ed., *Scholes Loves a Story* (Lulu.com, 2010). For a brief overview of Robert Scholes's scholarly life, see Sean Latham's "Robert Scholes: 1929–2016," https://www.brown.edu/academics/modern-culture-and-media/sites/ brown.edu.academics.modern-culture-and-media/files/uploads/Scholes_0.pdf.

6. Because of the pandemic, schools from pre-kindergarten to universities across the United States and much of the globe have mostly ended in-person teaching and, where possible, moved to online instruction. Various authorities are currently speculating about what is to come, but no one at the moment can say for certain what higher education, should it undergo drastic changes, will look like in the future. Our book was not and could not be about changes following the COVID-19 virus. But the thrust of the book's argument remains the same and, as we argue, pertinently so: it is necessary to understand how Pound's modernist advocacy for new methods of learning and different types of educational models were and still are ways to envision how we not lose the humanity of learning.

7. See Scholes's *Paradoxy of Modernism* (Yale University Press, 2006).

8. Although Pound was never quite the institutionally sanctioned schoolmaster, his lifetime of thinking about education—its failures and successes, its methods and possibilities—might be considered alongside the recent archival work of Rachel Sagner Buurma and Laura Heffernan and others. Studying the actual pedagogical history of the discipline by examining archives of reading lists, syllabuses, assignments, and other course material, Buurma and Heffernan have argued persuasively that the stories of our disciplinary history that we have passed along for generations are not altogether accurate. Their enlightening work has demonstrated how, for instance, T. S. Eliot's *Sacred Wood* was as much a product of the classroom (specifically a

working-class extension course) as it was the producer of the twentieth-century classroom ("The Classroom"). Essentially, they argue that the disciplinary methods derive from the experiences of students and teachers—what worked empirically rather than theoretically. (See also their "The Common Reader and the Archival Classroom," which explores the actual classroom experiences of Cleanth Brooks and Edmund Wilson.) While Pound could be more resistant to cultural and pedagogical pushback, he was, as we hope to demonstrate in this book, acutely aware of the student, particularly of the individuated one.

9. Paul Stasi and Josephine Park's excellent collection *Ezra Pound in the Present* demonstrates the continued relevance and seeming "newness" of Pound in our globalized economic age. Their aim, "situating Pound in ways that help us reimagine his work while simultaneously suggesting how that work might help us reimagine our present moment," is to demonstrate Pound's commitment to the "polyglot poetic form" of "world literatures" rather than the easily consumable "world literature," as many in popular culture and higher education problematically appropriate it today (vii).

10. Paulo Freire's *Pedagogy of the Oppressed* still remains one of the most influential texts in the field. John Dewey's thoughts on education would correspond better to Pound's time, if not his attitudes. For more recent developments, which often stress the emancipatory potential of educational methodologies, central texts include those of Jane Gallop, Henry Giroux, bell hooks, Peter McLaren, Jacques Rancière, Ira Shor, and Shirley Steinberg, among many, many others.

Introduction

1. The debate really got its legs in the 1970s. For the positive endorsement, see, for instance, Kenner, *The Pound Era* (Berkeley: University of California Press, 1971), and Brooke-Rose, *A ZBC of Ezra Pound* (Berkeley: University of California Press, 1971); and, for the negative take, see Harold Bloom, *A Map of Misreading* (1975; repr.; Oxford: Oxford University Press, 2003).

2. The quotation comes from Nadel's *Ezra Pound in Context* (5), an excellent collection of essays unapologetically negotiating the nuances of Pound's interconnected lives and voices.

3. Pound "delighted in cutting corners" and "get[ting] the 'feel' of a subject, picking up its jargon and the kind of questions that would interest real experts, thereby giving an impression of genuine knowledge" (Carpenter 55). Pound's early expertise sometimes had the feel of "here's what I read," and, as Carpenter argues, he was also very good at passing off knowledge regarding things he didn't actually read. Many people who met Pound at the time had equally contemptuous views about his posturing, but not everyone was as dismissive of his ambition.

4. Eliot continues, noting that Pound "has always been impelled . . . to pass on the benefit of his discoveries to others; not simply to make these benefits available, but to insist upon their being received. . . . One of the lessons to be learnt from his critical prose and from his correspondence is the lesson to care unselfishly for the art one serves" (xii).

5. Brooke-Rose notes how Pound's " 'one-man university' is inextricably linked with Pound as a poet" (5). Alan Golding sees Pound's "pedagogic stance . . . [as] inseparable from his literary avant-gardism and his commitment to the principle of 'discovery' or 'newness' " (87). Matthew Hofer sees the *Cantos* as "an expressly pedagogical objective" (80). "Indeed," he writes, "the tropes most frequently employed to understand the *Cantos*—including the luminous detail, the ideogram, the periplum, the Paideuma, and the requirement to 'make it new'—each reveal a trace of the Poundian pedagogy that takes ignorance, in any of its forms, as the enemy" (76). Peter Nicholls describes the bind of the poet-pedagogue: "the genuine poet is by definition in advance of his weaker contemporaries and derives his pedagogical legitimacy directly from his avant-gardism. Yet it is this avant-gardism that also makes him inimitable, remote from that mimetic relation of social reciprocity and identification in which learning in modern societies finds its usual ground" (148). See also Kenner, "Poets at the Blackboard," in *Ezra Pound and William Carlos Williams*, ed. Daniel Hoffman (Philadelphia: University of Pennsylvania Press, 1983), 3–13; and Harold K. Watt, *Ezra Pound and the Cantos* (London: Routledge and Kegan Paul, 1951).

6. McDonald's study situates Pound (closer to John Dewey) and Eliot (despite initial hesitation, eventually closer to Irving Babbitt) in the heart of public debates about the future of the American University. In her words, poetry, for Pound, "taught a kind of knowledge that other more obviously academic disciplines could not. Pound . . . decided to become [a teacher] of this different kind of knowledge" (44), and he would stress "the didactic motives and structures of the *Cantos* by choosing examples that refer overtly to the subject of pedagogy. Its heroes are model teachers and students, its villains 'obstructors of knowledge' " (143; internal quotation from Canto 14).

7. Daniel Swift's *The Bughouse: The Poetry, Politics, and Madness of Ezra Pound*, which draws on new material, is a recent popular entry to the collection.

8. In Canto 91, he writes, "*Democracies electing their sewage / till there is no clear thought about holiness / a dung flow from 1913 / and, in this, their kikery functioned, Marx, Freud / and the american beaneries / Filth under filth. . . .* (633–34; italics in original).

9. A letter to James Laughlin of January 6, 1936, has Pound declaring, "No real literature will come out of people who are trying to preserve a blind spot. that goes equally for ivory tower aesthetes, anti-propagandists, and communists who refuse to think: communize the product" (qtd. in Gordon 52). For a very different

take on the tangled relationship among Pound's modernist poetics, politics, and the more recent critical theory debates, see Leon Surette, "Pound, Postmodernism, and Fascism," *University of Toronto Quarterly* 59, no. 2 (Winter 1989–90): 334–55.

10. "SUPER SCHOOLMASTER" in *The Dial* (October 1920), 423. We return to this review in chapter 3.

11. Ghan Shyam Singh writes, "And if [Pound's] tone and approach were often those of a satirist and a polemicist rather than those of a moralist or a philosopher, it is because his interest in what he was discussing and analyzing was practical—even militantly so—rather than academic, and the history of culture and the history of criticism meant for him the history of ideas 'going into action' " (18–19).

12. Pound, "Raphaelite Latin" 31. Pound's early essay, a criticism leveled at the way he was being taught at Penn, was published in 1906. In it, he defends the study of ignored Latin writers who were contemporaneous with Raphael.

13. His correspondences with a young poet and future film scholar Iris Barry in 1916–17 and with Mary Barnard in 1934 present Pound as a very tough teacher, but also show him as one who was willing to listen. In a letter of April 17, 1916, he wrote to Barry: "It is rather difficult to respond to your request for criticism of your stuff. I am not quite satisfied with the things you have sent in. . . . The main difficulty seems to me that you have not yet made up your mind what you want to do or how you want to do it. I have introduced a number of young writers. . . . before I start I usually try to get some sense of their dynamics and to discern if possible which way they are going. . . . There's no use my beating about the bush with these enquiries. I get editorial notes from odd quarters blaming me that I have set off too many people. . . . If I am to hurl a new writer at the magazine with any sort of conviction I must have qualche cosa di speciale. I must have at least three or four pages of stuff which 'establish the personality.' At least I am not interested in the matter unless I can do that. Pentameter O.K. if it is interesting, but a lot of lines with no variety won't do. . . . Ah well, you may have got a worse overhauling than you wanted, but one can't criticize and be tactful all at once. And, at any rate, I shan't have kept you waiting six months for an answer" (Paige 76–78). Writing to Barnard almost two decades after, he was able to promote both his books and his method. One letter asserts "that at yr. tender age too much criticism is probably worse than none. Routledge promises to bring out my *ABC of Reading* by April or thereabouts. That contains *part* of the lessons" (January 22, 1934; Paige 252); a second letter confirms Pound's view that he "was certainly right in telling you to work on sapphics. Metric work, your only rock. . . . Keep at it. Have a care against spondee too often for second foot. The tension must be kept, and against the metric pattern struggle toward natural speech" (December 18, 1934; Paige 261). See also Jeffrey Meyers, "New Light on Iris Barry," *Paideuma* 13, no. 2 (Fall 1984): 285–89.

14. "Universities, with endowment and with provisions for fellowships in the dissection of every dead matter . . . [offered] no provision whatever for the fostering

of the creative energies" ("Patria Mia" in *Selected Prose* 132). In the words of K. L. Goodwin, "[Pound's] concern to secure publication for struggling writers; his appreciation of a wide variety of verse and prose, even if quite unlike his own; and his incessant campaign to educate the public have been, no matter how one attempts to explain them in terms of his personality, valuable and praiseworthy. His concern for the material welfare of writers, even if occasionally resented, has undoubtedly made life a good deal easier for scores of his friends and acquaintances" (218).

15. His dynamic sense of teacher-student relationships extended to his own family. Here are some words from Pound's (or "Babbo's") daughter: "At this stage it was always he who put questions to me. When I grew up he insisted I put questions to him" (67).

16. Speaking specifically of Pound's letter writing (or what Laughlin called Pound's "academy by mail"), Demetres Tryphonopoulos writes, "From Wabash College in Indiana to the Disciplinary Training Center in Pisa or St. Elizabeths Hospital in Washington, he wrote to defend, cajole, instruct, and inspire" ("Letters" 54). Pound's letters often had "reading assignments," which, more than mere suggestions from a friend, seemed akin to a schoolmaster's charge.

17. Gail McDonald makes the point that "The great books movement can be seen as an attempt to make a pedagogical method out of [Pound's] theory of the collaboration of past and present. All historical and cultural barriers removed, the text 'spoke for itself' directly to the student who assisted in the creation of the text's meaning" (187). See also Golding 88.

18. After our manuscript was completed, Modernist Cultures published a special issue (November 2017) on "*The Cantos* and Pedagogy." Michael Kindellan and Joshua Kotin intriguingly argue *against* the premise that *The Cantos* are one great pedagogical enterprise. They write, "Pound is not a teacher and we are not his students. The poem is not an attempt to help us acquire new knowledge about the world or ourselves, or to think critically about the knowledge we already possess" (346). Responding to this challenge in the same issue are Charles Altieri, Alan Golding, Marjorie Perloff, Steven G. Yao, and Michael Coyle. It should come as no surprise that the present authors would respond in kind. Our chapter 5 lays out our argument in a practical (rather than semantically nuanced) way.

19. Such reflection was preached by Pound: "A decent university wd/ consider the AIM of its existence. This, I take it, is to prepare the student to live IN the social order, and, where that social order is pustilent to ameliorate it" (letter of 1939; qtd. in Hungiville 467).

Chapter 1

1. Rather than lean on a single biography of Pound, we have drawn and benefited from the histories and contextualizations in both Carpenter's earlier and

Moody's recent (and excellent) biographies of Pound and also, though to a lesser degree, from Stock's earlier account. The biographies themselves are not without their own contexts and motivations. For a helpful overview of the many biographies (nonfictional and fictional) of Pound, see Ira B. Nadel, "The Lives of Pound," in *Ezra Pound in Context*, ed. Ira B. Nadel (Cambridge: Cambridge University Press, 2010), 159–67.

2. See Rebecca Beasley's "Pound's New Criticism" (esp. 652–59).

3. See also Moody I 16.

4. In a more nuanced take, Anne Birien argues that "[w]hat Pound had in mind was not the destruction of the philological establishment in its entirety, but a reform that would make it what he thought it was always meant to be: America's point of access to the foreign and its promises of a literary Renaissance" (24).

5. "Pound's much bruited animus against philology was more apparent than real," Smith writes. "It was directed more precisely against 'cold-storage,' the interpretive and evaluative stasis into which late-nineteenth-century academic authority seemingly locked old poems" (771).

6. Speaking of his own anthology *Confucius to Cummings* (which is discussed further in our third chapter), Pound remarks how the "book is intended . . . to arouse curiosity" and introduce work so that the student "can browse later with enjoyment" (322). The reason, he writes: "Faced with the all but total blackout of history in our schools and colleges, almost the sole chance of a pupil's learning anything useful by the age of twenty that he will be glad to know at forty or sixty, apart from mechanics and 'scientific developments,' some of dubious value, is via the courses in 'literature,' of which poetry is the most condensed form" (321–22). Marianne Moore, on this point, notes Pound's sense that "[i]nstruction should be painless . . . and his precept for writers is an epitome of himself: teach, stir the mind, afford enjoyment" (39–40).

7. Ruthven rightly notes that ". . . if Pound scorned the philological processing of literary texts under a Teutonic régime of scholarship it was not because he was no good at it but because he thought there were other and more important things to do with poems, and that he had earned the right to be a critic after submitting himself to the discipline of philology. This was to be the stand he would take later against any artist who moved straight into an avant-garde style without first having worked through the dominant traditional modes in a recapitulatory fashion" (23).

8. As did James Joyce—ironically enough for the author of *Ulysses*.

9. Carpenter (often) has a less charitable view of Pound, notably about his time at Penn: Pound, in his first year, "made only one friend" and "did 'little more than play chess' " (36; the latter words come from Pound himself). Pound would soon make another friend, a medical student named William Carlos Williams.

10. See Carpenter 46–58 and Moody I 18–27.

11. Peter Liebregts writes that Pound "object[ed] to the way Latin and Greek were taught as objects in themselves, rather than as keys to worlds whose discoveries

and philosophies about the human condition were still valid for an understanding of the modern world. His ultimate aim in reading and learning was not to live the scholar's life of texts, but to search for life in texts" (174).

12. Emily Mitchell Wallace calls Pound's failure "suspect," laying the blame on Penniman and Schelling ("America" 205–6). She notes, "For whatever combination of envy, arrogance, and fear of genius, Penniman and Schelling ridiculed their young student when he was most vulnerable and impressionable, and never invited him back to the campus, even for an hour's reading, though Pound had by 1920 at the age of thirty-five become an international celebrity . . . and had published more than all the University of Pennsylvania literature and languages faculty together" (206). Penniman, Carpenter writes, was "a careerist who later became Provost of the university; Ezra castigated him as one of 'those professors who regard their "subject" as a drill manual' " (68; *Essays* 15–16).

13. Ruthven writes, "he told his father that Hugo Rennert had assured him as long ago as 1911 that *The Spirit of Romance* would be acceptable in lieu of a thesis for the degree of Ph.D. [Wilhelm 1985, 154]; but when Homer Pound broached the matter with the Penn authorities, Felix Schelling, after canvassing opinion, recommended that the degree be not awarded because Pound had not satisfied all the Ph.D. requirements" (15; Wilhelm 154; Stock 88). Pound also asked the New York lawyer and patron John Quinn to secure a job at Columbia or City College (Reid 437). Next, Pound tried to get a degree based on the work he had done for his Cavalcanti book, but Penn, as Ruthven writes, believed "it was not an academically serious piece of work, and they again refused to award him a Ph.D. This second rejection proved to Pound that 'the "university" is dead': 'anyone interested in assessing the value of university degrees is invited to compare that volume with any batch of theses for Ph.D. that he fancies" (16; *Impact* 264).

14. See James Rader, "The Value of Testimony: Pound at Wabash," *Paideuma* 13, no. 1 (Spring 1984): 67–130; and E. L. Boyd, "Ezra Pound at Wabash College," *Journal of Modern Literature* 4, no. 1 (September 1974): 43–54.

15. See Moody I 58–61. Stock thinks there was one incident rather than two, the different (yet repetitive) stories being the result of Poundian embellishments over the years (70). See also James Longenbach's informative "Ezra Pound at Home" and the articles in *Paideuma* 13, no. 1 (Spring 1984).

16. Wallace, "EZRA THE TEACHER: 'gladly wolde he lerne, and gladly teche,' " *Ezra Pound and the Future(s) of the University* [MLA 2016 panel] (January 2016).

17. He told his mother that he had met "Miss Norton," the older woman who had befriended him in Venice, and "met several new people who wont do me any harm strategically" (133), and later related that he had had dinner with some friends of George Bernard Shaw, adding, that he thought he "might get into things before forever" (139).

18. Their correspondence can speak to an age. See Brita Lindberg-Seyersted's *Pound / Ford: The Story of a Literary Friendship*.

19. The "Preliminary Announcement" is reprinted from the Modernist Journals Project. It is available at https://modjourn.org/issue/bdr521181/.

20. Sayers, *Gaudy Night* (1936; repr., New York: Bourbon Street Books [Harper Collins], 2012), 15.

21. Discussions about reforming graduate programs—along the lines of what Pound suggests, as well as many other avenues he did not consider—are too numerous to list, but those seeking recent developments might try newer issues of *The Chronicle of Higher Education* and MLA's journal *Profession*.

22. Barker had sent Pound's father a letter, stating that the faculty's decision not to award the degree "was a just refusal" and that "an honorary degree is now out of the question" (*EPtP* 467). A subsequent letter clarifies that Pound was not rebuffed because of "conduct" but "because of what the professors thought was neglect of the work undertaken by him" (467).

Chapter 2

1. "If you want to find out something about painting," he later wrote, "you go to the National Gallery, or the Salon Carré, or the Brera, or the Prado, and LOOK at the pictures" (*ABC of Reading* 23).

2. All untitled numbers cited in this chapter refer to the 1968 edition, but all citations have been checked against the first edition.

3. As many critics have argued convincingly, though, Pound was not completely dismissive of the Arnoldian project. Hugh Witemeyer felt that Pound "belonged to the first generation of American literary aspirants to take Arnold's prescriptions to heart as educational imperatives" (44). In an even more "perversely incongruous" pairing, Andrew John Miller likens Pound to Lionel Trilling; both "participate in a culturally conservative discourse that translates Arnoldian imperatives into terms amenable to the ideology of American exceptionalism" (67). Anyone who has heard Pound recite his pedagogic poetry would have to agree that the schoolmaster is indeed trilling his three Rs.

4. While the phrase appears throughout many of Arnold's essays, it is used most notably in "The Study of Poetry": "In poetry, as in criticism of life under the conditions fixed for such a criticism by the laws of poetic truth and poetic beauty, the spirit of our race will find, we have said, as time goes on and as other helps fail, its consolation and stay. But the consolation and stay will be of power in proportion to the power of the criticism of life. And the criticism of life will be of power in proportion as the poetry conveying it is excellent rather than inferior, sound rather than unsound or half-sound, true rather than untrue or half-true"

(*Poetry and Prose* 664; originally published as the introduction to T. H. Ward, *The English Poets* [1880]).

5. Eliot's use of the expression, of course, is double-edged. If Dante wrote it about a poet who was a lesser figure in the world of letters than himself, and Eliot said it of Pound—where does that position Eliot? Rather high up the scale of poets, one would think. The better craftsman, in any case, is not necessarily the better artist. Pound helped Eliot a lot early in Eliot's career—helped him to get published and, of course, severely edited *The Waste Land* before it appeared in print. But the two poets were temperamentally very different, and they drifted apart, though they mainly continued to praise one another. As it happened, both had academic leanings. Eliot, however, finished his dissertation, while Pound never completed his. Their teaching styles, as represented in their critical writings, were completely different. Eliot's view was lofty, even when he looked at a music hall performer. Pound's was earthy, even when he looked at Dante's *Paradiso*.

6. Three metaphors for loving the unattainable, and, as Pound says, "his words run with an unperturbed order, almost that of prose" (38). In the next chapter on the culture and poetry of Provence, Pound points to the other side of troubadour verse—the actual singing of their words, in which simpler poems may have outdone the more complex ones favored by modern readers like himself, "so that the very faults which estrange the careful reader today may have contributed to the 'accord' of words and music, where the subtler effects of an Arnaut Daniel . . . might not have 'come over the footlights' when sung" (53).

7. For more on the complicated relationship between modernist aesthetics and performances of maleness in Pound, see Rachel Blau DuPlessis, "Propounding Modernist Maleness: How Pound Managed a Muse," in *Modernism / Modernity* 9, no. 3 (2002): 389–405; and Helen M. Dennis, "Pound, Women, and Gender," in *The Cambridge Companion to Ezra Pound*, ed. Ira B. Nadel (Cambridge: Cambridge University Press, 1999), 264–83.

8. After making this point, however, he moves on, taking us through the story of the *Cid*, describing characters and scenes, reporting actions, and translating key passages, before moving on to compare it to *The Song of Roland*, which he praises but still holds to be inferior to the Spanish poem: "Whatever the *Cid* owes to the *Roland*, it is an immeasurable advance in simplicity" (78). He then touches on the later medieval fashion for romances, discussing the work of Marie de France, Crestien de Troyes, and "the one immortal tale, the *Tristan*," which, he notes, came down to us in a number of versions, including an "excellent English version by Belloc" (79).

9. The chapter ends, in the 1910 edition, but not in the most recent version, with a horizontal line, followed by the words "Advenit Magister" (104). The later Pound may have felt that "The Master is Coming" was a bit flamboyant, but he certainly felt that way about Dante in 1910. For that matter, he felt a

strong kinship and admiration for Dante throughout his life, calling the magazine he edited in the late 1920s *The Exile* in homage to that great exile of Florence.

10. The Villon chapter is titled "Moncorbier, Alias Villon." The word "alias" in that title suggests Villon's criminality, and Pound does not hesitate to remind us that this "poet and gaol-bird" "walked the gutters of Paris" and said of himself what the earlier Provençal poets only said of one another. "What he sees, he writes," says Pound, and "Villon never forgets his fascinating, revolting self" (168). He had some of the learning of the schools, Pound tells us, "but his wisdom is the wisdom of the gutter" (173). In this short chapter, Pound uses translations of Villon by himself, Synge, Rossetti, and Swinburne to illustrate the power of Villon's verse, concluding that "Dante's vision is real, because he saw it. Villon's verse is real because he lived it" (178).

11. "THE art of literature and the art of the theatre are neither identical nor concentric. A part of the art of poetry is included in the complete art of the drama. Words are the means of the art of poetry; men and women moving and speaking are the means of drama. A play, to be a good play, must come over the footlights . . ." (179).

12. Many of Lope's plays have been lost, but three of those that survived are used by Pound for comparisons with versions by English playwrights of the same period. Lope wrote a version of the Romeo and Juliet story, a version of the Tamberlaine story used by Marlowe for his play, and a version of a story used by Shakespeare as a source for *The Tempest*. Pound follows his usual method of quotation and summary in discussing these and does not pull back from comparing Lope to the greatest writers, as in this comparison: "Dante and Shakespeare are like giants. Lope is like ten brilliant minds inhabiting one body. An attempt to enclose him in any formula is like trying to make one pair of boots to fit a centipede" (205). Finally, Pound gives up on trying to characterize Lope with the wonderful "He is not a man, he is a literature" (207), and moves on to mention a few other Spanish writers of that time, concluding with a long quotation from a travel book written in the seventeenth century that describes the public festivals and theatrical performances of the time.

13. Pound's chapter on Camoens generates important reflections on the art of poetry, which Pound places above that of literature in general, and the highest achievements in that art. Of Camoens and his epic of Portuguese discoveries, Pound concludes, "that part of the art of poetry which can be learned, he learned" (220) and finally dismisses him with a comparison to Henry Wadsworth Longfellow.

14. The articles Pound wrote under this title have been collected and published in the standard *Ezra Pound: Selected Prose 1909–1965*, edited by William Cookson, with a brief Foreword written by Pound in 1972. By removing these articles from their original situation in *The New Age* and leaving out things that have been collected in other places, Cookson's collection misses some important aspects of what

Pound was doing in this work, which are visible only in their original journalistic setting. We therefore refer not to this text but to the versions to be found in the digital editions of the magazine available on the website of the Modernist Journals Project (www.modjourn.org).

15. That crowd included the editor, A. R. Orage; his assistant, Beatrice Hastings; and a number of people who wrote for the magazine. Many years later, Hastings claimed that she was responsible for Pound becoming one of those writers, but, because she attacked him regularly and fiercely, that is by no means certain. What we do know is that Pound was one of the few writers who was paid for his contributions by Orage, getting a guinea a week when he contributed, which was frequent until 1920. Carpenter writes, "Orage proved an 'excellent friend' to [Pound], publishing nearly 300 of his articles and proving the most reliable of all his literary employers to date" (169). In return for Orage's support—he "did more to feed [Pound] than anyone else in England"—Pound was awfully dismissive: "To this day I haven't the faintest idea who *read* that paper" (qtd. in Carpenter 169).

16. For the accidentally serendipitous movement among Pound's "angles" and "angels," see Mutlu Blasing, "Pound's Soundtrack: 'Reading *Cantos* for What Is *on the Page*,'" in *Lyric Poetry: The Pain and the Pleasure of Words* (Princeton: Princeton University Press, 2007), 149–77.

17. Kenner writes, "Luminous Details are the transcendentals in an array of facts: not merely 'significant' nor 'symptomatic' in the manner of most facts" (152).

18. This was originally published in *Poetry* 2, no. 1 (April 1913): 12.

19. Eliot's more famous essay on the matter, "Tradition and the Individual Talent," speaks of this tension: "no poet, no artist of any art, has his complete meaning alone. His significance, his appreciation is the appreciation of his relation to the dead poets and artists. You cannot value him alone; you must set him, for contrast and comparison, among the dead" (*Selected Prose* 38).

20. This quasi-paradox is reminiscent of David Hume's sleight of hand regarding the "standard" of taste. See Hume, "Of the Standard of Taste" [1742], in *Essays Moral, Political, and Literary*, ed. Eugene F. Miller (Indianapolis: Liberty Classics, 1985), 226–49.

21. Pound begins to show how Arnaut complicates things and makes them more interesting, concluding with this statement about the translations he is about to provide: "The sound of the original is a little more clear and staccato than that of the words I have been able to find in English" (*NA* 10.11:249). The rhyming in these poems is different from what we are used to, because the pattern of similar sounds occurs not within the stanzas but across them, with, for example the fifth line in each stanza rhyming with all the other fifth lines—in one of Arnaut's poems, Pound's fifth lines are Birds, Curds, Girds, Herds, Words, and Thirds. Here are the first lines of the six main stanzas in that same poem:

The bitter air
So clear the flare
Amor, beware
If she but care
Sweet thou, ah fair
My song, prepare

22. Pound was very much a part of these early debates on free verse. See, for example, how they played out in the May 1913 issue of *Poetry* and thereafter. Especially significant are the defenses by Harriet Monroe and Alice Corbin Henderson.

23. His April 24, 1916, letter to Iris Barry advised as much: "Your practice with regular metres is a good thing; better to keep in mind that [it] is practice, and that it will probably serve to get your medium pliable. No one can do good free verse who hasn't struggled with the regular" (Paige 79).

24. Pound would later be a party to a rather infamous scrap regarding his translations. In March 1919, Harriet Monroe published in *Poetry Magazine* four of Pound's *Homage to Sextus Propertius* poems. A month later, she published "Pegasus Impounded," an acrimonious critique of Pound's translations by Professor William Gardner Hale of the University of Chicago. Hale had found sixty rather careless errors in Pound's work. "If Pound were a professor of Latin, there would be nothing left for him but suicide," Hale disturbingly wrote: "I do not counsel this. But I beg him to lay aside the mask of erudition" (*Poetry* 14.1:55). Pound, naturally, was incensed. He wrote angrily to Monroe, claiming that his own work was not a "translation" but a piece of artwork itself, and then wrote to the editor of the *English Journal*: "Hale's 'criticism' displayed not only ignorance of Latin but ignorance of English. . . . Miss Monroe appears to preserve the superstition that a man is learned, or, *me hercule*, infallible *because* he is a professor" (January 24, 1931; Paige 230–1). Rather than admit any mistakes, Pound became more vociferous, and the whole episode ended up confirming his opinion of the university and its stale philological approaches. Although his anger was unmistakably personal, the question he raised about translating literally as opposed to translating aesthetically still makes for much scholarly and artistic debate. Moreover, it seems to hint that translation, in his eyes, is a type of pedagogical exercise. As he writes in "Raphaelite Latin," defending his method, "Everywhere in the translation I have sacrificed the crystalized form of the Latin—and any desire I might have had for a classic English verse form—to ample rendering of the Latin thought" (33).

25. "The technique of art," Shklovsky writes, "is to make objects 'unfamiliar,' to make forms difficult, to increase the difficulty and length of perception because the process of perception is an aesthetic end in itself" (12). See "Art as Technique" [1917], in *Russian Formalist Criticism: Four Essays*, ed. and trans. Lee T. Lemon and Marion J. Reis (Lincoln: University of Nebraska Press, 1965), 12.

26. The phrases come from Arnold's important defense of the scholarly trade, "The Function of Criticism at the Present Time" (*Poetry and Prose* 361, 352).

27. The exception was a brief insult delivered by Beatrice Hastings, who quoted Pound's translation of a line from Arnaut Daniel and claimed that it did not capture the poet's "decivilised" nature adequately, so she offered an absurd alternative of her own. This was probably a clumsy joke, but Hastings, who ultimately published more than twenty poems in the magazine, may have felt threatened by Pound's description of what it took to be a good poet. Her attacks on him became fiercer and fiercer until she left the magazine in 1915, contributing very occasionally after that.

Chapter 3

1. The phrase is his own, and it comes from a 1913 letter to his mother. The letter is also quite disparaging toward Yeats, his host at the time (note the revealing word choice of "profitable"): "My stay in Stone cottage will not be in the least profitable. I detest the country. Yeats will amuse me part of the time and bore me to death with psychical research the rest. I regard the visit as a duty to posterity" (*EPtP 312*). A duty to posterity indeed. For an elucidation of a very different type of Poundian schooling, see Demetres P. Tryphonopoulos's "Ezra Pound's Occult Education."

2. See F. S. Flint's "Imagisme" (198–200) and Pound's "A Few Don'ts by an Imagiste" (200–6) in *Poetry* 1, no. 6 (March 1913). Pound insisted *Poetry* print 50000000000 copies of this piece and "insert [it] . . . in each returned msss. for the next decade" (Letter to Henderson, January 20, 1913; qtd. in Nadel 19).

3. Compare this to William Wordsworth's statement in his "Preface" to the *Lyrical Ballads* that "The knowledge both of the Poet and the Man of Science is pleasure; but the knowledge of the one cleaves to us as a necessary part of our existence, our natural and unalienable inheritance; the other is a personal and individual acquisition, slow to come to us, and by no habitual and direct sympathy connecting us with our fellow-beings" (606).

4. Hueffer claimed Pound played tennis like "an inebriated kangaroo" (qtd. in Lindberg-Seyersted, 87).

5. Ruthven notes the nuanced depiction of the reader in Pound's *The Treatise on Harmony*, where Pound "transforms his passive *élève* into 'mon contra-dicteur' . . . whose existence immediately threatens the authority of his discourse" (25; *Selected Prose* 83).

6. Reflecting back on the time, Woolf writes, "And now I will hazard a second assertion, which is more disputable perhaps, to the effect that on or about December 1910 human character changed. I am not saying that one went out, as one might into a garden, and there saw that a rose had flowered, or that a hen

had laid an egg. The change was not sudden and definite like that. But a change there was, nevertheless; and since one must be arbitrary, let us date it about the year 1910" (4).

7. Pound's circle (Wyndham Lewis, Gaudier-Brzeskaka, the painter and engraver Edward Wadsworth) initially had more contact with the Bloomsbury group than did Pound. In a letter to her friend, the painter and art critic Roger Fry, Woolf, who had just met "that strange young man Eliot," had tired of his constant mention of the "genius" of Pound. She wrote, ". . . Not that I've read more than 10 words of Ezra Pound," for her "conviction of his humbug is unalterable" (November 18, 1918; *Letters* II 295–96). In a letter four years hence, she charges his American eyes with being "perpetually shut" (572). Following a dispute between Lewis and Fry, Pound tired of the "Bloomsbuggars" and wrote to his father, speaking of "those washed-out Fry-ites" (Carpenter 244).

8. This was a moment in Anglo-American culture when Max Stirner's *The Ego and His Own* was being widely read, leading Dora Marsden to retitle her journal and call it *The Egoist*. Pound, who approved of that change, had a large emotional investment in individuality himself. One would be remiss in not mentioning the likely influence of George Meredith's 1879 novel *The Egoist*, central to modernist sentiments, and referenced in critical works such as E. M. Forster's *Aspects of the Novel*.

9. Compare this to the position of the New Critics, such as Cleanth Brooks, for whom poetry and the sciences were opposed: "there is a sense in which paradox is the language appropriate and inevitable to poetry. It is the scientist whose truth requires a language purged of every trace of paradox; apparently the truth which the poet utters can be approached only in terms of paradox" (3).

10. "After Gauthier, France produced, as nearly as I can understand, three chief and admirable poets: Tristan Corbière, perhaps the most poignant writer since Villon; Rimbaud, a vivid and indubitable genius; and Laforgue—a slighter, but in some ways a finer 'artist' than either of the others" (7). Pound then offers six poems from Laforgue, "one of the poets whom it is practically impossible to 'select'" (8), remarking that any other six by this poet might have done just as well. The poems are in French, untranslated, and accompanied by the occasional prod to encourage the reader's appreciation, concluding with a comparison between journalists, "who must think as their readers think" (15) and poets who offer readers something fresh—and pay a price in neglect. (Laforgue's collected poems only began to sell well after his death.)

11. Calling Laforgue "incontrovertible," Pound moved on to Tristan Corbière, whom he situated as "the greatest poet of the period" (19), noting that it still took more than a decade for his work to become widely known. With one long poem and some shorter quotations, he prods us to appreciate this Breton poet who came to Paris and captured something of the life of the city in his poems in a way that reminds Pound of Villon. Pound then moves on to the third of his trilogy of poets, Rimbaud, whose work, in Pound's view, shared certain qualities with the painting of Paul Cézanne.

12. And he praises, in particular, de Gourmont's incomparable rhythm in "Litanies de la Rose," warning us, before we are given the poem itself, that "It is not a poem to lie on the page, it must come to life in audition, or in the finer audition which one may have in imagining sound" (35).

13. He then sums up his conclusions to this point by insisting that "Corbière, Rimbaud, Laforgue are permanent; that probably some of De Gourmont's and Tailhade's poems are permanent, or at least reasonably durable; that Romains is indispensable, for the present at any rate" (76).

14. At this point in the *Instigations* Pound inserts a piece on "Unanisme" that actually appeared in a later issue of *The Little Review* than the original study of modern French poets. In it, he mainly lets Romains speak for himself, but translates his prose "Reflexions" for our benefit. There, Romains muses about the life of groups in the modern world—places, streets, squares, crowds at theaters or public places. Pound, who tells us that he retains his "full suspicion of agglomerates," nonetheless acknowledges that Romains "utters, in original vein, phases of consciousness whereinto we are more or less drifting, in measure of our proper sensibility" (83). He follows this with other pieces from his *Little Review* work, concluding with some thoughts about a Belgian magazine, *La Wallonie*, which began life as *L'Elan Littéraire* and lasted from 1885 to 1892. Its former editor wrote Pound about it, being, as Pound noted, "gracious enough to call it 'Notre *Little Review* à nous,' and to commend the motto on our cover" (88). We return to that motto, "MAKING NO COMPROMISE WITH THE PUBLIC TASTE" and to *La Wallonie* itself in the next chapter, but should note that Pound uses that journal's death notice for Jules Laforgue as a way of bringing closure to this whole "Study in French Poets."

15. (1) that there was emotional greatness in James's "hatred of tyranny," and (2) that his art was great because he captured racial characteristics rather than merely personal quirks in his writing. Pound himself had a strong sense of race, which was later to take a terrifying turn leading up to the Second World War.

16. Having said all this, Pound proceeds "for the reader of good-will" (129) to go through the works chronologically, offering his own opinions about their readability and importance, sometimes in a single phrase like "not important" and other times with pages of quotation and commentary. Sometimes he assumes the role of advocate, and on other pages he becomes a critic, but then he suggests that "All this critique is very possibly an exaggeration" (149).

17. Pound discusses not the novel but the notes, which demonstrate "this author's superiority, as conscious artist, over the 'normal' British novelist" (164). Pound calls them "simply the accumulation of his craftsman's knowledge" (165). He also criticizes the editor of the volume for putting the notes after the text of the unfinished work, thus depriving the reader of "the sport" of watching "the distinguished author" fleshing out the skeleton described in the notes.

18. But he does not only contrast de Gourmont with writers of the past. He compares the French writer's "sexual intelligence" favorably to Strindberg's "sexual

stupidity," and recommends that young men under thirty should read de Gourmont's novel of 1899, *Songe d'une femme* for an education in sexuality (173).

19. In the letter, de Gourmont agreed to work with Pound toward establishing a periodical that might connect the literary worlds of Paris, London, and New York. They both took a special interest in the "small reviews" that published the work of modern artists and writers. Pound even translates the last sentences of that letter so we cannot miss what de Gourmont says: "The aim of the *Mercure* has been to permit any man, who is worth it, to write down his thought frankly—this is a writer's sole pleasure. And this aim should be yours," adding, "[i]f only my great correspondent could have seen letters I received about this time from English alleged intellectuals!!!!!! The incredible stupidity, the ingrained refusal of thought!!!!!" (193). The *Mercure* was the name of a literary magazine and publishing house with ties to the symbolist movement.

20. Pound calls it Joyce's "profoundest work" and reminds us that he has gone beyond creating a character based on his own life to give us a second character who is quite different: "Bloom on life, death, resurrection, immortality. Bloom and the Venus de Milo. Bloom brings life into the book. All Bloom is vital" (210–11). For more on their fascinating correspondence, see Forrest Read's *Pound / Joyce: The Letters of Ezra Pound to James Joyce* (New York: New Directions, 1967).

21. It therefore seems natural at this moment in *Instigations* for him to move on from Joyce to Wyndham Lewis. Lewis's situation, though, offers problems, because he is a visual artist at least as much as a verbal one if not more, making it difficult to deal with his importance simply in words without illustrations. Having arranged for the publication of Lewis's novel *Tarr* in *The Egoist*, Pound turns to it here, praising it as "the most vigorous and volcanic English novel of our time" (215). Admitting that it has faults, he still insists that *Tarr* is of comparable quality to Joyce's *Portrait*, and he goes into considerable detail to demonstrate its vigor and appeal before moving on to other modernist writers he finds interesting: the Lytton Strachey of *Eminent Victorians*, and the now quite forgotten writers George S. Street and Frederic Manning.

22. The next part of *Instigations* is completely different, consisting of two creative efforts: a rather free version of Jules Laforgue's story of Salome from *Moralités légendaires*, and a commentary on the biblical book of Genesis, which claims to be a translation "from an eighteenth-century author" and is actually from Voltaire's critical commentary. Pound translates faithfully, adding a note at the end recommending Voltaire's "treatment of Ezekiel" as well.

23. The section on Provençal is mainly a return to Arnaut Daniel, with still more attention to his technique and rhyme schemes.

24. Fenollosa overestimated the iconic quality of the Chinese language, and both he and Pound would stress the visual over the phonetic. Steven G. Yao notes that Pound's "adherence to the evocative but vastly oversimplified theories of Ernest Fenollosa about the nature of the Chinese language merely allowed him to justify his

own ignorance and, indeed, see it as a positive trait" (Yao 12). Zhaoming Qian is a little more forgiving: "The aim of Fenollosa's essay is to push for concrete, natural thinking and writing as suggested by the primitive Chinese character. Nowhere in his essay does Fenollosa claim that '*all* Chinese characters are pictograms or ideograms.' What he states is that '*a large number of the primitive* Chinese characters, even the so-called radicals, are shorthand pictures of actions or processes" (Qian xix).

25. Prior to publishing this essay in *Instigations*, Pound also tried to place it several times in magazines before finally getting it published in *The Little Review* in four installments in the fall of 1919.

26. Bloom, *How to Read and Why* (New York: Touchstone, 2001). Alan Golding links Pound here more directly with the closer contemporary Mortimer J. Adler, great philosopher, teacher, and author of *How to Read a Book* (1940).

27. Ruthven points to Archibald MacLeish's humorous comment that Pound's next book "will be How to Dance or How to Vote Republican" (27). MacLeish was apparently unaware of Pound's own *New Age* piece on "How to look at a front house" (Zinnes 82). The MacLeish line comes from R. H. Winnick, ed., *Letters of Archibald MacLeish* (Boston: Houghton Mifflin, 1983), 258.

28. See Althusser, *Lenin and Philosophy and Other Essays* (New York: Monthly Review Press, 1971), 127–86.

29. Although comparative methodologies have infused many different disciplines, comparative literature departments in the United States have unfortunately had turbulent fortunes over the last few generations. See David Damrosch's *What Is World Literature?* (Princeton: Princeton University Press, 2003), Gayatri Spivak's *Death of a Discipline* (New York: Columbia University Press, 2003), and the recent essays in *Comparative Critical Studies*.

30. This was originally published in *Criterion*, April 1934.

31. See Orwell, "Politics and the English Language" [1946], *The Norton Reader*, 9th ed., ed. Linda H. Peterson (New York: W. W. Norton and Co., 1996), 617–28.

32. Hirsch's work itself is not without controversy. Although he is more thorough than Pound, his "minimum basis" can be quite lacking when it comes to assessing things of multicultural importance. See Hirsch's *Cultural Literacy: What Every American Needs to Know* (New York: Vintage, 1988).

33. Although the context is radically different, one might be reminded of Gayatri Chakravorty Spivak's negotiation of ideology, the aesthetic, and pedagogical spaces in "Reading the World: Literary Studies in the 80s," *College English* 43, no. 7 (November 1981): 671–79. The argument is later reimagined in her *A Critique of Postcolonial Reason: Toward a History of a Vanishing Present* (Cambridge: Harvard University Press, 1999).

34. In Lan's words, Confucianism "allowed [Pound] to bring together his previously fragmented beliefs, to reinstate their intelligibility, and to offer a coherent explanation of the relationships of humanity with nature and the divinity" (13). Lan is careful not to wed Pound's brand of Confucianism to his incipient fascism. Where

Pound's critical readers had tended to see Pound's interests in Western and Eastern culture as epitomizing binary oppositions, Lan sees a unity in the two, a unity that gave Pound a "deep conviction in the power of Confucianism for redeeming the troubled Western world" (326).

35. The great irony here is that Pound, who wanted to connect the dots of modern social life, sought a modern China that wanted to move away from Confucius. See the Fengchi Tang correspondence in Qian 23–39.

36. Dembo writes, "The aim of *The Cantos* is revelatory, and in the same general manner and the same general terms as Confucians traditionally perceived the aim of the Odes. The purpose of all poetry was the moral renovation of the mind, the radical condition from which the branches of an ordered state and an integrated Kultur would emerge" (20). Dembo can be overly Hegelian in a way Pound was not: "images are eventually, if not immediately, part of an organic whole, the signs by which Truth reveals itself" (17).

37. The linguistic order of "right naming" was also about a social order of people recognizing their right places. Pound, quoting from his translation of the *Analects*: "*To call people and things by their names, that is by the correct denominations, to see that the terminology was exact*" (*Guide to Kulchur* 16).

38. Marcella Spann articulates as much in her preface: "Courses in English literature can arouse curiosity and give the student a taste for reading things she or he would like to remember later in life" (vii). "The important thing," she later writes, ". . . is to get the student to look. All else will follow, that is, assuming the student has any intelligence at all. Agassiz, one of the greatest teachers of all time, was certainly aware of this. When asked what he considered his most important achievement, he said: 'I have taught men to observe'" (336).

39. Miller's syllabus contains a few bits of practical advice: "Shakespeare: *Plays*. Get a book you can read without a microscope and one you can carry. . . . [K]*now* a few of them. Don't read the notes. Don't read the critics. . . . Remember you are much better schooled than Shakespeare's audience and they understood him without any college professors" (332).

Chapter 4

1. See his book of the same name. Not everyone agrees with Kenner's diagnosis of the age. Harold Bloom (who sees Wallace Stevens as the paramount modernist) writes, "Gossip grows old and becomes myth; myth grows older and becomes dogma. Wyndham Lewis, Eliot, and Pound gossiped with one another; the New Criticism aged them into a myth of Modernism; now the antiquarian Hugh Kenner has dogmatized this myth into the Pound Era, a canon of accepted titans. Bloom, *A Map of Misreading* (New York: Oxford University Press, 1975), 28.

2. This section is a revised and amplified version of a chapter in Robert Scholes and Clifford Wulfman, *Modernism in the Magazines* (New Haven: Yale University Press, 2010). For more on the emergent periodical studies, see Suzanne W. Churchill and Adam McKible, eds., *Little Magazines and Modernism: New Approaches* (Aldershot: Ashgate, 2007); Jayne Marek, *Women Editing Modernism: "Little" Magazines & Literary History* (Lexington, KY: University Press of Kentucky, 1995); and Sean Latham and Robert Scholes, "The Rise of Periodical Studies" *PMLA* 121, no. 2 (March 2005): 517–31.

3. This series has finally been published together in a book. See Scholes and Wulfman's *Modernism in the Magazines*.

4. "Cat–piss and porcupines! . . ." begins his letter of resignation to Harriet Monroe (Moody I 354). Other letters follow this pattern.

5. "The fee was small—Orage himself said someone had nicknamed the paper the *No Wage*—but the guinea a week he paid Ezra was better than nothing, and Ezra once said that Orage 'did more to feed me than anyone else in England' " (Carpenter 169).

6. Ann L. Ardis's chapter on this journal (" 'Life is not composed of water-tight compartments': the *New Age*'s critique of modernist literary specialization") thoroughly details what was at stake in Orage's phrasing. See Ardis, *Modernism and Cultural Conflict*, 143–72.

7. See Frederick J. Hoffman, Charles Allen, and Carolyn F. Ulrich's *The Little Magazine: A History and a Bibliography* (Princeton: Princeton University Press, 1947).

8. Pound wrote to Henderson: "Of course the plain damn unvarnished fact is that Harriet is a fool, A noble, sincere, long struggling impeccable fool" (qtd. in Nadel 137).

9. In a letter from September 1912, Pound writes to Monroe, "We must be taken seriously at *once*. We must be *the voice* not only for the U.S. but inter-nationally" (Paige 10).

10. His letter of January 1915 goes on: "There must be no book words, no periphrases, no inversions. . . . There MUST be no interjections. No words flying off to nothing. . . . Rhythm must have meaning. It can't be merely a careless dash off, with no grip and no real hold to the words and sense, a tummy tum tumty tum tum ta. There must be no clichés, set phrases, stereotyped journalese . . ." (49).

11. Eunice Tietjens would officially end contact in April 1942: "The time has come to put a formal end to the countenancing of Ezra Pound. For a number of years, at the beginning of the magazine, he was associated with *Poetry*, and the association was valuable on both sides. Then he quarreled with us, as he has quarreled with everyone. . . . Now, so far as we and the rest of the English-speaking world of letters are concerned, he has written *finis* to his long career as inspired *enfant terrible*." After she uses her own hyperbole about "the rest of the English-speaking world," Tietjens goes on to label Pound "never a major poet himself" however

much "he probably did more than anyone else in his day to 'incite new impulses in poetry'" *Poetry* 61, no. 1 (April 1942): 38–39; the internal phrase is Sandburg's.

12. From "Vortex," one of Pound's contributions to the issue: "We use the words 'greatest efficiency' in the precise sense—as they would be used in a text book of MECHANICS" (153).

13. After *Blast* ended, Pound made another serious attempt to get control of a magazine in London, hoping to enlist John Quinn as a financial supporter. He wrote Quinn in May 1915, saying that "There is the faint chance, the faint nuance of a chance that I may get an ancient weekly to edit" (*Pound/Quinn*, 27). That weekly, *The Academy*, did not fall into his hands, but Pound continued writing to Quinn about starting a new magazine or taking over an old one, debating the merits of weekly versus monthly publication, citing the Parisian *Mercure de France* as a model of what a modern magazine should be, and wondering whether, in his ideal magazine, it might be necessary to include the work of "the better, populace-drawing writers from time to time" (*Pound/Quinn*, 35) in order to gain enough circulation to make the magazine economically viable. Pound referenced Hilaire Belloc as an example of the sort of writer he had in mind for this function. In this extraordinary series of letters that ran through most of 1915, Pound's plans became more and more specific and detailed as to costs, contributors, and numbers of subscribers, and more and more detached from the actual possibilities of magazine production, until they culminated in a bizarre plan for an all-male journal. Needless to say, these dreams never became a reality, and Pound had to settle for another role in an existing journal.

14. Ruthven aptly notes that Pound learned that literary criticism "is an aesthetic discourse which encodes a crypto-politics of reputation-mongering. What he failed to concede . . . is the part played by sexual politics" (108).

15. Pound's editorial choreographies with *The Literary Review* can be wonderfully traced in Thomas L. Scott and Melvin J. Friedman's *Pound / The Little Review*.

16. He wrote helplessly to his father, "Know anyone who wants to BUY the paper?" (qtd. in Monk 352).

17. Explaining "periodical studies" almost a century later, Latham and Scholes question the distinction between art and economics "as artificial, since high literature, art, and advertising have mingled in periodicals from the earliest years, and major authors have been published in magazines both little and big" (519).

18. The word "efficiency" rather than literary "merit" encapsulates Pound's critique of this commercialized culture: "Putting aside my personal preferences for 'literature,' thought, etc., and other specialised forms of activity, we (and again obviously *so*) will find here a display of technique, *of* efficiency. This . . . is manifestly what a vast number of people want; what a vast number of people spend the requisite 8d. to obtain. This is the 'solid and wholesome.' The ads. proclaim it. The absence of actresses' legs is a sign of power" (#5 *NA* 21.20:426).

19. One might be reminded of Universal Studios' "Sherlock Holmes" series (filmed during the Second World War, and starring Basil Rathbone), in which the Victorian icon is called into duty to fight the Nazis. For better or worse, for right or wrong, it is the reproducibility of the stock narrative that furthers the desire of the already interpellated mass public, which re-creates an aura of giants, myths, and finally religion.

20. Pound seems offended most by the favorable portrayal of the police: "Religious feeling shown in depiction of police (cf. guardians of the law, divine messengers, angels with flaming swords in earlier and more cumbrous religions)" (130). Aside from this and the other flaws he points out, this tale does not offend him because it has no godlike hero. It is simply "fiction" as defined by Oscar Wilde's Miss Prism (in *The Importance of Being Earnest*), with the good ending happily and the bad unhappily.

21. See, for example, Adorno and Max Horkheimer's *Dialectic of Enlightenment*, which takes in its crosshairs the "culture industry." *Dialectic of Enlightenment* [1944], trans. John Cumming (New York: Continuum, 1999).

22. Armour and Company was a giant meatpacking business located in Chicago. One might be reminded of Carl Sandburg's opening line "Hog butcher for the world" (*Poetry* 3, no. 6 [March 1914]: 191. As a footnote, two years after this poem, in February 1916, Sandburg called Pound "the best man writing poetry today," adding that "[t]he flair of great loneliness is there" (250, 257). See "The Work of Ezra Pound, *Poetry* 7, no. 5 (February 1916): 249–57.

23. See Peterson, *Magazines in the Twentieth Century* (Urbana: University of Illinois Press, 1956).

24. For an article specifically about teaching Pound on the internet, see Gail McDonald, "Hypertext and the Teaching of Modernist Difficulty," *Pedagogy* 2, no. 1 (2002): 17–30.

25. Pound often seemed to lose hope in teaching an older generation. In a letter to Harriet Monroe, he declares, "Of course there are several things I have been tryin to teach you for the past 20 yrs. I don't lay as much stock by teachin the elder generation as by teachin' the risin', and if one gang does without learnin' there is always the next" (December 27, 1931; Paige 238).

Chapter 5

1. Letter to Peter Whigham (qtd. in Carpenter 658). For a recent, comprehensive overview, see also Robert Spoo.

2. Carpenter relates, "A report to Washington later explained that 'extreme precautions were used to prevent suicide or escape,' and that it had been decided to place the prisoner 'in a small open cell with walls of steel grating in order that

he might be under constant observation.' Orders also went out that all DTC personnel, both prisoners and guards, should keep away from Ezra Pound's cell, and that no one was to speak to him" (657; internal quotations from William Van O'Connor and Edward Stone, eds., *A Casebook of Ezra Pound* [New York: Thomas Y. Crowell, 1959], 34). As Pound wrote about it himself years later, "Old Ez was a prize exhibit" (qtd. in Carpenter 658).

3. Carpenter writes, "most people who really knew him . . . could perceive that he was not insane at all. He could therefore scarcely be expected to 'recover' from a mental disturbance from which he was not suffering. Consequently he could not hope ever to be released from St Elizabeths. And if he were released, it would only be to stand trial all over again" (753). In addition to Stock (481–594), Carpenter (566–848), Kenner (460–95), and the countless excellent articles in *Paideuma*, see Omar Pound and Robert Spoo, eds., *Letters in Captivity 1945–1946* (New York: Oxford University Press, 1999); Julien Cornell, *The Trial of Ezra Pound* (London: Faber and Faber, 1967); Leslie Fiedler, "Traitor or Laureate: The Two Trials of the Poet," *New Approaches to Ezra Pound*, ed. Eva Hesse (London: Faber and Faber, 1970), 365–77; and the essays in William Van O'Connor and Edward Stone's *A Casebook on Ezra Pound*.

4. See Charles Bernstein's devastating but ambivalent take in his essay "Pounding Fascism," in *A Poetics* (Cambridge: Harvard University Press, 1992), 121–27; and Tim Redman's more comprehensive *Ezra Pound and Italian Fascism* (Cambridge: Cambridge University Press, 1991). Bernstein writes that Pound's "blindness to the meaning of his [own] work . . . contributed not only to the rabidness of his dogmatism but also to the heights of magnificent self-deception and elegiac confusion that is *The Cantos* at its best" (122).

5. In a letter to Archibald MacLeish, Pound interestingly attributes Mussolini's failure to a cultural deficiency and lays blame at his own (political) limitations as a teacher. "I did not think I could educate, beyond a certain point and given time, Muss/ in the sense you take it" (qtd. in Tryphonopoulos "Letters" 63).

6. While the historical reality of the situation has indeed enacted a closure, and while the dreams of the paradise seem shattered, the philosophical sense of this finality remains unclear. For Peter Stoicheff, "the emerging narrative of facism's destruction is thus redeemed by other texts that record and sustain a belief in divine purpose, in the process salvaging fascism from criticism and placing it in the context of man's continual blindness to what, according to the text of nature, is right" (128). Peter Nicholls sees this moment in Pound as "a refusal of recantation" (147).

7. What would become Pound's First Canto was initially part of Canto Three. See the June, July, and August 1917 issues (vol. 10, nos. 3–5) of *Poetry* for the original form of "Three Cantos."

8. Eliot brought this whimsical appellation to his *Old Possum's Book of Practical Cats* (from which the musical *Cats* would be based). See also Omar Pound

and Robert Spoo's *Ezra and Dorothy Pound: Letters in Captivity 1945–1946* for a whimsically apt newspaper cutout that Pound sent to Dorothy in May 1946 about an actual possum detained in an American police precinct (Image accompanying Letter 132, between pages 16 and 17).

9. Pound and Mussolini would meet, with Pound actually soliciting a journal contribution from the latter. For a not-completely overly judgmental account of Pound's enthusiasm for Mussolini, see Earle Davis's *Vision Fugitive* 147–70.

10. Many other moments in the author's life contradict such critical assertions. In a later letter to Hayden Carruth, Pound wrote that "The Jew book is the poison / that, since A.D. it has bitched everything it got into . . . The jew book has been filling bughouses with nuts ever since they set up such institutions" (qtd. in Torrey 226).

11. The process of rebuilding a culture—Pound's dream—resonated with the rebuilding of the Temple. Pound writes, "From the law, by the law, so build yr/ temple / with justice in meteyard and measure" ("Canto 74" 460; first slash in original).

12. For more on the composition history of these cantos, see Bush's " 'Quiet, Not Scornful?': The Composition of the *Pisan Cantos*," in *A Poem Including History: The Cantos of Ezra Pound*, ed. Lawrence Rainey (Ann Arbor: University of Michigan Press, 1996), 169–211.

13. Compare this especially to Pound's thoughts toward the end of this canto on the commercialization of modern art: "what art do you handle? / 'The best' And the moderns? 'Oh nothing modern / we couldn't sell anything modern' " (468).

14. The "Till" who was unceremoniously "hung yesterday" was Louis Till, father of Emmett Till, who was murdered in Mississippi in 1955 at age fourteen for speaking with a white woman. See Milton L. Welch's " 'Till Was Hung Yesterday': Louis Till as Lynching Topos in *The Pisan Cantos*."

15. In a November 1940 letter to the Japanese poet Kitasono Katsue [Katue Kitasono], Pound could still maintain that "when it comes to the question of transmitting from the East to the West, a great part of the Chinese sound is no use at all" (qtd. in Paige 347). This is not to say that, in his early work, Pound was indifferent to sound or poetic measure, but those were aspects of the lyric that could get lost in his fascination with the image.

16. Corresponding with Pound at St Elizabeths (February 1951), Achilles Fang asks the poet about his use of the ideogram here: "May one read 'ME' as the pronunciation of 莫 <mo or mu>? ME at the same time reminds one of μή, which in turn makes one think of οὐ. And OY TIΣ, 'Odessey,' → 'a man on whom the sun has gone down . . .' " (qtd. in Qian 57).

17. Pound corresponded with Tinkham, who visited Rapallo in the 1930s. Noting the didactic (as opposed to aesthetic) nature of his poetry, Pound wrote to Tinkham, "I don't care in the least whether you consider it as poetry or as telegraphic notes" (qtd. in Alec March 127).

18. Among others, see Cantos 54, 56, 96, and 99.

19. Moody states that Pound arranged to meet Santayana at the Hotel Danieli in Venice in December 1939. Santayana "sought enlightenment concerning the Chinese ideogram" but couldn't see the connections to European culture Pound wanted to make. "Possibly feeling rather talked at as by an over-excited teacher he told Pound an anecdote about how Henry Adams . . . had remarked, 'Teach? At Harvard? | Teach? It cannot be done'" (III 7).

20. See George Santayana, *Persons and Places: Critical Edition*, ed. Herman J. Saatkamp Jr. and William G. Holzberger (Cambridge: MIT Press, 1987).

21. See Leon Surette's *Pound in Purgatory* for a comprehensive, though debated, analysis.

22. The authors of *Super Schoolmaster* would like to thank Professor James Campbell for his suggestions and recontextualization of various aspects of this chapter.

23. Moody writes, "give the people the purchasing power to buy the things which industry needed to sell and which they needed for a decent life. That is what any enlightened government would do: distribute credit, not take it away in taxes" (Moody I 372). See also Carpenter, especially 356–59, 491–503.

24. In *ABC of Economics*, Pound called Keynes a "saphead" (70) and maintained (incorrectly) that, through Douglas's system, "[i]t is perfectly easy to increase the volume of money in circulation without debasing its value" (73). Surette is more generous toward Pound's economic vision than most economists would be: "since professional economists have been unable to settle the issue during the last two centuries, Pound's acceptance of Social Credit economics cannot count as evidence of his stupidity, venality, or malignity" ("Economics" 108).

For a quirky explanation of the problems with continual inflation, see Tim Harford's "What Babysitting Can Teach the World" (http://timharford.com/2012/06/what-babysitting-can-teach-the-world/).

25. Pound, "The Revolt of Intelligence" [IX], *New Age* 26, no. 19 (March 1920): 301. The article follows directly after Douglas's in the journal.

26. His (in)famous footnote in this Canto reads: "N.B. Usury: A charge for the use of purchasing power, levied without regard to production; often without regard to the possibilities of production. (Hence the failure of the Medici bank)" (230). According to Pound, the culture of usury was pervasive, infecting not just social history, but moreover artistic production and university scholarship. In *Guide to Kulchur*, he writes, "Usury endows no printing press. Usurers do not desire circulation of knowledge" (62).

27. Unrelatedly, but rather telling regarding Pound's as-yet uncertain future, the interview concludes by noting that "Mr. Pound said that he will keep clear of England and devote himself to his study of 12th-century music. . . . He is also writing a long poem, although he says that he realizes that one should not write long poems in the 20th-century" (310).

28. Even though this following letter to Douglas McPherson comes years later, it accurately reflects Pound's growing views about professors in higher education: "What is *needed* is 60 or 80 pages of *selections* of gists of the writings of Adams, Jefferson, VanBuren, Jackson, Johnson. Plus such data as [Willis A.] Overholser [whose *History of Money in the U.S.* is the "*only* American book that *needs* reading"] gives. You can't run volumes of the founders' series in a small mag, but you can demand 'em, and *damn* the lights out of the sons of bitches who aren't getting 'em into print, i.e., all these Hist. Profs" (September 2, 1939; Paige 325).

29. Or overly unclear with little support: "That may sound very vague, but it is nevertheless reducible to mathematical equations and can be scientifically treated" (52). One might pine for Pound's words from *How to Read*: "I cannot repeat too often or too forcibly my caution against so-called critics who talk 'all around the matter,' and who do not define their terms" (53).

30. For a more contemporary explanation of the relationships among super-abundance, individual freedoms, and state government, see the Nobel prize laureate Amartya Sen's *Development as Freedom* (1999).

31. Keynes famously makes his prediction in his 1930 "Economic Possibilities for Our Grandchildren." See Keynes, *Essays in Persuasion* (New York: Norton, 1963), 358–73. While the forecast makes logical sense, it has yet to materialize. Pound, for his part, works more with uncorroborated ideas in principle and little with actual quantitative data. Still, one cannot help but smile at Pound's concession that the individual would be willing "to work four hours a day between the ages of twenty and forty" (29), but might dispute his claim that "[i]t is idiotic to expect members of a civilized twentieth-century community to go on working eight hours a day" (59).

32. In describing the failures of planned economies, Friedrich Hayek (of the "Austrian School") demonstrated how information used by the price system is lost with a planned economy.

33. One of them was Sarah Perkins Cope: "It is like a Murkn college to decide that Eliot is a critic. . . . I have corrected the proofs of my *ABC of Reading*, and that may save you part of yr. Mawrterdom. I mentioned some books in *Instigations*. I wonder what is 'available' and what you have read already. Try Browning's *Sordello*. Are you still young enough to read ole Uncl. Willliam Yeats? . . . I don't know why you shd., at yr. time of life, take up all the ugliness that the generations before you *had* to *write* in order to cure. . . . [Y]our generation has got to understand how much of life can be cured by a very simple application of economic sense to reality" (Letter of April 22, 1934; Paige 257).

34. In the words of Ronald Duncan, "Ezra taught me more in one day than I had learned in a year at Cambridge. . . . And, like many other students at Rapallo, I continued to have, as it were, a post-graduate course by postcard from the Chancellor" (qtd. in Carpenter 525).

35. *Paris Review* 25:89 (Fall 1983); qtd. in Carpenter 528.

36. Nearly every book or article published on Pound today addresses his anti-Semitism. That is only a small price he has to pay, to borrow a word from Surette, for his canonical purgatory. Surette writes, "commentators tend to take one of two extreme positions: that since Pound was an anti-Semite, he and all his works should be shunned, or that his anti-Semitism was an 'aberration' and did not infect his poetry" (239). For an excellent earlier gloss, critiquing the quick dismissals of Pound's politics, see the first half of Andrew Parker, "Ezra Pound and the 'Economy' of Anti-Semitism," *boundary 2* 11, nos. 1–2 (Autumn 1982–Winter 1983), 103–28. (The second half of Parker's article offers a risky deconstructive reading of Pound.)

37. Zukofsky: "I never felt the least trace of anti-Semitism in his presence" (qtd. in O'Connor and Stone 10).

38. As reported (unconfirmed) by Michael Reck, Ginsberg visited Pound in Italy toward the end of Pound's life. Ginsberg: "The more I read your poetry, the more I am convinced it is the best of its time. And your economics are *right*. We see it more and more in Vietnam. You showed us who's making a profit out of war. . . ." Pound replied: "But the worst mistake I made was that stupid, suburban prejudice of anti-Semitism." "It's lovely to hear you say that," Ginsberg replied, adding that "anyone with any sense can see it as a humour . . . Anti-Semitism is your fuck-up . . . but it's part of the model . . . it's a mind like everybody's mind" (qtd. in Carpenter 899).

39. He continues, "Inasmuch as the Jew has conducted no holy war for nearly two millenia, he is preferable to the Christian and the Mahomedan." Pound, "Pastiche," *New Age* 26, no. 2 (November 13, 1919): 32. Pound's "last antithesis" included the following: ". . . the Jew, however, received a sort of roving commission from his 'Jhv' [Jehovah] to bash all and sundry." *New Age*, 26, no. 1 (November 6, 1919): 16.

40. Pound is writing in the January–March 1938 issue of the proto-fascist *British Union Quarterly* (qtd. in Carpenter 552).

41. He continues, "How long the whole Jewish people is to be sacrificial goat for the usurer, I know not" (*Selected Prose* 300n). In *Guide to Kulchur*, Pound writes that "Race prejudice is red herring" (242), and his Canto 52 distinguishes (not so convincingly) between Jews and "big" Jews: "poor yitts paying for Stink-schuld [Rothschild]/ paying for a few big jews' vendetta on goyim" (257). See also his letter to his father of November 1, 1927: "I hate SOME JEWS but I have a greater contempt for Christians. Look wot they dun to America: Bryan, Wilson, Volstead, all goyim. horrible goyim" (*EPtP* 638).

42. Here, Pound is critiquing T. S. Eliot, who "has not come through uncon-taminated by the Jewish poison" ("A Visiting Card" 1942 in *Selected Prose* 320). This is the same Eliot who could describe poetically how "the Jew squats on the window sill, the owner / Spawned in some estaminet of Antwerp" ("Gerontion" in *Selected Poems* 31) or in an essay write: "What is still more important is unity of religious background; and reasons of race and religion combine to make any large

number of free-thinking Jews undesirable" (*After Strange Gods*; qtd. in Christopher Ricks, *T. S. Eliot and Prejudice* [Berkeley: University of California Press, 1988], 41).

43. He wrote to Harriet Monroe, "Damn remnants in you of Jew religion, that bitch Moses and the rest of the tribal barbarians" (Letter of July 16, 1922; Paige 182).

44. Wyndham Lewis's not-so-subtle anti-Semitism and his support of fascist Germany in the early 1930s would fade toward the end of the decade, and he would retract most of his earlier political writings and characterizations.

45. Benjamin Friedlander writes, "The problem, in Pound's view, was not simply ignorance, but 'the crawling slime of a secret rule . . . that eats . . . like a cancer into the heart and soul of all nations.' Responding to that secret rule, Pound's pedagogical project became a form of counter-insurgency" (120; quoting Doob 73).

46. The perversity of the speeches is such that certain listeners—including critical ones from members of academia—even begin to hear ethical gradations in the "less" offensive lecture sections and end up praising Pound, in part, for not being *as* anti-Semitic as others. The Pound of March 21, 1943, says: "DON'T start a pogrom; the problem, the Chewisch problem, is not insoluble. . . . SELL 'em Australia. Don't go out and die in the desert for the sake of high kikery. . . . Don't GIVE 'em a national home. SELL 'em a national home." (Doob 255). Compared with other lectures, this excerpt feels less malicious, but that, in itself, is terrifyingly revealing, especially when the rest of the address is omitted: "The Jews have ruin'd every country they have got hold of. The Jews have worked out a system, very neat system, for the ruin of the rest of mankind, one nation after another. . . ."

47. Compare this sentiment with Pound's earlier claim in *ABC of Reading* that "[i]f the teacher is slow of wit, he may well be terrified by students whose minds move more quickly than his own" (85).

48. See Douglas Mao and Rebecca Walkowitz's "The New Modernist Studies," *PMLA* 123, no. 3 (May 2008): 737–48.

49. For the specifically tangled relationship with Olson, see *Charles Olson and Ezra Pound: An Encounter at St. Elizabeths* [1975], ed. Catherine Seelye (New York: Paragon House, 1991).

50. "The common denominator of them all was devout reverence toward their teacher" (Torrey 230).

51. According to some sources, he would still invoke *The Protocols of the Elders of Zion* "frequently to rationalize his bigotry, and he urged his disciples to read the book" (Torrey 226; see also Tytell 304). In his radio broadcasts, Pound could, without missing a beat, call *Mein Kampf* a book "slandered in England" (Doob 133; May 17, 1942), while naming the *Protocols* an "authentic" forgery. His April 20, 1943, speech offers: "If or when one mentions the Protocols alleged to be of the Elders of Zion, one is frequently met with the reply: Oh, but they are a forgery. Certainly they are a forgery, and that is the one proof we have of their authenticity" (Doob 283). See also his June 4, 1942, speech (Doob 158–61).

52. "Cut off by the layer of glass, the dust and filings rise and spring into order" (Pound, *Guide to Kulchur* 152). The final line, according to Surette, "would seem to mean those who have had some sort of visionary experience. Certainly it can hardly mean those whose memories have been wiped clean when so much of the *Pisan Cantos* is devoted to the sanctity of the remembered" (198). See also Terrell 388 and Cookson, *A Guide* 142 on these lines.

Afterword

1. For more on the method, see Lane Cooper's *Louis Agassiz as a Teacher*.

2. "All teaching of literature," he continues, "should be performed by the presentation and juxtaposition of specimens of writing and NOT by discussion of some other discusser's opinion *about* the general standing of a poet or author" (60). See also Golding, who connects Pound's pedagogic method to his poetic method of parataxis (92).

3. Gail McDonald aptly writes, "Pound's aim is to present education as an experience of navigation by periplus: 'not as land looks on a map / but as sea bord seen by men sailing.' We and Pound are not, as it were, outside the poem observing its shape in overview, but inside it, mapping its shape as we encounter it" (145; internal quotation from Canto 59, 324).

4. Scholes, in this text, is also, of course, coming to terms with the topical writings of Stanley Fish and "interpretive communities." See Fish's *Is There a Text in This Class?* (Cambridge: Harvard University Press, 1980).

5. I thank Rebecca Colesworthy for reminding me of another pedagogical fish-tale, namely the opening foray of David Foster Wallace's commencement speech at Kenyon College in 2005: "There are these two young fish swimming along and they happen to meet an older fish swimming the other way, who nods at them and says, "Morning, boys. How's the water?" And the two young fish swim on for a bit, and then eventually one of them looks over at the other and goes, "What the hell is water?" (3–4). Even though it offers what, in Wallace's words, is a "banal platitude," it still has a "life-or-death importance" (9). "The immediate point of the fish story," he relates, "is merely that the most obvious, ubiquitous, important realities are often the ones that are hardest to see and talk about" (8). And he connects this to liberal arts education in general, which "is not so much about filling you [students] up with knowledge as it is about, quote, 'teaching you how to think,'" or rather "about the choice of what to think about" (12, 14). I wonder why the young fish swim away without asking. Is their medium so different, or are they just so used to an institution that doesn't care to listen to their questions?

6. This question, of course, isn't new, however much it is continually renewed. For a diagnosis at the time, see Thorstein Veblen's *The Higher Learning in America* (New York: B. W. Huebsch, 1918); and for a general history of the debates, see

Gerald Graff's *Professing Literature: an Institutional History* (Chicago: University of Chicago Press, 1989).

7. "Pound's faults are not superficial, and absolutely nothing about our country in this century can be learned from him" (8), writes Bloom. Bloom, ed., *Modern American Poetry* (New York: Chelsea House, 2005), 18.

8. Buurma and Heffernan reject the assumption "that liberal education and vocational education" have historically belonged "to different worlds" ("Elite Colleges"). The different narratives, which are based on differing information (anecdotes from elite colleges versus data sets from vocational schools), "create the impression that students at elite institutions are individual learners connected to disciplines, while everyone else is a victim or vector of financialization in need of training, a bundle of responses to economic conditions." Looking through actual course archives at various colleges throughout the twentieth century, Buurma and Heffernan demonstrate how active liberal education has been in vocational schools. They warn that—given the undue influence of current administrative, political, commercial, and accreditation agency interests—such a history and democratizing curriculum is at risk.

9. Despite his frequent dismissals of higher education, the impact of good teachers on Pound was palpable. "Although Pound returned to the University of Pennsylvania," Charles Norman writes, "Hamilton was infinitely more important in shaping his life. It was there that Professor Shepard revealed to him the splendors of Provençal poetry, whose themes and images he made his own" (10). Norman finds T. S. Eliot's words about Irving Babbitt particularly apt to describe Shepard, who was not "merely a tutor or . . . [lecturer] but a man who directed . . . interests, at a particular moment, in such a way that the marks of that direction are still evident" (10).

10. One of my first classes in graduate school was with Robert Scholes. And he thought it would be a good idea—in the second week of the semester, mind you—to read Gertrude Stein's *Tender Buttons*. When we sat down and opened the text to page 1, he asked what we thought of it. So I answered, going on a ten-minute homily about the instability of the modernist signifier and the inability of literature to engage anymore with the meat of the world. And my teacher waited patiently for me to finish, smiling and nodding the whole time, as if he, too, understood my scholarly virtuosity and naturally agreed with what I had to say. And when I had concluded with my main course, he nodded politely and said, "ok . . . now what do you have to say about page 2?" I owe a lot to that day, and it is a lesson in pescatarianism I'm still digesting. It wasn't that we had to read the modernists on their own terms—simply that we had actually to *read* them. And one would be remiss not to mention here the generosity of Jo Ann Scholes, the dedicatee of our book—also a teacher—who, along with Robert Scholes, gave of her time and energy to afford students an opportunity to make the world their home.

11. He continues, "And pedagogy is rooted in a certain amount of faith in the political process as it has been developed in this country: far from perfect, mind you, and based on assumptions about the ability of people to learn enough

to make their own decisions, which are very idealistic assumptions. I'm still trying to help realize that enterprise by teaching reading and writing on a large scale at the highest possible level. My interpretive methods are based on their teachability more than anything else" (19).

12. See Rodrigo de Castro and Jerrold W. Grossman's "Famous Trails to Paul Erdős."

Works Cited

Adams, Henry. *The Education of Henry Adams: An Autobiography*. Boston: Houghton Mifflin, 1918.

Alexander, Michael. *The Poetic Achievement of Ezra Pound*. Berkeley: University of California Press, 1981.

Ardis, Ann L. *Modernism and Cultural Conflict, 1880–1922*. Cambridge: Cambridge University Press, 2002.

Arnold, Matthew. *Poetry and Prose*. Edited by John Bryson. Cambridge: Harvard University Press, 1956.

Bagwell, J. Timothy. "An Interview with Robert Scholes." *Iowa Journal of Literary Studies* 4 (1983): 13–20.

Barnhisel, Greg. *James Laughlin, New Directions, and the Remaking of Ezra Pound*. Amherst: University of Massachusetts Press, 2005.

Barry, Peter. *Beginning Theory: An Introduction to Literary and Cultural Theory*. Manchester: Manchester University Press, 2009.

Beasley, Rebecca. "Pound's New Criticism." *Textual Practice* 24, no. 4 (2010): 649–68.

Bernstein, Charles. *A Poetics*. Cambridge: Harvard University Press, 1992.

Birien, Anne. "Pound and the Reform of Philology." In *Ezra Pound and Education*, edited by Steven G. Yao and Michael Coyle, 23–45. Orono, Maine: National Poetry Foundation, 2012.

Bloom, Harold, ed. *Modern American Poetry*. New York: Chelsea House, 2005.

Boyd, E. L. "Ezra Pound at Wabash College." *Journal of Modern Literature* 4, no. 1 (September 1974): 43–54.

Brooke-Rose, Christine. *A ZBC of Ezra Pound*. Berkeley: University of California Press, 1971.

Brooks, Cleanth. *The Well Wrought Urn: Studies in the Structure of Poetry*. 1942. Reprint, San Diego: Harcourt Brace & Company, 1975.

Buurma, Rachel [Sagner], and Laura Heffernan. "The Classroom in the Canon: T. S. Eliot's Modern English Literature Extension Course for Working People and *The Sacred Wood*." *PMLA* 133, no. 2 (2018): 264–81.

———. "The Common Reader and the Archival Classroom: Disciplinary History for the Twenty-First Century." *New Literary History* 43, no. 1 (Winter 2012): 113–35.

———. "Elite Colleges Have No Monopoly on the Liberal Arts." *The Chronicle of Higher Education.* July 15, 2018.

Bush, Ronald. "Pisa." In *Ezra Pound in Context*, edited by Ira B. Nadel, 261–73. Cambridge: Cambridge University Press, 2010.

———. "'Quiet, Not Scornful?': The Composition of the *Pisan Cantos.*" In *A Poem Containing History: Textual Studies in* The Cantos, edited by Lawrence Rainey, 169–211. Ann Arbor: University of Michigan Press, 1996.

Carpenter, Humphrey. *A Serious Character: The Life of Ezra Pound.* Boston: Houghton Mifflin Company, 1988.

Churchill, Suzanne W., and Adam McKible, eds. *Little Magazines and Modernism: New Approaches.* Aldershot: Ashgate, 2007.

Coleman, Martin. "'It Doesn't . . . Matter Where You Begin': Pound and Santayana on Education." *Journal of Aesthetic Education* 44, no. 4 (Winter 2010): 1–17.

Cookson, William, ed. *Ezra Pound: Selected Prose 1909–1965.* New York: New Directions, 1973.

———. *A Guide to the Cantos of Ezra Pound.* New York: Anvil Press, 1985.

Cooper, Lane. *Louis Agassiz as a Teacher.* Ithaca, NY: Comstock Publishing Co., 1917.

Cornell, Julien. *The Trial of Ezra Pound.* London: Faber and Faber, 1967.

Davis, Earle. *Vision Fugitive: Ezra Pound and Economics.* Lawrence: University Press of Kansas, 1968.

De Castro, Rodrigo, and Jerrold W. Grossman. "Famous Trails to Paul Erdős." *The Mathematical Intelligencer* 21, no. 3 (September 1999): 51–63.

de Rachewiltz, Mary. *Discretions.* 1971. New York: New Directions, 2005.

de Rachewiltz, Mary, A. David Moody, and Joanna Moody, eds. *Ezra Pound to His Parents: Letters 1895–1929.* Oxford: Oxford University Press, 2010.

Doob, Leonard W., ed. *"Ezra Pound Speaking."* Westport: Greenwood Press, 1978.

Duncan, Ronald. *All Men Are Islands.* London: Rupert Hart-David, 1964.

Eliot, T. S. "Introduction." In *Literary Essays of Ezra Pound*, edited and introduction by T. S. Eliot, ix–xv. New York: New Directions, 1968.

———. *Selected Poems.* San Diego: Harcourt Brace, 1962.

———. *The Selected Prose of T. S. Eliot.* Edited by Frank Kermode. New York: Harcourt Brace Jovanovich, 1975.

Fiedler, Leslie. "Traitor or Laureate: The Two Trials of the Poet." In *New Approaches to Ezra Pound*, edited by Eva Hesse, 365–77. London: Faber and Faber, 1970.

Friedlander, Benjamin. "Radio Broadcasts." In *Ezra Pound in Context*, edited by Ira B. Nadel, 115–24. Cambridge: Cambridge University Press, 2010.

Gallup, Donald. *Ezra Pound: A Bibliography.* Charlottesville: University Press of Virginia, 1983.

Golding, Alan. "From Pound to Olson: The Avant-Garde Poet as Pedagogue." *Journal of Modern Literature* 34, no. 1 (Fall 2010): 86–106.

Goodwin, K. L. *The Influence of Ezra Pound*. London: Oxford University Press, 1966.

Gordon, David M., ed. *Ezra Pound and James Laughlin: Selected Letters*. New York: Norton, 1994.

Hale, William Gardner. "Pegasus Impounded." *Poetry* 14, no. 1 (April 1919): 52–55.

Hofer, Matthew. "Education." In *Ezra Pound in Context*, edited by Ira B. Nadel, 75–84. Cambridge: Cambridge University Press, 2010.

Hoffman, Frederick J., Charles Allen, and Carolyn F. Ulrich. *The Little Magazine: A History and a Bibliography*. Princeton: Princeton University Press, 1947.

Houen, Alex. "Anti-Semitism." In *Ezra Pound in Context*, edited by Ira B. Nadel, 391–401. Cambridge: Cambridge University Press, 2010.

Hungiville, Maurice. "Ezra Pound, Educator: Two Uncollected Pound Letters." *American Literature* 44, no. 3 (November 1972): 462–69.

Kenner, Hugh. *The Pound Era*. Berkeley: University of California Press, 1971.

Kindellan, Michael, and Joshua Kotin. "*The Cantos* and Pedagogy." *Modernist Cultures* 12, no. 3 (2017): 345–63.

Lan, Feng. "Confucius." In *Ezra Pound in Context*, edited by Ira B. Nadel, 324–34. Cambridge: Cambridge University Press, 2010.

———. *Ezra Pound and Confucianism: Remaking Humanism in the Face of Modernity*. Toronto: University of Toronto Press, 2005.

Latham, Sean, and Robert Scholes. "The Rise of Periodical Studies." *PMLA* 121, no. 2 (March 2005): 517–31.

Laughlin, James. *Pound as Wuz: Essays and Lectures on Ezra Pound*. St. Paul, MN: Graywolf, 1987.

Liebregts, Peter. "The Classics." In *Ezra Pound in Context*, edited by Ira B. Nadel, 171–80. Cambridge: Cambridge University Press, 2010.

Lindberg-Seyersted, Brita, ed. *Pound / Ford: The Story of a Literary Friendship*. New York: New Directions, 1982.

Longenbach, James. "Ezra Pound at Home." *Southwest Review* 94, no. 2 (2009): 147–59.

MacNiven, Ian S. *"Literchoor Is My Beat": A Life of James Laughlin, Publisher of New Directions*. New York: Macmillan, 2014.

Marsh, Alec. " 'Ezratic "Reeducation" ': Pound and the Solons." In *Ezra Pound and Education*, edited by Steven G. Yao and Michael Coyle, 121–34. Orono, Maine: National Poetry Foundation, 2012.

———. "Politics." In *Ezra Pound in Context*, edited by Ira B. Nadel, 96–105. Cambridge: Cambridge University Press, 2010.

Marek, Jayne. *Women Editing Modernism: "Little" Magazines & Literary History*. Lexington, KY: University Press of Kentucky, 1995.

Materer, Timothy, ed. *Pound/Lewis*. New York: New Directions, 1985.

McDonald, Gail. *Learning to Be Modern: Pound, Eliot and the American University*. Oxford: Clarendon Press, 1993.

Miller, Andrew John. "Dreaming the Super-College: Ezra Pound, Lionel Trilling, and the Arnoldian Ideal." In *Ezra Pound and Education*, edited by Steven G. Yao and Michael Coyle, 67–93. Orono, Maine: National Poetry Foundation, 2012.

Monk, Craig. "Little Magazines." In *Ezra Pound in Context*, edited by Ira B. Nadel, 345–55. Cambridge: Cambridge University Press, 2010.

Monroe, Harriet. *A Poet's Life: Seventy Years in a Changing World*. New York: Macmillan, 1938.

Moody, A. David. *Ezra Pound: Poet, a Portrait of the Man and His Work*. *Volumes I–III*. Oxford: Oxford University Press, 2007, 2014, 2015.

Moore, Marianne. "Teach, Stir the Mind, Afford Enjoyment." 1955. In *Ezra Pound: A Collection of Criticism*, edited by Grace Schulman, 39–44. New York: McGraw-Hill, 1974.

Nadel, Ira B., ed. *The Cambridge Companion to Ezra Pound*. Cambridge: Cambridge University Press, 1999.

———, ed. *Ezra Pound in Context*. Cambridge: Cambridge University Press, 2010.

———, ed. *The Letters of Ezra Pound to Alice Corbin Henderson*. Austin: University of Texas Press, 1993.

Nichols, John G. "Editor, Anthologist." In *Ezra Pound in Context*, edited by Ira B. Nadel, 65–74. Cambridge: Cambridge University Press, 2010.

Nicholls, Peter. " 'You in the Dinghy Astern There': Learning From Ezra Pound." In *Ezra Pound and Education*, edited by Steven G. Yao and Michael Coyle, 137–61. Orono, Maine: National Poetry Foundation, 2012.

Norman, Charles. *Ezra Pound*. Rev. ed. New York: Funk & Wagnalls, 1969.

O'Connor, William Van, and Edward Stone, eds. *A Casebook of Ezra Pound*. New York: Thomas Y. Crowell, 1959.

Olson, Charles. *Charles Olson and Ezra Pound: An Encounter at St. Elizabeths*. 1975. Reprint, edited by Catherine Seelye. New York: Paragon House, 1991.

Orage, A. R. "Journals Insurgent." *New Age* 13, no. 15 (August 7, 1913): 414–15.

Paige, D. D. *The Letters of Ezra Pound 1907–1941*. New York: Harcourt, 1950.

Parker, Andrew. "Ezra Pound and the 'Economy' of Anti-Semitism." *boundary 2* 11, nos. 1–2 (Autumn 1982–Winter 1983): 103–28.

Pound, Ezra. *ABC of Reading*. Norfolk, CT: New Directions, 1934.

———. *ABC of Economics*. Tunbridge Wells, UK: Peter Russell, 1933.

———. "America: Chances and Remedies." *The New Age* 13, no. 4 (May 22, 1913): 83.

———. *The Cantos of Ezra Pound*. New York: New Directions, 1998.

———. "Data." *The Exile* 4 (Autumn 1928): 104–17.

———. *How to Read*. London: Desmond Harmsworth, 1931.

———. *I Gather the Limbs of Osiris*. *The New Age* 10, nos. 5–16 (November 1911–February 1912).

———. *Impact: Essays on Ignorance and the Decline of American Civilization*. Edited and introduction by Noel Stock. Chicago: Henry Regnery, 1960.

———. "In a Station of the Metro." *Poetry* 2, no. 1 (April 1913): 12.

———. *Instigations*. New York: Boni and Liveright, 1920.

———. *Jefferson and/or Mussolini: L'idea Statale Fascism as I Have Seen It*. 1935. Reprint, New York: Liveright, 1970.

———. *Literary Essays of Ezra Pound*. Edited and introduction by T. S. Eliot. New York: New Directions, 1968.

———. *Make It New*. New Haven: Yale University Press, 1935.

———. "Murkn Magzeens." *New English Weekly* 5, no. 10 (June 21, 1934): 235–36.

———. "Patria Mia." *The New Age* 11, no. 25 (October 17, 1912): 587–88.

———. *Pavannes and Divisions*. New York: Alfred A. Knopf, 1918.

———. "Raphaelite Latin." *Book News Monthly* 25, no. 1 (September 1906): 31–34.

———. "The Renaissance" [III]. *Poetry* 5, no. 5 (May 1915): 84–91.

———. "The Revolt of Intelligence" [IX]. *New Age* 26, no. 19 (March 1920): 301–2.

———. *Selected Prose 1909–1965*. Edited and introduction by W. Cookson. London: Faber & Faber, 1973.

———. "Small Magazines." *The English Journal* 19, no. 9 (November 1930): 689–704.

———. *The Spirit of Romance*. London: J. M. Dent, 1910.

———. *The Spirit of Romance*. New York: New Directions, 1968.

———. "Studies in Contemporary Mentality." *The New Age* 21, no. 16–22, no. 11 (August 1917–January 1918).

———. "The Teacher's Mission." *Literary Essays of Ezra Pound*. Edited and introduction by T. S. Eliot, 58–63. New York: New Directions, 1968; originally published in the *English Journal* in 1934.

———. "Vortex." *Blast* 1. 1914. Reprint, Santa Rosa: Black Sparrow Press, 1997.

Pound, Ezra, trans. *Confucius: The Great Digest, the Unwobbling Pivot, the Analects*. New York: New Directions, 1969.

Pound, Ezra, and Marcella Spann, eds. *Confucius to Cummings*. New York: New Directions, 1963.

Pound, Omar, and Robert Spoo, eds. *Ezra and Dorothy Pound: Letters in Captivity 1945–1946*. Oxford: Oxford University Press, 1999.

Putnam, Samuel. *Paris Was Our Mistress: Memoirs of a Lost and Found Generation*. New York: Viking Press, 1947.

Qian, Zhaoming. *Ezra Pound's Chinese Friends: Stories in Letters*. Oxford: Oxford University Press, 2008.

Rabaté, Jean-Michel. *Language, Sexuality, and Ideology in Ezra Pound's Cantos*. Albany: State University of New York Press, 1986.

Read, Forrest, ed. *Pound/Joyce*. New York: New Directions, 1967.

Redman, Tim. *Ezra Pound and Italian Fascism*. Cambridge: Cambridge University Press, 1991.

Reid, B. L. *The Man from New York: John Quinn and his Friends*. Oxford: Oxford University Press, 1968.

Robbins, J. A., ed. *EP to LU: Nine Letters Written to Louis Untermeyer by Ezra Pound*. Bloomington: Indiana University Press, 1963.

Ruthven, K. K. *Ezra Pound as Literary Critic*. London: Routledge, 1990.

Sandburg, Carl. "Chicago." *Poetry* 3, no. 6 (March 1914): 191–92.

———. "The Work of Ezra Pound." *Poetry* 7, no. 5 (February 1916): 249–57.

Scholes, Robert. *Textual Power: Literary Theory and the Teaching of English*. New Haven: Yale University Press, 1985.

Scott, Thomas L., and Melvin J. Friedman, eds. *Pound / The Little Review: The Letters of Ezra Pound to Margaret Anderson:* The Little Review *Correspondence*. New York: New Directions, 1988.

Sicari, Stephen. *Joyce's Modernist Allegory:* Ulysses *and the History of the Novel*. Columbia: University of South Carolina Press, 2001.

Sieburth, Richard, ed. *The Pisan Cantos*. New York: New Directions, 2003.

Singh, G. *Ezra Pound as Critic*. New York: St. Martin's Press, 1994.

Smith, J. Mark. "The Energy of Language(s): What Pound Made of Philology." *ELH* 78, no. 4 (Winter 2011): 769–800.

Spoo, Robert. "Introduction." *Ezra and Dorothy Pound: Letters in Captivity 1945–1946*, edited by Omar Pound and Robert Spoo, 1–36. Oxford: Oxford University Press, 1999.

Stasi, Paul, and Josephine Park, eds. *Ezra Pound in the Present*. New York: Bloomsbury, 2016.

Stock, Noel. *The Life of Ezra Pound*. New York: Avon Books, 1970.

Stoicheff, Peter. *The Hall of Mirrors:* Drafts & Fragments *and the End of Ezra Pound's* Cantos. Ann Arbor: University of Michigan Press, 1995.

Surette, Leon. "Economics." In *Ezra Pound in Context*, edited by Ira B. Nadel, 106–14. Cambridge: Cambridge University Press, 2010.

———. *A Light from Eleusis: A Study of Ezra Pound's* Cantos. Oxford: Clarendon Press, 1979.

———. *Pound in Purgatory: From Economic Radicalism to Anti-Semitism*. Urbana: University of Illinois Press, 1999.

———. "Pound, Postmodernism, and Fascism." *University of Toronto Quarterly* 59, no. 2 (Winter 1989–90): 334–355.

Swift, Daniel. *The Bughouse: The Poetry, Politics, and Madness of Ezra Pound*. New York: Farrar, Straus and Giroux, 2017.

Terrell, Carroll F. *A Companion to* The Cantos *of Ezra Pound*. Berkeley: University of California Press, 1993.

Torrey, E. Fuller. *The Roots of Treason: Ezra Pound and the Secret of St. Elizabeths*. San Diego: Harcourt Brace Jovanovich, 1984.

Tryphonopoulos, Demetres P. "Ezra Pound's Occult Education." *Journal of Modern Literature* 17, no. 1 (Summer 1990): 73–96.

———. "Letters." In *Ezra Pound in Context*, edited by Ira B. Nadel, 54–64. Cambridge: Cambridge University Press, 2010.

Tytell, John. *Ezra Pound: The Solitary Volcano*. New York: Doubleday, 1987.

Wallace, David Foster. *This Is Water: Some Thoughts, Delivered on a Significant Occasion, about Living a Compassionate Life*. New York: Little, Brown and Company, 2009.

Wallace, Emily Mitchell. "America." In *Ezra Pound in Context*, edited by Ira B. Nadel, 202–20. Cambridge: Cambridge University Press, 2010.

Watt, Harold K. *Ezra Pound and the Cantos*. London: Routledge and Kegan Paul, 1951.

Welch, Milton L. " 'Till Was Hung Yesterday': Louis Till as Lynching Topos in *The Pisan Cantos*." In *Ezra Pound and Education*, edited by Steven G. Yao and Michael Coyle, 163–82. Orono, Maine: National Poetry Foundation, 2012.

Wilhelm, J. J. *The American Roots of Ezra Pound*. New York: Garland, 1985.

Witemeyer, Hugh. "Early Poetry 1908–1920." In *The Cambridge Companion to Ezra Pound*, edited by Ira B. Nadel, 43–58. Cambridge: Cambridge University Press, 1999.

Woolf, Virginia. *The Letters of Virginia Woolf*, vol. II: 1912–1922. Edited by Nigel Nicolson and Joanne Trautmann. New York: Harcourt Brace Jovanovich.

———. *Mr. Bennett and Mrs. Brown*. London: The Hogarth Press, 1924.

Wordsworth, William. *The Major Works*. Edited and introduction by Stephen Gill. Oxford: Oxford University Press, 1984.

Yao, Steven G. *Translation and the Languages of Modernism: Gender, Politics, Language*. New York: Palgrave Macmillan, 2002.

Yao, Steven G., and Michael Coyle, eds. *Ezra Pound and Education*. Orono, Maine: National Poetry Foundation, 2012.

Zinnes, Harriet, ed. *Ezra Pound and the Visual Arts*. New York: New Directions, 1980.

Index

Achebe, Chinua, 142
Adams, Henry, 115, 122–123, 174n19
Adams, John, 118, 175n28
Adams, John Quincy, 119
Adler, Mortimer J., 167n26
Adorno, Theodor, 110
Adorno, Theodor and Max
    Horkheimer, 171n21
Aeschylus, 75
Agassiz, Louis, xv, 76, 137, 139, 146,
    149n3, 168n38, 178n1
Aiken, Conrad, 123, 133
Aldington, Richard, xv, 62, 97, 99
Alexander, Michael, 120
Alighieri, Dante, 16, 36–37, 40–42,
    47, 50, 52, 59, 79, 84, 118, 120,
    159n5, 159–160nn9–10, 160n12
Allen, Charles. See Hoffman, Frederick
    J., Charles Allen, and Carolyn F.
    Ulrich
Althusser, Louis, 78, 167n28
Altieri, Charles, 155n18
Alvarez, Al, 133
America: Chances and Remedies. See
    Pound, Ezra: America: Chances
    and Remedies
Anderson, Margaret, 92, 97
Answers, 101
Apuleius, 36
Ardis, Ann L., 169n6

Aristotle, 142
Arnold, Matthew, 34–35, 43, 59,
    158–159nn3–4, 163n26
Atheling, William [Pound pseudonym],
    60, 91
The Athenaeum, 92–93
The Atlantic, 110
Ávila, Saint Teresa de, 84
Aucassin and Nicolette, 40
Auden, W. H., 123

Babbitt, Irving, 153n6, 179n9
Bacon, Kevin, 145
"Ballad of the Goodly Fere." See
    Pound, Ezra: "Ballad of the
    Goodly Fere"
Barker, Wharton, 32, 158n22
Barnard, Mary, 154n13
Barnhisel, Greg, 127
Barry, Iris, 154n13, 162n23
Barry, Peter, 11
Barthes, Roland, 137
Baudelaire, Charles, 96
Beasley, Rebecca, 156n2
Belloc, Hilaire, 23, 159n8, 170n13
Bergson, Henri, 22, 60
Bernstein, Charles, 172n4
The Bibelot, 90
Binyon, Lawrence, 21
Birien, Anne, 156n4

Bishop, Elizabeth, 127, 133
Blackwood's, 93
Blake, William, xii
Blasing, Mutlu, 161n16
Blast, 92, 95–96, 111, 170nn12–13
Bloom, Harold, 1, 77, 141, 152n1,
     167n26, 168n1, 179n7
Blum, W. C. *See* Watson Jr., James
     Sibley
Bogan, Louise, 123
Book of Genesis, 150, 166n22
The Bookman, 101–102
Book News Monthly, 17, 91
Born, Bertran de, 59
Boyd, E. L., 157n14
Bradbury, Malcolm, 133
Brandt, Herman, 14
Breen, Stella. *See* Seymour, George, S.
The British Weekly, 101
Bronner, Milton, 96
Brooke-Rose, Christine, 1, 128, 152n1,
     153n5
Brooks, Cleanth, 152n8, 164n9
Brooks, Van Wyck, 146–147
Browning, Robert, 40, 42, 75,
     175n33
Bryan, William Jennings, 176n41
Buinicelli, Guido, 40
Bunting, Basil, 84, 121
Burne-Jones, Edward, 42
Bush, Ronald, 120, 173n12
Busoni, Ferruccio, 54
Buurma, Rachel Sagner and Laura
     Heffernan, 142, 151–152n8,
     179n8
Byington, Steven, 96

Caesar, Julius, xiv
Cairns, Huntington, 133
Camoens, Luís de, 43, 160n13
The Cantos. *See* Pound, Ezra: *The
     Cantos*

Canzoni. *See* Pound, Ezra: *Canzoni*
Carpenter, Humphrey, 5, 9, 15,
     17–18, 115, 123–125, 134,
     152n3, 155n1, 156nn9–10,
     157n12, 161n15, 164n7,
     169n5, 171–172nn1–3, 174n23,
     175nn34–35, 176n38, 176n40
Carruth, Hayden, 173n10
Castro, Rodrigo de and Jerrold W.
     Grossman, 147, 180n12
Cathay. *See* Pound, Ezra: *Cathay*
Catholic Anthology, 94
Catullus, Gaius Valerius, 17
Cavalcanti, Guido, 40, 47–49, 84
Central High School [Philadelphia],
     17
Century Illustrated, 110
Cézanne, Paul, 164n11
Chambers' Journal, 101
Chambers, Robert W., 107
Chanson de Roland, 38, 159n8
Chapin, Katherine Garrison 123
Chaucer, Geoffrey, 52, 65, 151n4
Cheltenham Military Academy, 17
Chester, Carlos Tracy, 13
Chopin, Frederic, 54
The Christian Herald, 101
Churchill, Suzanne W. and Adam
     McKible, 169n2
Churchill, Winston, 118, 130
Church Review, 101
The Church Times, 101
Le Cid. *See* Corneille, Pierre
Coleman, Martin, 122
Colesworthy, Rebecca, 178n5
College English, 110
Comley, Nancy R., 146
Condé Nast, 111
Confucius / Confucianism, 80, 82–83,
     118–119, 167–168nn34–37
Confucius to Cummings. *See* Pound,
     Ezra: *Confucius to Cummings*

Cookson, William, 128, 160n14, 178n52
Cooper, Lane, xv, 149n3, 178n1
Cope, Sarah Perkins, 175n33
Corbière, Tristan, 68, 80, 164nn10–11, 165n13
Corelli, Marie. *See* Mackay, Mary
Corneille, Pierre, 14, 38–40, 44, 159n8
Cornell, Julien, 172n3
Cosmopolitan, 91
Coyle, Michael. *See* Yao, Steven G. and Michael Coyle
Crabbe, George, 151n4
The Criterion, 111, 167n30
Cromwell, Oliver, 79
Cummings, E. E., 84, 121, 127, 133

Damrosch, David, 167n29
Daniel, Arnaut, 36–37, 49–53, 57–59, 159n6, 161–162n21, 163n27, 166n23
Dante. *See* Alighieri, Dante
Davis, Earle, 173n9
Debussy, Claude, 61
Defoe, Daniel, xii
della Gherardesca, Ugolino, 120
Dembo, L. S., 82, 168n36
Dennis, Helen M., 159n7
de Rachewiltz, Mary. *See* Rachewiltz, Mary de
Descartes, René, 14
Dewey, John, 152n10, 153n6
The Dial, 4, 67, 74, 92, 98, 111, 154n10
Dias, B. H. [Pound pseudonym], 60, 91, 112–113
Dickens, Charles, 150n4
Dickey, James, 133
Dickinson, Emily, 95
Dolmetsch, Arnold, 63
Donne, John, 151n4

Doob, Leonard W., 1. *See also* Pound, Ezra: *Ezra Pound Speaking*
Doolittle, Hilda. *See* H.D.
Douglas, [Major] C. H., xv, 116, 123–125, 128–129, 174n24, 174n25
Douglas, Gavin, 150–151n4
Doyle, Sir Arthur Conan, 108–109, 171n19
Duncan, Robert, 126
Duncan, Ronald, 175n34
DuPlessis, Rachel Blau, 159n7

Edinburgh Review, 101
The Egoist, 25–29, 65, 91–92, 96–97, 130–131, 158n19, 164n8, 166n21
Eisenhower, Dwight D., 118
L'Elan Littéraire. See [*La*] *Wallonie*
Eliot, Charles William, 19
Eliot, George, 142, 150n4
Eliot, T. S., xii, xv, 1, 13, 25, 36, 47, 63, 73–74, 84, 88–89, 94, 96, 98, 111, 118, 122–123, 133, 151–152n8, 153n4, 153n6, 159n5, 161n19, 164n7, 168n1, 172–173n8, 175n33, 176–177n42, 179n9
Emerson, Ralph Waldo, 15
English Journal, xi, 100, 110, 162n24
The English Review, 22, 92–93, 101, 111
Erdős, Paul, 145
Everybody's Magazine, 91
The Exile, 92, 98, 100, 160n9
Ezra Pound: Poet, a Portrait of the Man and His Work. See Moody, A. David
"Ezuversity," xii, 126–127, 133, 175n34

The Family Herald, 101, 106

Fang, Achilles, 82, 173n16
Fauré, Gabriel, 61
Fenollosa, Ernest, 69–70, 74, 75–77,
    82, 166–167n24
Fiedler, Leslie, 172n3
Fish, Stanley, 178n4
Fitch, Edward, 16
Fitzgerald, Edward, 64, 151n4
Flaubert, Gustave, 71, 88–89, 96
Fletcher, John Gould, 96
Flint, F. S., 22, 46, 163n2
Ford, Ford Madox. *See* Hueffer, Ford
    Madox
Forget-Me-Not, 101, 109
Forster, E. M., 164n8
France, Marie de, 159n8
Freeman, Edward, 11
The Freewoman, xii, 20. See also *The
    New Freewoman*
Freire, Paulo, 152n10
Freud, Sigmund, 3
Friedlander, Benjamin, 177n45
Friedman, Melvin J. *See* Scott, Thomas
    L. and Melvin J. Friedman
Frobenius, Leo, 4
Frost, Robert, xv, 95
Fry, Roger, 164n7

Gaipa, Mark, 146
Gallop, Jane, 152n10
Gallup, Donald, 90–91
Galsworthy, John, 107
Gates, Bill, 143
Gaudier-Brzeska, Henri, xv, 28, 73,
    164n7
Gauthier, Théophile, 68, 164n10
Gesell, Silvio, 128
Gilbert, Stuart, 134
Ginsberg, Allen, 128, 176n38
Giroux, Henry, 152n10
Goethe, Johann Wolfgang von,
    131–132

Golding, Alan, 153n5, 155n17,
    155n18, 167n26, 178n2
Golding, Arthur, 64–65, 150–151n4
Goodwin, K. L., 155n14
Gourmont, Remy de, 62–63, 68,
    72–73, 111, 165nn12–13,
    165–166nn18–19
Graff, Gerald, 179n6
Grant, Ulysses S., 110
Green, Geoffrey, 151n5
Grossman, Jerrold W. *See* de Castro,
    Rodrigo and Jerrold W. Grossman
Guare, John, 145
Guggenheim, John Simon, 137–138
Guide to Kulchur. See Pound, Ezra:
    Guide to Kulchur

Hale, William Gardner, 162n24
Hamilton, David, 146
Hardy, Thomas, 40, 72
Harford, Tim, 174n24
Harper's, 87, 110
Hastings, Beatrice, 93, 161n15, 163n27
Hawthorne, Nathaniel, 150n4
Hayek, Friedrich, 175n32
H.D. [Hilda Doolittle], xv, 62, 84, 95
Heap, Jane, 97–98
Hearst, William Randolph, 74
Heffernan, Laura. *See* Buurma, Rachel
    Sagner and Laura Heffernan
Hegel, Georg Wilhelm Friedrich,
    168n36
Hemingway, Ernest, 99
Henderson, Alice Corbin, 94, 162n22,
    163n2, 169n8
Herrick, Robert, 151n4
Hirsch, E. D., 80, 167n32
Hofer, Matthew, 153n5
Hoffman, Daniel, 153n5
Hoffman, Frederick J., Charles Allen,
    and Carolyn F. Ulrich, 93, 111,
    169n7

Holmes, Sherlock. *See* Doyle, Sir
  Arthur Conan
Homer, 52, 75, 79
hooks, bell, 152n10
Horkheimer, Max. *See* Adorno,
  Theodor and Max Horkheimer
Houen, Alex, 134
Hound and Horn, 113
Hueffer, Ford Madox, 22–23, 92–93,
  95–96, 111, 121, 163n4
Hugo, Victor, 127
Hulme, T. E., 22, 46, 95
Hume, David, 161n20
Huneker, James, 96
Hunt, Violet Hunt, 22–23, 96

Ibbotson, Joseph Darlington [Bib],
  14–16, 45
ideogram 58, 81, 83, 119–120, 129,
  153n5, 166–167n24, 168n37,
  173nn15–16, 174n19, *passim*. *See
  also* Fenollosa
I Gather the Limbs of Osiris. *See*
  Pound, Ezra: *I Gather the Limbs
  of Osiris*
Imagism / *Imagisme*, 22, 46, 61–62,
  77, 81, 95, 138–139, 163n2
"In a station of the metro." *See* Pound,
  Ezra: "In a station of the metro"
Instigations. *See* Pound, Ezra:
  Instigations

Jackson, Andrew, 175n28
James, Henry, 67, 70–72, 165nn15–17
Jefferson and/or Mussolini. *See* Pound,
  Ezra: *Jefferson and/or Mussolini*
Jefferson, Thomas, 119, 175n28
Jepson, Edgar, 121
Jonson, Ben, 135, 151n4
Joyce, James, xii, xv, 13, 22, 63,
  72–74, 88–89, 92, 95–98, 121,
  134, 146, 156n8, 166nn20–21

Kain, Richard, 146
Kasper, John, 134
Keats, John, 73
Kellogg, Robert L., 146
Kenner, Hugh, 1–2, 87, 128, 133–
  135, 152n1, 153n5, 161n17,
  168n1, 172n3
Ker, W. P., 37
Keynes, John Maynard, 124, 126,
  174n24, 175n31
Kindellan, Michael and Joshua Kotin,
  155n18
King James Bible, 150n4
Kitasono, Katue, 173n15
Klaus, Carl H., xv, 146
Kotin, Joshua. *See* Kindellan, Michael
  and Joshua Kotin

Ladies' Home Journal, 74
Laforgue, Jules, 68, 164nn10–11,
  165nn13–14, 166n22
Lan, Feng, 76, 82, 167–168n34
Lang, Andrew, 39
Latham, Sean, 146, 151n5, 169n2,
  170n17
Laughlin, James, xii–xiii, 5, 9, 83,
  126–128, 153n9, 155n16
Lawrence, D. H., xv
Leacock, Stephen, 107
Leavis, F. R., 78
Leavis, Q. D., 78
Le Guin, Ursula K., 147
Lewis, Wyndham, xv, 22, 28, 69,
  72–73, 84, 88–89, 92, 95–96,
  100, 102, 164n7, 166n21, 168n1,
  177n44
Liebregts, Peter, 156–157n11
The Life of Ezra Pound. *See* Stock,
  Noel
Lincoln, Abraham, 103
Lindberg-Seyersted, Brita, 158n18
Li Po, 84

The Little Review, 22, 68, 70, 72–73, 91–93, 97–99, 111, 165n14, 167n25, 170n15
Longenbach, James, 157n15
Longfellow, Henry Wadsworth, 160n13
Lowell, Amy, 68–69
Lowell, Robert, 123, 133
Loy, Mina, 73
"luminous detail," xx, 5–7, 33, 46–50, 57–59, 78, 121, 153n5, 161n17

Mackail, John William, 36
Mackay, Mary [Marie Corelli], 107
Mackintosh, George Lewes, 18
MacLeish, Archibald, 133, 167n27, 172n5
MacNiven, Ian, 126–127
Malatesta, Sigismondo, 97
Mani [Manes], 117
Manning, Frederic, 166n21
Marek, Jayne, 169n2
Marlowe, Christopher, 40, 160n12
Marsden, Dora, xii, 20, 25, 65, 92, 96–97, 164n8
Marsh, Alec, 128
Martial [Marcus Valerius Martialis], 17
Marx, Karl, 3
Matthews, Charles Elkin, 21
McAlmon, Robert, 99
McClure's, 91–92
McDonald, Gail, 2, 153n6, 155n17, 171n24, 178n3
McKible, Adam. *See* Churchill, Suzanne W. and Adam McKible
McLaren, Peter, 152n10
McLuhan, Marshall, 133
McPherson, Douglas, 175n28
"Melopoeia, Phanopoeia, and Logopoeia," 79, 149n3
Melville, Herman, 150n4
Mencius, 82
Mencken, H. L., 92, 133

Mercure de France, 111, 166n19, 170n13
Meredith, George, 164n8
Meyers, Jeffrey, 154n13
Miller, Andrew John, 158n3
Miller, Henry, 127
Miller, Vincent, 84, 168n39
Milton, John, 42, 64–65, 79, 149–150n4
Modernist Journals Project, xviii
Monroe, Harriet, 61, 87, 92, 94–95, 97–98, 110, 113, 122, 162n22, 162n24, 169n4, 169nn8–9, 171n25, 177n43
Moody, A. David, xi, 9, 13–15, 17–18, 82–84, 90, 93, 96, 115–116, 123, 125, 135, 156n1, 156n3, 156n10, 157n15, 169n4, 174n19, 174n23. *See also* Pound, Ezra: *Ezra Pound to His Parents: Letters 1895–1929*
Moody, Joanna, xi. *See also* Pound, Ezra: *Ezra Pound to His Parents: Letters 1895–1929*
Moore, Marianne, 73, 84, 127, 133, 156n6
Morris, Gouverneur, 107
Mozart, Wolfgang Amadeus, 54
Mullins, Eustace, 134
Munsey's, 90–91
"Murkn Magzeens." *See* Pound, Ezra: "Murkn Magzeens"
Murry, J. Middleton, 92
Mussolini, Benito, 63, 82, 116–120, 128, 172n5, 173n9

Nadel, Ira B., 1, 152n2, 156n1
Nash's Magazine, 101, 107–108
National Council of Teachers of English, xi, 110
The New Age, xv, 3, 6, 22, 24–25, 29–31, 37, 44–60, 89, 91–93, 100–110, 113, 123–124, 160n14,

161n15, 161–162n21, 163n27,
167n27, 169nn5–6, 170n18,
171n20, 174n25, 176n39
"The New Criticism," 13, 16, 41, 44,
50, 164n9, 168n1
New Democracy, 113
New Directions Press, xii–xiii, 5, 127
New English Weekly, 100, 112
The New Freewoman, 65, 92, 96–97
The New Review, 20, 92, 99
Nicholls, Peter, 153n5, 172n6
Nichols, John G., 83
Nietzsche, Friedrich, 96, 105–106
Norman, Charles, 179n9
Norton, Charles Eliot Norton, 19

O'Connor, William Van and Edward
Stone, 171–172nn2–3
Old Moore's Almanac, 101
Olson, Charles, 133, 177n49
Orage, A. R., xv, 92–93, 100, 102,
112–113, 124, 161n15, 169n5
Orwell, George, 79, 167n31
Others: An Anthology of the New Verse,
73
Outlook, The, 91
Overholser, Willis A., 175n28
Ovid, xiv, 64–65, 68, 151n4
Oxford Book of Verse, 151n4

"Paideuma," 4, 82, 145, 153n5
Paine, Thomas, 103
Paris Review, 127
Park, Josephine. *See* Stasi, Paul and
Josephine Park
Parker, Andrew, 176n36
Pascal, Blaise, 14
Patria Mia. See Pound, Ezra: *Patria
Mia*
Pauline Epistles, 150n4
Pavannes and Divisions. See Pound,
Ezra: *Pavannes and Divisions*

Péladan, Joséphin, 17
Penniman, Josiah, 18, 32, 157n12
Peritz, Janice, 146
Perloff, Marjorie, 155n18
Personae. See Pound, Ezra: *Personae*
Pervigilium Veneris, 36
Peterson, Theodore, 111, 171n23
Petrarch [Francesco Petrarca], 37
Phelan, James, 146
Plarr, Victor, 121
Poetry Magazine, 62, 91–98, 110, 113,
161n18, 162n22, 162n24, 163n2,
169n9, 171n22, 172n7
Poet's Club, 21, 23
Pope, Alexander, 151n4
Porter, Katherine Anne, 133
Possum. *See* Eliot, T. S.
Pound, Dorothy, 173n8
Pound, Ezra
  Academic Institutions
  Baliol College, Oxford, 19
  City College New York, 157n13
  Columbia University, 157n13
  Cornell University, 15
  Hamilton College, xiii, 13–17,
    32–33, 130,179n9
  Hobart College, 24
  London Polytechnic, 20–23, 33, 78
  Princeton University, 22–23
  Temple University, 22
  Trinity College [Hartford,
    Connecticut], 22
  University of Pennsylvania, xiii, 5,
    10–15, 17–18, 20, 23–24, 31–33,
    51, 80, 91, 130, 139, 154n12,
    156n9, 157nn12–13, 179n9
  Wabash College, xii, 18–19, 139,
    155n16
  Wyncote Public School, 9–10
  Works
  ABC of Economics, xiv, 125–126,
    149n2, 174n24, 175n29

Pound, Ezra
  Works *(continued)*
  ABC of Reading, xiii–xv, 2, 78,
    81–83, 125, 127, 139–140, 146,
    150–151n4, 154n13, 158n1,
    175n33, 177n47, 178n2
  America: Chances and Remedies, 24
  "Ballad of the Goodly Fere," 22,
    150n4
  "Canto 1," 117, 172n7
  "Canto 3," 75
    "Canto 14," 153n6
  "Canto 45," 13, 124, 174n26
  "Canto 52," 176n41
  "Canto 53," 83
  "Canto 54," 174n18
  "Canto 56," 174n18
  "Canto 59," 178n3
  "Canto 74," 115–123, 135, 173n11,
    173nn114, 173n16, 178n52
  "Canto 91," 153n8
  "Canto 96," 174n18
  "Canto 99," 174n18
  "Canto 116," 30
  The Cantos, 7, 12–13, 30, 75, 83,
    99, 115–124, 127, 133, 135,
    153n5, 153n8, 155n18, 168n36,
    172n7, 173nn11–14, 173n16,
    174n18, 174nn26–27, 176n41,
    178n52, 178n3
  Canzoni, 47
  Cathay, 76
  Confucius to Cummings, 6, 83–85,
    134–135, 156n6, 168nn38–39
  Ezra Pound Speaking, xi, 88–89,
    130–132, 177nn45–46, 177n51
  *Ezra Pound to His Parents: Letters
    1895–1929*, xi–xii, 9–10, 14–15,
    17–24, 31–32, 76, 91, 140,
    149n1, 157n17, 163n1, 176n41
  Guide to Kulchur, 3–4, 12, 93,
    121, 143–144, 174n26, 176n41,
    178n52

Homage to Sextus Propertius, 162n24
How to Read, xiii–xiv, 6, 12–13,
    77–81, 129, 144, 150n4, 175n29
I Gather the Limbs of Osiris, 6, 33,
    44–60, 160n14
"In a station of the metro," xvii,
    46–47, 161n18
Instigations, 6, 62, 67–77, 164–
    166nn10–23, 167n25, 175n33
Jefferson and/or Mussolini, 119
Literary Essays, 1, 15
Make It New, xiii–xiv, 88–89, 103
"Murkn Magzeens," 100, 112–113
"New Method in Scholarship," 6,
    45–46, 49, 58
Patria Mia, 24, 154–155n14
Pavannes and Divisions, 6, 61–67,
    96
Personae, 21–22
Pisan Cantos. See Pound, Ezra: *The
    Cantos*
"Raphaelite Latin," 11–12, 154n12,
    162n24
"The Renaissance," 12
"The Seafarer" [translation] 45, 49,
    57
"The Serious Artist," 96
"Sestina Altaforte," 22
"Small Magazines," xi, 100, 110–112
*The Sonnets and Ballate of Guido
    Cavalcanti*, 157n13
The Spirit of Romance, xv, 6, 16,
    20, 23, 32–47, 53, 83, 157n13,
    159n6, 159–160nn8–11
"Studies in Contemporary
    Mentality," xiv, 88–89, 91,
    100–110, 113
"The Teacher's Mission," 139, 143
Pound, Homer, 157n13. See also
    *Ezra Pound to His Parents: Letters
    1895–1929*
Pound, Omar and Robert Spoo,
    172n3, 172–173n8

Price, John, 98
Propp, Vladimir, 106
Punch, 22, 101, 106
Putnam, Samuel, 92, 99

Qian, Zhaoming, 167n24
Quarterly Review, 101
Quinn, John, 97, 157n13, 170n13
The Quiver, 101, 104–105

Rabaté, Jean-Michel, 119
Rabkin, Eric S., 146
Rachewiltz, Mary de, xi, 155n15. *See also* Pound, Ezra: *Ezra Pound to His Parents: Letters 1895–1929*
Rader, James, 157n14
Rancière, Jacques, 152n10
Rankin's Head Ointment, 106
"Raphaelite Latin." *See* Pound, Ezra: "Raphaelite Latin"
Ravel, Maurice, 61
Read, Forrest, 89, 166n20. *See also* Pound, Ezra: *Pound/Joyce*
Reagan, Ronald, 143
Reck, Michael, 176n38
Redman, Tim, 172n4
"The Renaissance." *See* Pound, Ezra: "The Renaissance"
Rennert, Hugo, 17–18, 20, 38, 43, 157n13
Richardson, Samuel, 150n4
Rickert, Edith, 40
Rimbaud, Arthur, 68, 164nn10–11, 165n13
Rodker, John, 99
Romains, Jules, 69, 104, 165nn13–14
Roosevelt, Franklin D., 119, 121
Rossetti, Dante Gabriel, 40, 64, 75, 160n10
Rothschild, Mayer Amschel, 119
Ruthven, K. K., 11–13, 16, 77, 83, 130, 156n7, 157n13, 163n5, 167n27, 170n14

Sandburg, Carl, 170n11, 171n22
Santayana, George, 122–123, 174nn19–20
Sappho, 84
Sayers, Dorothy, 31, 158n20
Schelling, Felix Emmanuel, 137–138, 157nn12–13
Scholes, Robert, xvii–xxi, 6, 137–140, 144–147, 149n3, 151n5, 151n7, 169nn2–3, 170n17, 178n4, 179–180nn10–11
Scott, Thomas L. and Melvin J. Friedman, 170n15
Scribner's Magazine, 90–91, 110
"The Seafarer." *See* Pound, Ezra: "The Seafarer"
Sen, Amartya, 175n30
"The Serious Artist." *See* Pound, Ezra: "The Serious Artist"
A Serious Character: The Life of Ezra Pound. See Carpenter, Humphrey
"Sestina Altaforte." *See* Pound, Ezra: "Sestina Altaforte"
Seymour, George, S., 99
Shakespear, Olivia, 21
Shakespeare, William, xii, 40, 42, 52, 59, 65, 77, 84, 151n4, 160n12, 168n39
Shapiro, Karl, 123
Shaw, George Bernard, 23, 105–106, 157n17
Shelley, Percy Bysshe, 42, 79
Sheppard, William [Bill] Pierce, 14–15, 140, 144, 179n9
Shklovsky, Viktor, 58, 162n25
Shor, Ira, 152n10
Sicari, Stephen, 119
Sidney, Sir Philip, 66, 79
Sieburth, Richard, 117
Silverman, Michael, 146
Sinclair, May, 22
Singh, Ghan Shyam, 154n11
Sir Gawain and the Green Knight, 151n4

Slusser, George E., 146
"Small Magazines." *See* Pound, Ezra: "Small Magazines"
The Smart Set, 91–93, 111
Smith, J. Mark, 11, 156n5
Sommers, Nancy, 146
Spann, Marcella, 6, 83–85, 168n38
Spectator, 102
Spellings Commission Report (2006), 3
Spender, Stephen, 133
The Spirit of Romance. See Pound, Ezra: *The Spirit of Romance*
Spivak, Gayatri Chakravorty, 167n29, 167n33
Spoo, Robert, 171n1. *See also* Pound, Omar and Robert Spoo
Stasi, Paul and Josephine Park, xix, 152n9
Stein, Gertrude, 127, 179n10
Steinberg, Shirley, 152n10
Stendhal, Marie-Henri, 96
Stevens, Wallace, 95, 168n1
Stirner, Max, 66, 96, 164n8
Stock, Noel, 2, 18, 125, 128, 130, 133–134, 156n1, 157n13, 157n15, 172n3
Stoicheff, Peter, 172n6
Stone, Edward. *See* O'Connor, William Van and Edward Stone
Strachey, Lytton, 166n21
Strand, 102, 108–109
Street, George S., 166n21
Strindberg, August, 165–166n18
Stryker, Melanchthon Woolsey, 13–14
Sullivan, Rosemary, 146
Surette, Leon, 7, 116, 120, 154n9, 174n21, 174n24, 176n36, 178n52
Swift, Daniel, 153n7
Swinburne, Algernon Charles, 40, 64, 72, 160n10
Synge, John Millington, 40, 160n10

Tacitus, Publius Cornelius, xiv
Tailhade, Laurent, 165n13
Tate, Allen, 123, 133
"The Teacher's Mission." *See* Pound, Ezra: "The Teacher's Mission"
Terrell, Carroll F., 178n52
Thackeray, William Makepeace, 150n4
Thayer, Scofield, 92, 98
Theocritus, 16
Tietjens, Eunice, 169–170n11
Till, Emmett, 173n14
Till, Louis, 120, 173n14
Tinkham, George Holden, 121, 173n17
T.J.V. [Pound pseudonym], 93
Torrey, E. Fuller, 133, 177nn50–51
Towne, Charles Hanson, 107
transatlantic review, 111
Trilling, Lionel, 158n3
Trollope, Anthony, 150n4
Troyes, Chrétien [Crestien] de, 159n8
Tryphonopoulos, Demetres, 155n16, 163n1
Twain, Mark, 150n4
Tytell, John, 177n51

Ulmer, Gregory L., 146
Ulrich, Carolyn F. *See* Hoffman, Frederick J., Charles Allen, and Carolyn F. Ulrich
Untermeyer, Louis, 10, 33

Van Buren, Martin, 119, 175n28
Veblen, Thorstein, 178n6
Vega, Lope de, 17, 42–44, 160n12
Vendler, Helen, 1
Villon, François, 42, 160n10, 164nn10–11
Vivaldi, Antonio, 127
Volstead, Andrew 176n41
Voltaire [François-Marie Arouet], 103, 150n4, 166n22

Wadsworth, Edward, 164n7

Wallace, David Foster, 178n5
Wallace, Emily Mitchell, 19, 157n12, 157n16
La Wallonie, 111, 165n14
Watson Jr., James Sibley, 4, 67, 69, 74, 92, 154n10
Watt, Harold K., 153n5
Weaver, Harriet Shaw, 25, 92, 97
Welch, Milton L., 173n14
Wescott, Glenway, 95
West, Rebecca, 22, 95–97
Weston, Jesse, 39
Whigham, Peter, 171n1
Whistler, James, 42, 67
Whitman, Walt, 94
Wilcox, E. W., 107
Wilde, Oscar, 171n20
Wilder, Thornton, 133
Wilhelm, J. J., 157n13
Williams, William Carlos, xv, 74, 84, 95, 123, 127, 133, 156n9
Wilmot, John, Earl of Rochester, 151n4

Wilson, Edmund, 152n8
Wilson, T. C., 18
Wilson, Woodrow, 176n41
Winters, Yvor, 95
Witemeyer, Hugh, 158n3
Wood, Frank Hoyt, 14
Woolf, Virginia, xii, 13, 63, 163–164nn6–7
Wordsworth, William, 42, 163n3
Wright, W. H., 92, 111
Wulfman, Clifford, xviii, xx, 6, 146, 169nn2–3

Yao, Steven G., 166–167n24
Yao, Steven G. and Michael Coyle, 2–3, 143, 155n18
Yeats, William Butler, 16, 20–22, 28, 72, 99, 121, 163n1, 175n33

Zabel, Morton, 113
Zukofsky, Louis, xv, 99, 126–128, 133, 176n37